File for Divorce in Washington

(+ CD-ROM)

Tara K. Richardson
Edward A. Haman

Attorneys at Law

SPHINX® PUBLISHING
AN IMPRINT OF SOURCEBOOKS, INC.®
NAPERVILLE, ILLINOIS
www.SphinxLegal.com

First Edition: 2005

Published by: **Sphinx® Publishing, An Imprint of Sourcebooks, Inc.®**

Naperville Office
P.O. Box 4410
Naperville, Illinois 60567-4410
(630) 961-3900
Fax: 630-961-2168
www.sourcebooks.com
www.SphinxLegal.com

This publication is designed to provide accurate and authoritative information in regard to the subject matter covered. It is sold with the understanding that the publisher is not engaged in rendering legal, accounting, or other professional service. If legal advice or other expert assistance is required, the services of a competent professional person should be sought.

*From a Declaration of Principles Jointly Adopted by a Committee of the
American Bar Association and a Committee of Publishers and Associations*

This product is not a substitute for legal advice.

Disclaimer required by Texas statutes.

Library of Congress Cataloging-in-Publication Data
Richardson, Tara K.
  File for divorce in Washington + CD-ROM / by Tara K. Richardson and Edward A. Haman.-- 1st ed.
    p. cm.
  Includes index.
  ISBN-13: 978-1-57248-522-8 (pbk. : alk. paper)
  ISBN-10: 1-57248-522-1 (pbk. : alk. paper)
  1. Divorce--Law and legislation--Washington (State)--Popular works. I. Haman, Edward A. II. Title.

KFW100.Z9R53 2005
346.79701'66--dc22
                                                          2005022310

Printed and bound in the United States of America.
BG — 10 9 8 7 6 5 4 3 2 1

Dedication

To Chad, who will never need to read this book.

Contents

How to Use the CD-ROM ix

Using Self-Help Law Books. xiii

Introduction xvii

Chapter 1: Marriage Ins and Outs. 1
    Marriage
    Divorce
    Annulment
    Legal Separation
    Wanting a Divorce
    Alternatives to Divorce

Chapter 2: The Legal System 11
    Theory versus Reality
    Divorce Law and Procedure
    Legal Research

Chapter 3: Lawyers. **21**
  Wanting a Lawyer
  Selecting a Lawyer
  Evaluating a Lawyer
  Working with a Lawyer

Chapter 4: Evaluating Your Situation **31**
  Your Spouse
  Gathering Information
  Property and Debts
  Parenting Plans
  Child Support
  Spousal Support
  Which Procedure to Use

Chapter 5: General Procedures. **55**
  An Introduction to Legal Forms
  Filing with the Court Clerk
  Notifying Your Spouse
  Setting a Court Hearing
  Courtroom Manners
  Negotiating

Chapter 6: Consent Divorce **65**
  Petition for Dissolution
  Finalizing
  Decree of Dissolution
  Findings of Fact and Conclusions of Law
  Order of Child Support
  Parenting Plan

Chapter 7: Uncontested Divorce **87**
  Summons
  Petition for Dissolution
  Motion and Declaration of Default
  Order of Default

Chapter 8: Contested Divorce 93
Forms
Property and Debts
Child Custody and Visitation
Child Support
Spousal Support
If You Reach a Settlement

Chapter 9: The Trial 99
General Procedures
Preparing the Final Pleadings

Chapter 10: When You Cannot Find
Your Spouse 107
The Diligent Search
You Know Where Your Spouse Lives
You Do Not Know Where Your Spouse Lives

Chapter 11: Temporary Orders 113
Types of Forms
Temporary Orders
Ex Parte Orders
Entering Orders

Chapter 12: Special Circumstances 125
When You Cannot Afford Court Costs
Protecting Yourself and Your Children
Taxes
Pension Plans
Relocation

Glossary 131

Appendix A: Washington Child Support
Guidelines 137

Appendix B: Worksheets **155**

Appendix C: Blank Forms **159**

Index **253**

How to Use the CD-ROM

Thank you for purchasing *File for Divorce in Washington (+CD-ROM)*. We have included every document in the book on the CD-ROM, which is attached to the inside back cover of the book.

You can use these forms just as you would the forms in the book. Print them out, fill them in, and use them however you need. You can also fill in the forms directly on your computer. Just identify the form you need, open it, click on the space where the information should go, and input your information. Customize each form for your particular needs. Use them over and over again.

The CD-ROM is compatible with both PC and Mac operating systems. (While it should work with either operating system, we cannot guarantee that it will work with your particular system and we cannot provide technical assistance.) To use the forms on your computer, you will need to use Adobe® Reader®. The CD-ROM does not contain this program. You can download this program from Adobe's website at **www.adobe.com**. Click on the "Get Adobe® Reader®" icon to begin the download process and follow the instructions.

Once you have Adobe® Reader® installed, insert the CD-ROM into your computer. Double-click on the icon representing the disc on your desktop or go through your hard drive to identify the drive that contains the disc and click on it.

Once opened, you will see the files contained on the CD-ROM listed as "Form #: [Form Title]." Open the file you need through Adobe® Reader®. You may print the form to fill it out manually at this point, or your can use the "Hand Tool" and click on the appropriate line to fill it in using your computer.

Any time you see bracketed information [ ] on the form, you can click on it and delete the bracketed information from your final form. This information is only a reference guide to assist you in filling in the forms and should be removed from your final version. Once all your information is filled in, you can print your filled-in form.

NOTE: *Adobe® Reader® does not allow you to save the PDF with the boxes filled in.*

• • • • •

Purchasers of this book are granted a license to use the forms contained in it for their own personal use. By purchasing this book, you have also purchased a limited license to use all forms on the accompanying CD-ROM. The license limits you to personal use only and all other copyright laws must be adhered to. No claim of copyright is made in any government form reproduced in the book or on the CD-ROM. You are free to modify the forms and tailor them to your specific situation.

The author and publisher have attempted to provide the most current and up-to-date information available. However, the courts, Congress, and your state's legislatures review, modify, and change laws on an ongoing basis, as well as create new laws from time to time. By the very nature of the information and due to the continual changes in our legal system, to be sure that you have the current and best information for your situation, you should consult a local attorney or research the current laws yourself.

• • • • •

This publication is designed to provide accurate and authoritative information in regard to the subject matter covered. It is sold with the understanding that the publisher is not engaged in rendering legal, accounting, or other professional service. If legal advice or other expert assistance is required, the services of a competent professional person should be sought.

> —*From a Declaration of Principles Jointly Adopted by a Committee of the American Bar Association and a Committee of Publishers and Associations*

This product is not a substitute for legal advice.

> —*Disclaimer required by Texas statutes*

Using Self-Help
Law Books

Before using a self-help law book, you should realize the advantages and disadvantages of doing your own legal work and understand the challenges and diligence that this requires.

The Growing Trend

Rest assured that you will not be the first or only person handling your own legal matter. For example, in some states, more than 75% of the people in divorces and other cases represent themselves. Because of the high cost of legal services, this is a major trend and many courts are struggling to make it easier for people to represent themselves. However, some courts are not happy with people who do not use attorneys and refuse to help them in any way. For some, the attitude is, "Go to the law library and figure it out for yourself."

We write and publish self-help law books to give people an alternative to the often complicated and confusing legal books found in most law libraries. We have made the explanations of the law as simple and easy to understand as possible. Of course, unlike an attorney advising an individual client, we cannot cover every conceivable possibility.

Cost/Value Analysis

Whenever you shop for a product or service, you are faced with various levels of quality and price. In deciding what product or service to buy, you make a cost/value analysis on the basis of your willingness to pay and the quality you desire.

When buying a car, you decide whether you want transportation, comfort, status, or sex appeal. Accordingly, you decide among such choices as a Neon, a Lincoln, a Rolls Royce, or a Porsche. Before making a decision, you usually weigh the merits of each option against the cost.

When you get a headache, you can take a pain reliever (such as aspirin) or visit a medical specialist for a neurological examination. Given this choice, most people, of course, take a pain reliever, since it costs only pennies; whereas a medical examination costs hundreds of dollars and takes a lot of time. This is usually a logical choice because it is rare to need anything more than a pain reliever for a headache. But in some cases, a headache may indicate a brain tumor and failing to see a specialist right away can result in complications. Should everyone with a headache go to a specialist? Of course not, but people treating their own illnesses must realize that they are betting on the basis of their cost/value analysis of the situation. They are taking the most logical option.

The same cost/value analysis must be made when deciding to do one's own legal work. Many legal situations are very straightforward, requiring a simple form and no complicated analysis. Anyone with a little intelligence and a book of instructions can handle the matter without outside help.

But there is always the chance that complications are involved that only an attorney would notice. To simplify the law into a book like this, several legal cases often must be condensed into a single sentence or paragraph. Otherwise, the book would be several hundred pages long and too complicated for most people. However, this simplification necessarily leaves out many details and nuances that would apply to special or unusual situations. Also, there are many ways to interpret most legal questions. Your case may come before a judge who disagrees with the analysis of our authors.

Therefore, in deciding to use a self-help law book and to do your own legal work, you must realize that you are making a cost/value analysis. You have decided that the money you will save in doing it yourself outweighs the chance that your case will not turn out to your satisfaction. Most people handling their own simple legal matters never have a problem, but occasionally people find that it ended up costing them more to have an attorney straighten out the situation than it would have if they had hired an attorney in the beginning. Keep this in mind while handling your case, and be sure to consult an attorney if you feel you might need further guidance.

Local Rules   The next thing to remember is that a book which covers the law for the entire nation, or even for an entire state, cannot possibly include every procedural difference of every jurisdiction. Whenever possible, we provide the exact form needed; however, in some areas, each county, or even each judge, may require unique forms and procedures. In our state books, our forms usually cover the majority of counties in the state, or provide examples of the type of form which will be required. In our national books, our forms are sometimes even more general in nature but are designed to give a good idea of the type of form that will be needed in most locations. Nonetheless, keep in mind that your state, county, or judge may have a requirement or use a form that is not included in this book.

You should not necessarily expect to be able to get all of the information and resources you need solely from within the pages of this book. This book will serve as your guide, giving you specific information whenever possible and helping you to find out what else you will need to know. This is just like if you decided to build your own backyard deck. You might purchase a book on how to build decks. However, such a book would not include the building codes and permit requirements of every city, town, county, and township in the nation; nor would it include the lumber, nails, saws, hammers, and other materials and tools you would need to actually build the deck. You would use the book as your guide, and then do some work and research involving such matters as whether you need a permit of some kind, what type and grade of wood are available in your area, whether to use hand tools or power tools, and how to use those tools.

Before using the forms in a book like this, you should check with your court clerk to see if there are any local rules of which you should be aware, or local forms you will need to use. Often, such forms will require the same information as the forms in the book but are merely laid out differently or use slightly different language. They will some-times require additional information.

Changes in the Law

Besides being subject to local rules and practices, the law is subject to change at any time. The courts and the legislatures of all fifty states are constantly revising the laws. It is possible that while you are reading this book, some aspect of the law is being changed.

In most cases, the change will be of minimal significance. A form will be redesigned, additional information will be required, or a waiting period will be extended. As a result, you might need to revise a form, file an extra form, or wait out a longer time period; these types of changes will not usually affect the outcome of your case. On the other hand, sometimes a major part of the law is changed, the entire law in a particular area is rewritten, or a case that was the basis of a central legal point is overruled. In such instances, your entire ability to pursue your case may be impaired.

To help you with local requirements and changes in the law, be sure to read the section in Chapter 2 on "Legal Research."

Introduction

Going through a divorce is one of the most trying and stressful times in any person's life. You may feel lost, confused, depressed, and angry all at the same time. These feelings are perfectly valid. Do not be reluctant to seek help from a counselor or therapist—you will best handle the legal requirements of your situation if you are as emotionally strong as possible.

This book is designed to help you make sense of the legal process from start to finish. It is divided into easy-to-understand chapters and includes most of the commonly needed mandatory forms. Chapters 1 and 3 are intended to help you decide what type of family law proceeding, if any, is right for you and to give you an overview of what issues are addressed in a divorce. Chapters 2 and 4 introduce you to the legal resources available to you, from case books to websites to helping you decide if you should retain an attorney.

Once you have decided that you want to represent yourself (*pro se*) in the divorce process, Chapter 5 begins your introduction to the necessary legal forms and how to conduct yourself in court. The following three chapters (Chapters 6 through 9) explain the different steps to take if you and your spouse agree to everything, if your spouse does not respond at all to your requests, or if your spouse contests one or more of the things you want. The final chapter in this grouping, Chapter 10, addresses how to proceed when your spouse cannot be found.

Wrapping things up, Chapters 11 and 12 explain what to do if you need the court to make some provisions for you and your family prior the entry of a final decree. They also address specific issues, such as tax considerations.

Thank you for purchasing this book. We hope that it will make the divorce process that much easier for you to negotiate, and ultimately assist you in moving forward with your life.

chapter 1

Marriage Ins and Outs

Several years (or maybe only months) ago, you made a decision to get married. This chapter discusses, in a very general way, what you got yourself into and how you can get yourself out. As discussed in the next section, marriage involves several different types of agreements. This book focuses on the agreements created by the law of the State of Washington. Throughout this book you will see references to Washington laws. The laws passed by the Washington Legislature are compiled in a set of books called the *Revised Code of Washington Annotated*, which is abbreviated RCWA. (See the section in Chapter 2 on "Legal Research" for more information.)

MARRIAGE

Marriage is frequently referred to as a contract. It is a legal contract, and for many it is also a religious contract. This book deals only with the legal aspects. The wedding ceremony involves the bride and groom reciting certain vows, which are actually mutual promises about how they will treat each other.

Although the ceremony's focus is on the emotional and romantic aspects of the relationship, legal papers are also signed, such as a marriage license and a marriage certificate. These formalities create certain rights and obligations for the husband and wife. These financial rights, property rights, and obligations cannot be broken without a legal proceeding.

Marriage will give each of the parties certain rights in property and create certain obligations with respect to the support of any children they have or adopt together. Unfortunately, most people do not fully realize that these rights and obligations are being created until it comes time for a divorce.

DIVORCE

In Washington, a divorce is legally referred to as a *dissolution of marriage*. Since this is a phrase most people are not familiar with, throughout this book we will use the terms "divorce" and "dissolution" interchangeably.

A divorce is the most common method of terminating or breaking the marriage contract. In a divorce, the court declares that the marriage is irretrievably broken, divides the parties' property and debts, and decides if either party should receive *spousal maintenance* (formally known as *alimony*).

If children are involved, the court also makes a determination of *primary residential placement* (the parent with whom the children will reside the majority of the time) and creates a residential schedule (**PARENTING PLAN**), which sets forth specific dates and times that the children will live with each parent. Finally, the court calculates child support.

Traditionally, a divorce could only be granted under exceptional circumstances, such as adultery or mental cruelty. Today, a divorce may be granted simply because one or both parties want one. Washington is what is called a *no-fault* state. This means that either party's conduct during the marriage, unless it impacts the safety and well-being of the other party or the children, has no bearing on the dissolution process.

ANNULMENT

The basic difference between a divorce and an *annulment* is that a divorce says, *this marriage is broken* and an annulment says, *there never was a marriage*. An annulment is more difficult and often more complicated to prove, so it is not used very often. Annulments are only possible in a few circumstances, usually when one party has deceived the other. If you decide that you want an annulment, consult an attorney. If you are seeking an annulment for religious reasons and need to go through a church procedure (rather than, or in addition to, a legal procedure), consult your clergyman.

A divorce is generally easier to get than an annulment because all you need to prove to get a divorce is that your marriage is irretrievably broken or defunct. How do you prove this? Simply by saying it. In the **PETITION FOR DISSOLUTION** (see form 2, p.163), all you must do is check the box that states: "The marriage is irretrievably broken."

Keep in mind that only one party need allege that the marriage is irretrievably broken. In other words, even if your spouse does not agree that the marriage is defunct, your dissolution can still go forward.

In order to get an annulment, however, you will need to prove more. This proof will usually involve introducing various documents into evidence and having other people come to testify at the court hearing.

Grounds   Annulments can only be granted based on one of the following grounds.

- One or both of the parties is *too young*. The minimum age for marriage without parental or court approval is 18. If a party is under the age of 18, proof of age is required (birth certificate or driver's license). Additionally, the parent or guardian must be present to sign the application form. If a party is under age 17, written permission from the family court must be obtained.

- If one party is *still married to another* individual.

- Reasons of *consanguinity*. Consanguinity is the degree of relationship of family members who share at least one common ancestor. For example, uncle and niece, nephew and aunt, and first cousins are prohibited from marrying.

✪   If a party lacked the *mental capacity* to consent to the marriage because he or she either lacked the mental capacity or was under the influence of alcohol or other incapacitating substances.

✪   If a party was forced to enter the marriage by *force*, *duress*, or *fraud* involving the essentials of marriage.

In addition to one or more of these reasons, in order to obtain an annulment, the parties must not have ratified the marriage by living together after reaching the age of consent (16), after attaining the capacity to consent, or after the force or duress has ended or the fraud was discovered.

If your spouse wants to stop an annulment, there are several arguments he or she can make to further complicate the case. This area of the law is not as well-defined as divorce. The annulment procedure is much less common than divorce and can be extremely complicated. Do not attempt this without consulting a lawyer.

LEGAL SEPARATION

A *legal separation* is used to divide property and provide for child support and custody in cases in which the husband and wife live separately, but remain married. This is usually used to divide the financial rights and obligations of a couple when their religion does not permit divorce, when the parties are not psychologically ready for a divorce, or when one party has health issues that require continued insurance coverage. Most employer-provided insurance policies allow the employee to keep his or her spouse on that policy even after a legal separation. While COBRA coverage is available to divorced spouses, it is often prohibitively expensive and is only available for a relatively short period of time. In Washington, to begin the legal separation process a person files a *Petition for Legal Separation*. Virtually all of the processes and procedures one must undertake in a marital dissolution apply to a legal separation action.

WANTING A DIVORCE

Getting a divorce is one of the most emotionally stressful events in a person's life. It will also have an impact on several aspects of your life and can change your entire lifestyle. Before you begin the process of getting a divorce, take some time to think about how it will affect your life. This section helps you examine these things and offers alternatives in the event you want to try to save your relationship. Even if you feel absolutely sure that you want a divorce, you should still read this section so you are prepared for what may follow.

Legal Divorce

The legal divorce is simply the breaking of your matrimonial bonds—the termination of your marriage contract and partnership. The stress of going through a court system procedure, when compared to the other aspects of divorce, does not last that long. However, the legal divorce can be the most confrontational and emotionally explosive stage.

There are generally four matters to be resolved in the legal divorce:

1. the divorce of two people—basically, this gives each the legal right to marry someone else;

2. the division of their property (and responsibility for debts);

3. the determination of the primary residential parent and the creation of a **PARENTING PLAN** for their children; and,

4. the calculation of child support.

Although it is possible for the legal divorce to be concluded within a few months, the legalities most often continue for years. This is mostly caused by emotional battles over the children.

Social and Emotional Divorce

Long after you are legally divorced, divorce will have a tremendous impact on your social and emotional life. The social and emotional strains of a divorce may include some or all of the following.

Lack of companionship. Even if your relationship is quite stormy, you are probably still accustomed to having your spouse around. You may be able to temporarily put aside your problems and at least somewhat support each other in times of mutual adversity (such as dealing with a death in the family, the illness of your child, or tornado damage to your home). You may also feel a little more secure at night knowing that you are not alone in the house. Even if your marriage is miserable, you may still notice a little emptiness, loneliness, or solitude after the divorce. It may not be that you miss your spouse in particular, but just miss another person being around.

Grief. Divorce may be viewed as the death of a marriage. Like the death of anyone you have been close to, you will feel a sense of loss. This aspect can take you through all of the normal feelings associated with grief, such as guilt, anger, denial, and acceptance. You may get angry and frustrated over the years you have wasted. You may feel guilty because you failed to make the marriage work. You may find yourself saying, "I can't believe this is happening to me." And, for months or even years, you might spend a lot of time thinking about your marriage. It can be extremely difficult to put it all behind you and get on with your life.

Dating. If you want to avoid solitary evenings in front of the TV, you will find yourself trying to get back into dating. This will probably involve a change in friends and lifestyle. Your current married friends may no longer find that you, as a single person, fit in with their circle. Gradually (or even quickly) you may find yourself dropped from their guest list. Now you have to start making an effort to meet single people at work, going out on the town, and dating. This experience can be frightening, tiring, and frustrating, especially after years of being away from this lifestyle. It can also be very difficult if you have custody of the children.

Financial Divorce

In financial terms, a divorce can be a very long and drastic adjustment. Divorce has a significant financial impact in almost every case. Many married couples are just able to make ends meet. After getting divorced, there are suddenly two rent payments, two electric bills, etc. For the spouse without custody, there is also child support to be paid.

Once you have divided your property, each of you will need to replace the items the other person got to keep. If she got the bedroom furniture and the pots and pans, he will need to buy his own. If he got the television and the sofa, she will need to buy her own television and sofa. For at least one spouse (and often for both) money becomes even tighter than it was before the divorce.

Children and Divorce

The effect of a divorce on your children—and your relationship with them—can be the most painful and long-lasting aspect of divorce. Your family life will be permanently changed. Even if you remarry, stepparents rarely bring back that same family feeling. Your relationship with your children may become strained as they work through their feelings of blame, guilt, disappointment, and anger. This strain may continue for many years. Your children may even need professional counseling. Also, as long as there is child support and visitation involved, you will have at least some contact with your ex-spouse.

ALTERNATIVES TO DIVORCE

By the time you have purchased this book and read this far, you have probably already decided that you want a divorce. However, if what you have just read and thought about has changed your mind or made you want to make a last effort to save your marriage, there are a few basic approaches you can try. More detailed suggestions can be offered by professional marriage counselors.

Talk to Your Spouse

Choose a good time (not when your spouse is trying to unwind after a day at work or trying to quiet a crying baby) and talk about your problems. Establish a few ground rules, such as:

- ✪ talk about how you feel instead of making accusations that may start an argument;

- ✪ each person listens while the other speaks (no interrupting); and,

- ✪ each person must say something that he or she likes about the other and about the relationship.

Change Your Thinking

As you talk, you may want to discuss things such as where you would like your relationship to go, how it has changed since you got married, and what can be done to bring you closer together.

Many people get divorced because they will not change something about their outlook or their lifestyle. Once they get divorced, they sometimes find they have made that same change they resisted for so long.

Example:

George and Wendy were unhappy in their marriage. They did not seem to share the same lifestyle. George felt bored and overburdened with responsibility. He wanted Wendy to be more independent and outgoing, to meet new people, to handle the household budget, and to go out with him more often. But Wendy was more shy and reserved, was not confident in her ability to find a job and succeed in the business world, and preferred to stay at home. Wendy wanted George to give up some of his frequent nights out with the guys, to help with the cooking and laundry, to stop leaving messes for her to clean up, and to stop bothering her about going out all the time. But neither would try to change, and eventually all of the little things built up into a divorce.

After the divorce, Wendy was forced to get a job to support herself. Now she has friends at work, she goes out with them two or three nights a week, she is successful and happy at her job, and she is quite competent at managing her own budget. George now has his own apartment, cooks his own meals (something he finds he enjoys), and does his own laundry. He has also found it necessary to clean up his own messes and keep the place neat, especially if he is going to entertain guests.

Both George and Wendy have changed in exactly the way the other had wanted. It is too bad they did not make these changes before they got divorced. If you think some change may help, give it a try. You can always go back to the divorce option if things do not work out.

Marriage Counseling

Counseling is not the same as giving advice. A counselor should not tell you what to do. A counselor's job is to assist you in figuring out what you really want to do and to ask questions that will get you thinking.

Talking things out with your spouse is a form of self-counseling. The only problem is that it is difficult to remain objective and nonjudgmental. You both need to be able to calmly analyze what the problems are and discuss possible solutions.

Very few couples seem to be able to self-counsel successfully, which is why there are professional marriage counselors. As with doctors and lawyers, good marriage counselors are best discovered by word of mouth. You may have friends who can direct you to someone who helped them. You can also check with your family doctor or your clergyman for a referral. You can even check the Yellow Pages under "Marriage and Family Counselors" or some similar category. You can see a counselor either alone or with your spouse. It may be a good idea to see a counselor, even if you are going through with the divorce.

Another form of individual counseling is talking to a close friend. Just remember the difference between counseling and giving advice. Do not let your friend tell you what you should do.

Trial Separation   Before going to the time, expense, and trouble of getting a divorce, you and your spouse may want to try just getting away from each other for awhile. This can be as simple as taking separate vacations or as complex as actually separating into different households for an indefinite period of time. This may give each of you a chance to think about how you will like living alone, how important or trivial your problems are, and how you really feel about each other.

The Legal System

This chapter gives you a general introduction to the legal system. There are some things you need to know in order to obtain a divorce (or help your lawyer get the job done) and to get through any encounter with the legal system with minimal stress.

THEORY VERSUS REALITY

Our legal system is a system of rules. There are basically three types of rules.

1. *Rules of law.* The basic substance of the law, such as a law telling a judge how to go about dividing your property.

2. *Rules of procedure.* These outline how matters are to be handled in the courts, such as requiring court papers to be in a certain form or filed within a certain period of time.

3. *Rules of evidence.* These set forth the manner in which facts are to be proven.

These rules allow each side to present evidence most favorable to that side so an independent person or persons (the judge or jury) can figure out the truth. Then, certain legal principles are applied to that truth, which will give a fair resolution of the dispute between the parties.

Legal principles should be relatively unchanging, so that people know what will happen in any given situation and can plan their lives accordingly. This provides order and predictability to society. Any change in the legal principles is supposed to occur slowly, so that the expected behavior in society is not unclear from day to day. Unfortunately, the system does not really work this way. What follows are only some of the problems in the real legal system.

The System is not Perfect

Contrary to how it may seem, legal rules are not made just to complicate things and confuse everyone. They are attempts to make the system fair and just. They have been developed over several hundred years, and in most cases, they do make sense. Unfortunately, our efforts to find fairness and justice have resulted in a complex set of rules.

The legal system affects our lives in important ways. It is not a game; however, it can be compared to a game in some ways. The rules are designed to apply to all people, in all cases. There are also cases in which one side wins by cheating. Sometimes the rules do not seem to give a fair result in a certain situation, but are still followed. Just as a referee can make a bad call, so can a judge.

Judges do not Always Follow the Rules

Many judges make a decision simply based on what they think seems fair under the circumstances. Unfortunately, what seems fair to a particular judge may depend upon his or her personal ideas and philosophy. For example, there is nothing in the divorce laws that gives one parent priority in child custody. However, a vast majority of judges believe that a child is generally better off with his or her mother. All other things being equal, these judges will find a way to justify awarding custody to the mother.

The System is often Slow

Even lawyers get frustrated at how long it can take to get a case completed. Whatever your situation, things will take longer than you expect. Patience is required to get through the system with minimal stress. Do not let your impatience or frustration show. No matter what happens, keep calm and be courteous.

**No Two Cases
are Alike**

Just because your friend's case went a certain way does not mean yours will have the same result. Even if your coworker makes a similar income and has the same number of children, you cannot assume you will be ordered to pay the same amount of child support. There are usually other circumstances your coworker does not tell you about and possibly does not understand.

**Half of the
People Lose**

Remember, there are two sides to every legal issue and usually only one winner. Do not expect to have every detail go your way, especially if you let the judge decide.

DIVORCE LAW AND PROCEDURE

This section gives you a general overview of the law and procedures involved in getting a divorce. To most people, the law appears very complicated and confusing. Fortunately, many areas of the law can be broken down into simple and logical steps. Divorce is one of those areas.

The Players

Law and the legal system are often compared to games, and just like with games, it is important to know the players.

The judge. The judge has the power to decide whether you can get divorced, how your property will be divided, which of you will get custody of the children, and how much the other will pay for child support. The judge is the last person you want to make angry. In general, judges have large caseloads and like it best when your case can be concluded quickly and without much hassle. This means that the more you and your spouse agree upon and the more complete your paperwork is, the more the judge will like it. Most likely, your only direct contact with the judge will be at the final hearing, which may last as few as five minutes. (See Chapter 5 for more about how to deal with the judge.)

The judge's clerk, or bailiff. The judge's clerk or bailiff sets the hearings for the judge, and can frequently answer many of your questions about the procedure and what the judge likes or requires. You do not want to make an enemy of the judge's clerk or bailiff. Do not call often or ask too many questions, though a few questions are okay. You may want to start off saying that you just want to make sure you have everything in order for the judge. You will get much farther by being nice.

The court clerk. While the judge's clerk usually only works for one judge, the court clerk handles the files for all of the judges. The clerk's office is the central place where all of the court files are kept. The clerk files your court papers and keeps the official records of your divorce.

Most people who work in the clerk's office are friendly and helpful. While they cannot give you legal advice (such as telling you what to say in your court papers), they can help explain the system and the procedures (such as telling you what type of papers must be filed). The clerk has the power to accept or reject your papers, so you do not want to anger the clerk either. If the clerk tells you to change something in your papers, just change it. Do not argue or complain.

Lawyers. Lawyers serve as guides through the legal system. They try to guide their own client while trying to confuse, manipulate, and out-maneuver their opponent. In dealing with your spouse's lawyer (if he or she has one), try to be polite. You will not get anywhere by being difficult. Generally, the lawyer is just doing his or her job—trying to get the best situation for the client.

Some lawyers cannot be reasoned with, and you should not try. If your spouse gets one of these lawyers, it is a good idea for you to also get a lawyer. (Chapter 3 provides more information to help you decide if you want a lawyer.)

This book. This book serves as your map through the legal system. In most cases, the dangers along the way are relatively small. If you start getting lost, or the dangers seem to be getting worse, you can always hire a lawyer to jump to your aid.

The Law The law relating to divorce, as well as to any other area of law, comes from two sources. The first source is the laws passed by the Washington Legislature. These laws may be found in a set of books called *Revised Code of Washington Annotated* (RCWA).

The other source of law is the past decisions of the Washington courts. These decisions are much more difficult to locate and follow. For most situations, the law is clearly spelled out in the statutes, and the past court decisions are not all that important. However, if you wish to learn more about how to find these court decisions, see the section of this chapter on page 17 entitled "Legal Research."

The law is really very simple in most divorce cases. You will need to show the following four things:

1. that the marriage is *irretrievably broken* (done by simply stating this fact, which means that your marriage relationship is broken and cannot be saved);

2. how your property should be divided between you and your spouse;

3. who should be primary residential parent of your children and what sort of **PARENTING PLAN** should be implemented; and,

4. who should pay child support and how much that child support payment should be.

Residency requirement. One basic law is that either you or your spouse must establish residency in Washington before a **PETITION FOR DISSOLUTION** can be filed. (see form 2, p.163) can be filed. This generally entails living in Washington for six months. You will also need to file in either the county where you reside or in the county where your spouse resides.

Residency, in this context, is a term of art. If your spouse challenges the county in which you have filed, you will need to show the court why you should be considered a resident of that county and why there is no great hardship to the spouse who lives outside the filing county for the case to proceed in the county where you have filed. For example, you will need to show that you have a job in the filing county, your children are enrolled in school there, or you have purchased a residence in the county in which you have filed. If your spouse challenges either your state or county residency, you should consult an attorney for assistance.

The Procedure   The basic uncontested divorce process may be viewed as a five-step process.

1.   File court papers asking the judge to grant a divorce, which includes dividing your property and deciding who will take care of the children.

2.   Notify your spouse that you are filing for divorce.

3.   Prepare final court documents explaining what you and your spouse have agreed to do. Both of you need to sign these documents.

4.   Obtain a hearing date.

5.   Attend a hearing with the judge and have the judge sign a judgment granting the divorce.

(Later chapters provide more details and tell you how to carry out these steps.)

Petition for Dissolution. The **PETITION FOR DISSOLUTION** is simply a written request to grant you a divorce, divide your property and debts, and make provisions for your children. A **PETITION FOR DISSOLUTION** form is provided with full instructions for preparing it in Chapter 6 in Appendix C (see form 2, p.163) Once the **PETITION FOR DISSOLUTION** is completed, it is taken to the court clerk to be filed.

Notifying your spouse. After you have prepared the **PETITION FOR DISSOLUTION**, you need to officially notify your spouse. Even though your spouse may already know that you are filing for divorce, you still need to have him or her officially notified. This is done by having a copy of your **PETITION FOR DISSOLUTION** delivered to your spouse. (See Chapter 5, "Notifying Your Spouse," for more details.) This step is eliminated in the consent divorce procedure.

Obtaining a hearing date. Once all of your paperwork has been filed, you need to set a date for a hearing. A *hearing* is simply a meeting with the judge so that he or she can give you a divorce. This is usually done by contacting the judge's bailiff or clerk, or the court clerk, and asking for a hearing date. This can often be done over the telephone.

The hearing. Finally, you go to the hearing. The judge will review the papers you have submitted and will take short testimony from you about the agreements in the final court documents. Assuming everything is in order, the judge will simply approve your agreement and sign the final documents.

LEGAL RESEARCH

This book is designed so that you do not need to do your own legal research. However, if you need or want to find out more about the divorce law in Washington, this section gives you some guidance. Most of the books discussed cannot be found at your local public library. To find them, you will probably need to go to a specialized law library. Most counties have a law library affiliated with the circuit court. Your court clerk's office can probably tell you where to find the law library.

If you live near a law school, you can also find a law library there. Law school libraries are usually much more extensive than county law libraries. Just like court clerks, law librarians cannot give you legal advice. However, they can show you where to find the books you will need to help you.

Online Research   You can obtain a lot of legal information online. The *Revised Code of Washington* can be found online at:

www.leg.wa.gov/rcw/index.cfm

The domestic relations laws are contained in Title 26 of the RCWA. Dissolution statutes are contained in Title 26, Chapter 9 (cited as RCWA 26.09). Specific child support provisions are contained in Title 26, Chapters 18 and 19 (cited as RCWA 26.18 and RCWA 26.19). Within the chapters are the individual statutes. For example, the statute that defines the terms relating to dissolution laws is RCWA 26.09.010.

In Washington, 99.9% of anything that needs to be filed with the court in a divorce case is done by filing a *mandatory form*. In other words, the legislature has attempted to make it easier for people to represent themselves by having one set of standard forms that everyone uses.

These forms can be found at **www.courts.wa.gov**. From the index on the left of that website, select "Court Forms." Under "Related Links" select "List of All Forms." You will then be directed to a page containing every mandatory form produced by the court. The forms that you need are contained under the "Domestic Relations" subheading. The "Court Forms" page also contains sections entitled "Court Form Instructions" and "Washington Law Help," which provide additional information to complete the forms and answers to frequently asked questions.

Also, most county courts in Washington have their own websites from which you can access court information and download the mandatory family law forms. Finally, at the courthouse, you can usually purchase a packet that contains all the mandatory divorce forms. (This does not mean that you need to use all the forms in the packet.)

Another source of legal information is **www.findlaw.com**. To obtain Washington information, click on "Search Cases & Codes," then click on "US State Laws." Scroll down to and click on "Washington." This will bring you to a page with listings for various sources. Clicking on "Revised Code of Washington" will take you to the site for the Washington Legislature previously discussed. You can then click on the chapter of the Revised Code of Washington you want to see. (More information about obtaining forms online can be found at the beginning of Appendix C.)

Washington Statutes   The main source of information on Washington divorce law is the laws passed by the Washington Legislature, which are found in a set of books called *Revised Code of Washington Annotated* (RCWA). The word *annotated* means that after each section of the law, you will find additional information, such as how that section has been interpreted by the courts. The RCWA can sometimes be found at the regular public library, although you will need to check to be sure they have the most recent information. These books are updated each year using a *supplement* that will be found in the back of each volume. These updates are called *pocket parts*, because they slide into a pocket on the inside back cover.

In addition to the laws passed by the legislature, law is also made by the decisions of the judges in various cases each year. You will definitely not find this case law at the regular public library, so you will need to go to a law library. In addition to the annotation portion of the RCWA, case law may be found in the reference materials that follow.

Digests   *Digests* are sets of books that give short summaries of cases and references to the place where you can find the court's full written opinion. Washington's digest is titled *West's Washington Digest 2nd*. The information in the digest is arranged alphabetically by subject. Find the chapter on divorce, then look for the subject you want.

Pacific Reporter   The *Pacific Reporter* is where the Washington appeals courts publish their written opinions on the cases they hear. There are two series of the *Pacific Reporter*, the older cases being found in the *Pacific Reporter* (abbreviated P.) and newer cases being found in the *Pacific Reporter 2d Series* (P.2d). For example, if the digest refers you to *Smith v. Smith*, 149 P.2d 721 (1987), this tells you that the case of *Smith v. Smith* can be found in Volume 149 of the *Pacific Reporter 2d Series*, on page 721. The number in parentheses is the year in which the case was decided.

Case law can also be researched online at **www.courts.wa.gov**. From the index on the left side of this website, select "Court Opinions."

Legal Encyclopedia   A *legal encyclopedia* is similar to a regular encyclopedia. You simply look up the subject you want (*divorce,* in this case), in alphabetical order, and it gives you a summary of the law on that subject. It will also refer to specific court cases, which can then be found in the *Pacific Reporter*. There are legal encyclopedia sets that give general information for the the entire United States, but you will get more helpful information from the legal encyclopedia sets specifically relating to Washington law. These can be found in books entitled *Washington Practice,* at Volumes 19–22.

Washington Rules of Court

The *Washington Rules of Court* are the rules that are applied in the various courts in Washington. They also contain some approved forms. These rules mainly deal with forms and procedures. You are primarily concerned with the *Rules of Civil Procedure* (CR).

These rules are contained in a book called *Washington Court Rules—State*, which can be found in your county court's law library. State court rules can also be found at **www.courts.wa.gov**. From the index on the left side of the page, select "Court Rules."

Many counties also have local court rules that specifically apply to divorce cases. These rules are contained in a book called *Washington Court Rules—Local*, which can be found in your county court's law library. These local rules are often listed on the county court's website. In researching the court rules, be sure to inquire as to whether any such local rules apply in your county and whether they have been changed or updated recently.

Washington Family Law Deskbook

Another resource is the *Washington State Family Law Deskbook*. The Deskbook is divided into three volumes. It provides an overview of all areas of family law and citations to relevant case law.

Family Law Facilitators

Nearly every county court has a family law facilitator's office that can provide you with basic information and assist you with obtaining and filling out forms. Check with the clerk of the county court or **www.courts.wa.gov/court_dir/?fa=court_dir.facils** to determine if your county court has such an office.

Lawyers

chapter 3

Whether you need an attorney will depend upon many factors, including:

- ✪ how comfortable you feel handling the divorce yourself;

- ✪ whether your situation is more complicated than usual;

- ✪ how much opposition you get from your spouse; and,

- ✪ whether your spouse has an attorney.

It may also be advisable to hire an attorney if you encounter a judge with a hostile attitude or if your spouse gets a lawyer who wants to fight. There are no court-appointed lawyers in divorce cases, so if you want an attorney, you will have to hire one.

Consider hiring an attorney whenever you reach a point where you no longer feel comfortable representing yourself. This point is different for each person, so there is no way to be more definite.

Rather than asking if you *need* a lawyer, a more appropriate question to ask yourself is if you *want* a lawyer. The next section discusses some of the pros and cons of hiring a lawyer, and some of the things you may want to consider in making this decision.

WANTING A LAWYER

One of the first questions you will want to consider is *How much will an attorney cost?* Attorneys come in all price ranges. For a very rough estimate, you can expect an attorney to charge anywhere from $500 to $1,000 for an uncontested divorce, and from $1,500 and up for a contested divorce. Lawyers usually charge an hourly rate for contested divorces, ranging from about $75 to $300 per hour. Most new (and therefore, less expensive) attorneys would be quite capable of handling a simple divorce, but if your situation became more complicated, you may prefer a more experienced lawyer.

Advantages to Hiring a Lawyer

Some advantages to hiring a lawyer include the following.

Judges may take you more seriously if you have an attorney represent you. Most judges prefer both parties to have attorneys. They feel this helps the case move in a more orderly fashion, because both sides will know the procedures and relevant issues. People representing themselves often waste a lot of time on matters that have absolutely no bearing on the outcome of the case.

A lawyer will serve as a buffer between you and your spouse. This can lead to a quicker passage through the system by reducing the chance for emotions to take control and confuse the issues.

Attorneys prefer to deal with other attorneys for the same reasons as judges. If you become familiar with this book, however, and conduct yourself in a calm and proper manner, you should have no trouble. (Proper courtroom manners are discussed in Chapter 5.)

You can let your lawyer worry about all of the details. By having an attorney, you only need to be generally familiar with the contents of this book, as it will be your attorney's job to file the proper papers in the correct form and to deal with the court clerk, the judge, the process server, your spouse, and your spouse's attorney.

Lawyers provide professional assistance with problems. In the event your case is complicated or suddenly becomes complicated, it is an advantage to have an attorney who is familiar with your case. It can also be comforting to have a lawyer to turn to for advice and to get your questions answered.

Advantages to Representing Yourself

Some advantages to representing yourself include the following.

Sometimes judges feel more sympathetic toward a person not represented by an attorney. This sometimes results in the unrepresented person being allowed a certain amount of leeway with the rules of procedure.

The procedure may be faster. Two of the most frequent complaints about lawyers received by the bar association involve delays in completing the case and failure to return phone calls. Most lawyers have a heavy caseload that sometimes results in cases being neglected for various periods of time. If you are following the progress of your own case, you will be able to push it along the system diligently.

Selecting an attorney is not easy. As the next section shows, it is hard to know whether you are selecting the right attorney.

Middle Ground

You may want to look for an attorney who will be willing to accept an hourly fee to answer your questions and give you help as you need it. This way, you will save some legal costs, but still get professional assistance.

SELECTING A LAWYER

Selecting a lawyer is a two-step process. First, you need to decide which attorney to make an appointment with. Then, you need to decide if you want to hire that attorney. There are several ways to go about finding a lawyer.

Ask a Friend   The most common—and frequently the best—way to find a lawyer is to ask someone you know to recommend one to you. This is especially helpful if the lawyer represented your friend in a divorce or other family law matter.

Lawyer Referral Service   You can find a referral service by looking in the phone directory under "Attorney Referral Services" or "Attorneys." This service, usually operated by a bar association, is designed to match a client with an attorney handling cases in the area of law the client needs. The referral service does not guarantee the quality of work, or the level of experience or ability, of the attorney. Finding a lawyer this way will at least connect you with one who is interested in divorce and family law matters, and probably has some experience in this area.

Yellow Pages   Check under the heading for "Attorneys" in the Yellow Pages. Many of the lawyers and law firms will place display ads there indicating their areas of practice and educational backgrounds. Look for firms or lawyers that indicate they practice in areas such as divorce, family law, or domestic relations.

Ask Another Lawyer   If you have used the services of an attorney in the past for some other matter, such as to prepare a will or a real estate closing, you may want to call and ask if he or she could refer you to an attorney in the area of family law.

EVALUATING A LAWYER

From your search, you should select three to five lawyers worthy of further consideration. Your first step will be to call each attorney's office, explain that you are interested in seeking a divorce, and ask the following questions.

- Does the attorney (or firm) handle this type of matter?

- How much can you expect it to cost? (Do not expect to get much of an answer.)

- How soon can you get an appointment?

If you like the answers you get, ask if you can speak to the attorney. Some offices will permit this, but others will require you to make an appointment. Make the appointment if that is required. Once you begin contact with the attorney (either on the phone or at the appointment), ask the following questions.

- ✪ How long has the attorney been in practice?

- ✪ How long has the attorney been in practice in Washington?

- ✪ What percentage of the attorney's cases involve divorce cases or other family law matters? (Do not expect an exact answer, but you should look for an attorney whose rough estimate is at least 20%.)

- ✪ How long will it take? (Do not expect an exact answer, but the attorney should be able to give you an average range and discuss the factors that may make a difference.)

If you get acceptable answers to these questions, it is time to ask yourself the following questions about the lawyer.

- ✪ Do you feel comfortable talking to the lawyer?

- ✪ Is the lawyer friendly toward you?

- ✪ Does the lawyer seem confident in him- or herself?

- ✪ Does the lawyer seem to be straightforward and able to explain things so that you understand?

If you get satisfactory answers to all of these questions, you probably have a lawyer that you will be able to work with easily. Most clients are happiest with an attorney who makes them feel comfortable.

WORKING WITH A LAWYER

In general, you will work best with your attorney if you keep an open, honest, and friendly attitude. You should also consider the following suggestions.

Ask Questions

If you want to know something or if you do not understand something, ask your attorney. If you do not understand the answer, tell your attorney, and ask him or her to explain it again. There are many points of law that even many lawyers do not fully understand, so you should not be embarrassed to ask questions. Many people who say they had a bad experience with a lawyer either did not ask enough questions or had a lawyer who would not take the time to explain things to them. If your lawyer is not taking the time to explain what he or she is doing, it may be time to look for a new lawyer.

Give Complete Information

It is important to give your lawyer complete information. Anything you tell your attorney is confidential. An attorney can lose his or her license to practice if he or she reveals information without your permission, so do not hold back. Tell your lawyer everything, even if it does not seem important to you. There are many things that seem unimportant to a nonattorney but can actually change the outcome of a case.

Also, do not hold something back because you are afraid it will hurt your case. It will definitely hurt your case if your lawyer does not find out about it until he or she hears it in court from your spouse's attorney. If he or she knows in advance, your attorney can plan to eliminate or reduce damage to your case.

Accept Reality

Listen to what your lawyer tells you about the law and the system. It will not do you any good to argue because the law or the system does not work the way you think it should. For example, if your lawyer tells you that the judge cannot hear your case for two weeks, do not try demanding that he or she set a hearing tomorrow. By refusing to accept reality, you are only setting yourself up for disappointment. It is not your attorney's fault that the system is not perfect or that the law does not say what you would like it to say.

Be Patient

You will be much happier if you can be patient with the system (which is often slow), and with your attorney. Do not expect your lawyer to return your phone call within an hour. He or she may not even be able to return it the same day. Most lawyers are very busy and often overworked.

Talk to the Secretary

Your lawyer's secretary can be a valuable source of information, so be friendly and get to know him or her. Often, the secretary will be able to answer your questions (and you will not get a bill for this time).

Let Your Attorney Deal with Your Spouse

It is your lawyer's job to communicate with your spouse or with your spouse's lawyer. One of the biggest advantages to hiring a lawyer is that you do not have to deal with your spouse. Let your attorney do this job. Many clients lose or damage their cases when they independently decide to say or do something.

Be on Time

You should always be on time, both to appointments with your lawyer and to court hearings.

Keep Your Case Moving

Many lawyers operate on the old principle of *the squeaking wheel gets the oil*. Work on a case tends to get put off until a deadline is near, an emergency develops, or the client calls. Your task is to become a squeaking wheel that does not squeak so much as to become annoying to the attorney and his or her staff. Whenever you talk to your lawyer, ask the following questions.

   ✪   What is the next step?

   ✪   When do you expect it to be done?

   ✪   When should I talk to you next?

If you do not hear from the lawyer when you expect to, call him or her the following day and ask how the case is going.

Save Money

Of course, you do not want to spend unnecessary money for an attorney. Here are a few things you can do to avoid excess legal fees.

   ✪   Do not make unnecessary phone calls to your lawyer.

   ✪   Give information to the secretary whenever possible.

✪ Direct your question to the secretary first. He or she will refer your question to the attorney if necessary.

✪ Plan your phone calls so you can get to the point and take less of your attorney's time.

✪ Do some of the legwork yourself. For example, pick up and deliver papers yourself. Ask your attorney what you can do to assist with your case.

✪ Be prepared for appointments. Have all related papers with you, plan your visit to get to the point, and make an outline of what you want to discuss and what questions you want to ask.

Pay Your Attorney's Bill When It is Due

No client gets prompt attention like a client who pays his or her lawyer on time. However, you are entitled to an itemized bill that shows what the attorney did and how much time it took. Many attorneys will have you sign an agreement that states how you will be charged, what is included in the hourly fee, and what is extra. Review your bill carefully.

There are numerous stories of people paying an attorney $500 or $1,000 in advance, only to have the attorney make a few phone calls to the spouse's lawyer, then ask for more money. If your attorney asks for $500 or $1,000 in advance, be sure that you and the lawyer agree on what is to be done for this fee. For $500, you should at least expect to have a petition prepared, filed with the court, and served to your spouse (although the filing and service fees will probably be extra).

Firing Your Lawyer

If you find that you can no longer work with your lawyer or do not trust your lawyer, it is time to either go it alone or get a new attorney. You will need to send your lawyer a letter stating that you no longer desire his or her services and are discharging him or her from your case.

Also state that you will be coming by his or her office the following day to pick up your file. The attorney does not have to give you his or her own notes or other work in progress, but he or she must give you the essential contents of your file (such as copies of papers already filed or prepared and billed for, and any documents you provided). If

he or she refuses to give you your file for any reason, contact the
Washington State Bar Association about filing a complaint or *grievance* against the lawyer, at:

Washington State Bar Association
2101 Fourth Avenue
Suite 400
Seattle, WA 98121-2330
206-443-9722
800-945-9722
Fax: 206-727-8319
www.wsba.org

NOTE: *You will need to settle any remaining fees or charges.*

chapter 4

Evaluating Your Situation

Before actually starting the divorce procedures, you need to take a few moments to do some preliminary work. This includes preparing yourself for your spouse's reaction and gathering information that will be needed in court. Matters concerning your finances and your children should be thought through at the onset, before the judicial process takes control.

YOUR SPOUSE

First, evaluate your situation with respect to your spouse. Have you both already agreed to get a divorce? If not, what kind of reaction do you expect from him or her? The expected reaction can determine how you proceed. If he or she reacts in a rational manner, you can probably use the consent or uncontested procedure discussed in later chapters. If you expect an extremely emotional and possibly violent reaction, you will need to take steps to protect yourself, your children, and your property. (See Chapter 12 for more information about how to handle these situations.) In this case, expect to use the contested procedure.

Unless you and your spouse have already decided together to get a divorce, you may not want your spouse to know you are thinking about filing for divorce. This is a defense tactic, although it may not seem that way at first. If your spouse thinks you are planning a divorce, he or she may do things to prevent you from getting a fair result. These things include withdrawing money from bank accounts, hiding information about income, and hiding assets. Do not let on what you are planning until you have collected all the information you will need and are about to file with the court, or until you are prepared to protect yourself from violence, if necessary.

– Caution –

Tactics such as withdrawing money from bank accounts and hiding assets are dangerous. If you try any of these things, you risk looking like the bad guy before the judge. This can result in anything from having disputed matters resolved in your spouse's favor to being ordered to produce the assets (or be jailed for contempt of court).

If you suspect your spouse may hide assets, try to keep evidence of them (such as photographs, sales receipts, or bank statements) to present to the judge. Then your spouse will be the bad guy. However, once your spouse has taken assets and hidden them, or sold them and spent the money, even a contempt order may not get the money or assets back. If you determine that you need to get the assets in order to keep your spouse from hiding or disposing of them, be sure you keep them in a safe place and disclose them on any financial statements you may be required to submit to the judge. Do not dispose of the property. If your spouse claims you took them, you can explain to the judge why you were afraid that your spouse would dispose of them and that you merely got them out of his or her reach.

GATHERING INFORMATION

It is very important that you collect any financial information you can get, including originals or copies of the following.

- ✪ Your most recent income tax return (and your spouse's, if you filed separately).

- ✪ The most recent W-2 tax forms for yourself and your spouse.

✪   Any other income reporting papers (such as interest, stock dividends, etc.).

✪   Your spouse's most recent paystub, hopefully showing year-to-date earnings. (Otherwise try to get copies of all paystubs since the beginning of the year).

✪   Deeds to all real estate and titles to cars, boats, or other vehicles.

✪   Your and your spouse's wills.

✪   Life insurance policies.

✪   Stocks, bonds, or other investment papers.

✪   Pension or retirement fund papers and statements.

✪   Health insurance cards and papers.

✪   Bank account or credit union statements.

✪   Your spouse's Social Security number and driver's license number.

✪   Names, addresses, and phone numbers of your spouse's employer, close friends, and family members.

✪   Credit card statements, mortgage documents, and other credit and debt papers.

✪   A list of vehicles, furniture, appliances, tools, etc., owned by you and your spouse. (See the next section for forms and a detailed discussion of what to include).

✪   Copies of bills or receipts for recurring, regular expenses, such as rent, electric, gas, or other utilities, car insurance, etc.

✪   Copies of bills, receipts, insurance forms, or medical records for any unusual medical expenses (including for recurring or

continuous medical conditions) for yourself, your spouse, or
your children.

✪   Any other papers showing what you and your spouse earn,
own, or owe.

Make copies of as many of these papers as possible, and keep them in
a safe and private place (where your spouse will not be able to get
them). Try to make copies of new papers as they come in, especially
as you get close to filing court papers and to a court hearing.

PROPERTY AND DEBTS

This section is designed to help you get a rough idea of where things
stand regarding the division of your property and to prepare you for
completing the court papers you will need to file. The following
sections deal with your debts, child support, **PARENTING PLAN**, and
maintenance. If you are still not sure whether you want a divorce,
these sections may help you to decide.

Property   Washington law divides property in a divorce according to the principle of *equitable distribution*. Basically, this means a just and
equitable distribution under all of the circumstances. The judge has a
great amount of discretion in dividing property.

According to statute, when dividing property and liabilities, the court
shall consider all relevant factors (except marital misconduct), including but not limited to:

✪   the nature and extent of the community property;

✪   the nature and extent of the separate property;

✪   the duration of the marriage; and,

✪   the economic circumstances of each spouse at the time the
division of property is to become effective, including the desir-
ability of awarding the family home or the right to live therein
for reasonable periods to a spouse with whom the children
reside the majority of the time.

Generally, an inheritance or a gift is considered the separate property of the spouse who inherited or received it. The same holds true for property owned by one spouse prior to the marriage—it remains the separate property of that spouse. Also, a court award for pain and suffering in a personal injury lawsuit is considered separate property.

However, all property, whether community or separate property, is before the court for distribution. In certain very limited circumstances, the court can award the separate property of one spouse to the other.

This section basically assists you in completing a **PROPERTY INVENTORY**. (see worksheet 1, p.156.) This worksheet is a list of all of your property and key information about that property. This will help you organize your case. You will notice that it is divided into nine columns, designated as follows.

- ❖ Column (1): Check the box in this column if you believe that that piece of property should be considered *separate* property. This might be property that you or your spouse acquired before you were married, was given to you or your spouse separately, or was inherited by you or your spouse separately.

- ❖ Column (2): Describe the property. A discussion regarding what information should go in this column is on page 36.

- ❖ Column (3): Write the serial number, account number, or other number that will help clearly identify that piece of property.

- ❖ Column (4): Write the current market value of the property.

- ❖ Column (5): Write how much money is owed on the property, if any.

- ❖ Column (6): Subtract the "Balance Owed" (Column 5) from the "Value" (Column 4). This will show how much the property is worth to you (your *equity*).

◈ Column (7): Indicate the current legal owner of the property. (H) designates the husband, (W) the wife, and (J) for jointly owned property (in both of your names).

◈ Column (8): In this column, check those pieces of property you expect the husband will keep.

◈ Column (9): In this column, check the property you expect the wife will keep.

Use columns (1) through (9) to list your property, including the following.

Cash. List the name of the bank, credit union, etc., as well as the account number for each account. This includes savings accounts, checking accounts, and certificates of deposit (CDs). The balance of each account should be listed in the columns entitled "Value" and "Equity." (Leave the "Balance Owed" column blank.) Make copies of the most recent bank statements for each account.

Stocks and bonds. All stocks, bonds, or other paper investments should be listed. Write down the number of shares and the name of the company or other organization that issued them. Also, copy any notation such as *common* or *preferred* stock or shares. This information can be obtained from the stock certificate itself or from a statement from the stock broker. Make a copy of the certificate or the statement.

Real estate. List each piece of property you and your spouse own. The description might include a street address for the property, a subdivision name and lot number, or anything that lets you know what piece of property you are describing. There probably will not be an ID number, although you might use the county's tax number.

Real estate (or any other property) may be in both of your names (joint), in your spouse's name alone, or in your name alone. The only way to know for sure is to look at the deed to the property. (If you cannot find a copy of the deed, try to find mortgage papers or payment coupons, homeowners' insurance papers, or a property tax assessment notice.) On the deed, the owners of property are usually referred to as the *grantees*.

In assigning a value to the property, consider the market value, which is the amount for which you could probably sell the property. This might be what similar houses in your neighborhood have sold for recently. You might also consider how much you paid for the property or for how much the property is insured. *Do not* use the tax assessment value, as this is usually considerably lower than the market value.

Vehicles. This category includes cars, trucks, motor homes, recreational vehicles (RVs), motorcycles, boats, trailers, airplanes, and any other means of transportation for which the state requires a title and registration. Your description should include the following information (which can usually be found on the title or on the vehicle itself):

   ✪   year it was made;

   ✪   make (name of the manufacturer, such as *Ford*, *Honda*, *Chris Craft*, etc.);

   ✪   model; and,

   ✪   serial number/vehicle identification number (VIN).

Make a copy of the title or registration. Regarding a value, you can go to the public library and ask to look at the *blue book* for cars, trucks, or whatever it is you are trying to find. A *blue book* (which may actually be yellow, black, or any other color) gives the average values for used vehicles. Your librarian can help you find what you need. You can also go online and type "blue book" into any search engine to find websites for valuing your vehicle.

Another source is to look in the classified advertising section of a newspaper to see what the prices are for similar vehicles. You might also try calling a dealer to see if it can give you a rough idea of the value. Be sure you take the condition of the vehicle into consideration.

Furniture. List all furniture as specifically as possible. Include the type of piece (such as sofa, coffee table, etc.), the color, and if you know it, the manufacturer, line name, or style. Furniture usually will not have a serial number, although if you find one, be sure to write it on the list. Unless you just know what it is worth, estimate a value.

Appliances, electronic equipment, yard machines, etc. This category includes things such as refrigerators, lawn mowers, and power tools. Again, simply estimate a value (unless you are familiar enough with them to simply know what they are worth). There are too many different makes, models, accessories, and age factors to be able to figure out a value otherwise. These items will probably have a make, model, and serial number on them. You may have to look on the back, bottom, or other hidden place for the serial number, but try to find it.

Jewelry and other valuables. You can plan on keeping your own personal watches, rings, etc. However, if you own an expensive piece you should include it in your list, along with an estimated value. You do not need to list inexpensive or costume jewelry. Be sure to include silverware, original art, gold, coin collections, etc. Again, be as detailed and specific as possible.

Life insurance with cash surrender value. This is any life insurance policy that you can cash in or borrow against, and therefore has value. If you cannot find a cash surrender value in the papers you have, you can call the insurance company and ask.

Other big ticket items. This is simply a general reference to anything of significant value that does not fit in one of the categories already discussed. Examples might be a portable spa, an above-ground swimming pool, golf clubs, guns, pool tables, camping or fishing equipment, farm animals, or machinery.

Pensions and military benefits. The division of pensions, military, and retirement benefits can be a complicated matter. Whenever these types of benefits are involved, you will need to consult an attorney or a CPA to determine the value of the benefits and how they should be divided. (see Chapter 12.)

What not to list. You will not need to list your clothing and other personal effects. Pots, pans, dishes, and cooking utensils ordinarily do not need to be listed, unless they have an unusually high value.

Division of property. Once you have completed your list, go back through it and try to determine who should end up with each item.

The ideal situation is for both you and your spouse to go through the list together and divide things fairly. If this is not possible, you will need to offer a reasonable settlement to the judge. Consider each item and make a checkmark in either column (8) or (9) to designate whether that item should go to the husband or wife.

You may make the following assumptions.

- ✪ Your separate property will go to you.

- ✪ Your spouse's separate property will go to your spouse.

- ✪ You should get the items that only you use.

- ✪ Your spouse should get the items that only he or she uses.

- ✪ The remaining items should be divided, evening out the total value of all the marital property and taking into consideration who would really want each item.

To somewhat equally divide your marital property, you first need to know the total value of your property. (Do not count the value of the separate property items.) Add the remaining amounts in the "Equity" column of worksheet 1, which will give you an approximate value of all marital property.

Debts   This section relates to the **DEBT INVENTORY**, which will list your debts. (see worksheet 2, p.163.) Although there are cases in which, for example, the wife gets a car but the husband is ordered to make the payments, generally whoever gets the property also gets the debt owed on that property. This seems to be a fair arrangement in most cases. On worksheet 2, you will list each debt owed by you or your spouse. As with separate property, there is also separate debt. This is any debt incurred before you were married that is yours alone. Worksheet 2 contains a column for *S* debts, which should be checked for each separate debt. Generally, you will be responsible for your separate debts, and your spouse will be responsible for his or hers.

To complete the **DEBT INVENTORY** (worksheet 2), list each debt as follows.

⬦ Column (1): Check if this is a separate debt. (Separate debts would be those related to separate property, or those that for any other reason you believe should not be considered as your joint responsibility. Keep in mind that you may need to convince the judge why these debts should be considered separate.)

⬦ Column (2): Write in the name and address of the creditor (the bank, company, or person to which the debt is owed).

⬦ Column (3): Write in the account, loan, or mortgage number.

⬦ Column (4): Write in any notes to help identify the purpose of the loan (such as Christmas gifts, vacation, etc.).

⬦ Column (5): Write in the amount of the monthly payment.

⬦ Column (6): Write in the balance still owed on the loan.

⬦ Column (7): Write in the approximate date when the loan was made.

⬦ Column (8): Note whether the account is in the husband's name (H), the wife's name (W), or jointly in both names (J).

⬦ Columns (9) and (10): These columns note who will be responsible for the debt after the divorce. As with your property, each of you will keep your separate debts and the remainder should be divided, taking into consideration who will keep the property the loan was for and equally dividing the debt. (See Chapter 8 for information on dividing debts in contested cases.)

PARENTING PLANS

As a general rule, Washington does not use the terms "custody" or "visitation" when it comes to children. Instead, the parent with whom the child resides the majority of the time is called the *primary residential parent*. Instead of *visits*, the other parent has *residential time*.

However, since most people still think in terms of custody and visitation, this book will use these terms interchangeably.

The arrangements between the parents as to who is the primary residential parent and who has residential time are embodied in the **PARENTING PLAN**. (see form 6, p.203.) The **PARENTING PLAN** also designates arrangements such as for transportation.

As with everything else in divorce, ideally, both parties can agree on a **PARENTING PLAN** for the children. Generally, the judge will accept any agreement you reach, provided that your agreement is specific enough to be enforced and it does not appear that it will cause harm to your children.

If you and your spouse cannot agree on how these matters will be handled, you will be leaving this important decision to a complete stranger—the judge. The judge cannot possibly know your child as well as you and your spouse do, so try to work this out yourselves.

Factors to Consider   If a judge has to decide your **PARENTING PLAN** for you, according to statute he or she will consider the following factors with the first factor being given the greatest weight.

- ✪ The relative strength, nature, and stability of the child's relationship with each parent, including whether one parent has taken greater responsibility for performing functions relating to the daily needs of the child.

- ✪ The agreements of the parties, provided they were entered into knowingly and voluntarily.

- ✪ Each parent's past and potential for future performance of parenting functions.

- ✪ The emotional needs and developmental level of the child.

- ✪ The child's relationship with siblings and with other significant adults, as well as the child's involvement with his or her physical surroundings, school, or other significant activities.

✪ The wishes of the parents and the wishes of a child who is sufficiently mature to express reasoned and independent preferences as to his or her residential schedule.

> **NOTE:** *A word of warning as to this factor—there is no age in Washington in which a child has an absolute right to pick which parent he or she resides with, and most courts deeply frown on having a child testify.*

✪ Each parent's employment schedule.

Restrictions   In addition, under certain circumstances, a court may impose restrictions on a parent's residential time with the children. In general, those circumstances involve the following:

✪ willful abandonment, neglect, or substantial nonperformance of parenting functions;

✪ domestic violence against a spouse;

✪ physical, sexual, or emotional abuse of a child;

✪ a long-term emotional or physical impairment, or impairment from alcohol or substance abuse that interferes with parenting;

✪ the absence or substantial impairment of emotional ties between a parent and child; or,

✪ abusive use of conflict that creates the danger of serious damage to the child's psychological development.

50/50 Plans   Under certain circumstances, Washington law authorizes **PARENTING PLANS** in which the children frequently alternate between households. This is usually an arrangement in which the children reside with both parents for an equal amount of time. The factors the court considers are as follows:

✪ there are no statutory bases for the court to limit a parent's residential time under the **PARENTING PLAN** and

✪   the parties have knowingly and voluntarily entered into such a **Parenting Plan**; or

✪   the parties have a history of cooperation and shared parenting and such a **Parenting Plan** is geographically feasible and

✪   the provisions are in the best interests of the child.

Again, you and your spouse can always agree to this type of **Parenting Plan**. However, in a contested case, it is usually quite difficult to convince a judge that a 50/50 **Parenting Plan** should be implemented.

Bear in mind that once a final **Parenting Plan** is filed with the court, it is a permanent plan. 50/50 **Parenting Plans** often seem like a *fair* way to allocate residential time with the children but can ultimately prove unworkable. If one parent later wants to change the **Parenting Plan** and the other does not, it is a difficult process to get the court to grant a change.

It is difficult to predict the outcome of a **Parenting Plan** battle. There are too many factors and individual circumstances to make such a guess. Do not make allegations about your spouse and his or her parenting skills unless you can prove them. Judges are not impressed with unfounded allegations, and they can do more harm than good. In highly contested cases, the court may appoint a *guardian ad litem* (GAL) to conduct a parenting investigation and make recommendations to the court.

Allowing Your Child to Decide   There is no age in Washington in which a child has the right to decide with which parent he or she would like to live the majority of the time. Most courts will not want to hear direct testimony from your child on this or any other issue. It is generally accepted that involving children in the divorce process in this way is psychologically harmful to them.

CHILD SUPPORT

The following information and the Washington State Child Support Schedule (see Appendix A, p.137 and form 5, p.191) are used to calculate the standard amount of basic child support. Absent specific circumstances, the basic child support calculations must be used.

Additional information on calculating child support, and frequently asked questions about the calculation and collection of child support, can be found at **www.courts.wa.gov**. From the index on the left side of the website, select "Court Forms." On the "Court Forms" page, click on "Washington LawHelp." Then, click on "Family Law."

If you and your spouse reach an agreement on child support that *deviates* (is lower than) from the amount under the child support formula, the judge may only go along with your agreement if he or she determines that using the formula would be unjust or inappropriate. He or she must state the reasons on the record. The *Revised Code of Washington Annotated* lists factors for the judge to consider in deviating from the formula. While there are a host of reasons set forth in RCWA 26.17.075 that may form a basis for the court to deviate from the standard calculation, the most common reasons are as follows.

- ✪ Per the **PARENTING PLAN**, the children spend a significant amount of time with the parent obligated to pay child support. There is no set definition of *significant amount of time*, but it is generally thought to be at least ninety-one overnights per year.

- ✪ The spouse obligated to pay child support must also pay support for children from another relationship.

- ✪ The special medical, educational, or psychological needs of a child.

The judge may also *extrapolate* (set child support at an amount higher than the child support formula) if one parent possesses extreme wealth and the basic child support amount under the child support formula is not enough to support the lifestyle to which the child has become accustomed. Extrapolating support is not, however, a very common occurrence. If you believe that you may be a candidate for extrapolated child support, you should consult an attorney so that your best case for extrapolated support can be made.

How Child Support is Determined

Child support is based on the number of children for whom support is being determined and the combined net monthly incomes of the parents. Washington uses a formula to calculate child support based on these factors. The current formula is found in Appendix A to this book. This formula has not been revised in quite some time. You will see that the formula *caps* at a combined net monthly income of $7,000. This means that the basic amount of child support is the same for all parents whose combined incomes exceed $7,000. Only the parents' proportionate shares of that basic support will change (see the later section on "Calculating Child Support").

In filling out the worksheets, be sure to convert everything to monthly amounts. The following steps are used in determining the proper amount of support to be paid by the noncustodial parent.

1.   You and your spouse each provide proof of your gross monthly income.

2.   Taxes and other deductions are allowed to determine each of your net incomes.

3.   Your net incomes and the number of children you have are used to establish basic support. (This is done by using a table or chart.)

4.   The net income of the parent without custody is divided by the combined income. (This gives that parent's percentage of the combined income.)

5.   That percentage is multiplied by the basic support figure to determine the paying parent's basic child support transfer payment (the monthly amount the paying, or *obligor*, parent pays to the receiving, or *obligee*, parent).

Income Determination   The first thing you will need to do is determine your gross income. This is basically your income before any deductions for taxes, Social Security, etc. The following sources are considered part of gross income:

❂   salaries or wages;

❂   commissions;

❂   deferred compensation;

- overtime;

- contract-related benefits;

- income from second jobs;

- dividends;

- interest;

- trust income;

- severance pay;

- annuities;

- sick pay or disability benefits;

- capital gains;

- pension retirement benefits;

- workers' compensation;

- unemployment benefits;

- spousal maintenance actually received;

- bonuses (to the extent they are recurring);

- Social Security benefits; and,

- disability insurance benefits.

The following are not considered income for the purposes of child support:

- income of a new spouse or income of other adults in the household;

- child support received from other relationships;

✪   gifts and prizes;

✪   aid to families with dependent children;

✪   supplemental security income;

✪   general assistance; or,

✪   food stamps.

If you voluntarily reduce your income or quit your job, the judge can refuse to recognize the reduction or loss of income. This is true even if you are not employed or employed part-time in order to stay home and care for your child. If this question comes up, the judge will decide whether you need to stay home, so be ready to explain your reasons. If the court refuses to recognize your reduction in income, it will impose an amount for you called *imputed income*. If the court decides to impute income, it will usually do so according to the following chart.

MALE	AGE	FEMALE
$1,363	15-24	$1,222
$2,154	25-34	$1,807
$2,610	35-44	$1,957
$2,846	45-54	$2,051
$2,880	55-64	$1,904
$2,828	65 +	$1,940

Fill in the gross amount of your income and your spouse's income at lines 1a through 1e and put the total at line 1f of the child support worksheets.

Net income. Net income is determined by subtracting certain deductions from your gross income. The following deductions are allowed:

✪   federal and state income taxes;

✪   Social Security and Medicare deductions;

- ✪ mandatory pension plan payments or voluntarily pension plan payments up to $2,000 per year ($167 per month) so long as those pension plan payments were made monthly for the prior two years;

- ✪ mandatory union or professional dues; and,

- ✪ normal business expenses and self-employment taxes for self-employed persons.

Fill in the allowable deductions for yourself and your spouse at lines 2a through 2g, then write in the totals on line 2h. Now, subtract the total deductions (line 2h) from the gross income (line 1f), and write the answers on line 3.

Combined income. Combined income is simply your monthly adjusted net income added to your spouse's monthly adjusted net income. Add your amount from line 3 to your spouse's amount from line 3, and write the total on line 4. This is your combined income.

Example:
Your net income is $2,000 per month. Your spouse's net income is $3,000 per month. Your combined income would be $5,000 ($2,000 + $3,000).

Next, divide your net income from line 3 by the combined income from line 4. Fill in the answer on line 6. This is your percentage of the combined income. Then, divide your spouse's net income from line 3 by the combined income from line 4. Fill in the answer on line 6. This is your spouse's percentage of the combined income.

Example:
You and your spouse have a combined income of $5,000 per month. To get your share, divide your net income by the combined income ($2,000 divided by $5,000). The answer is .4, or 40%. The figure .40 would go on line 6. Next divide your spouse's net income by the combined income ($3,00 divided by $5,000). The answer is .6, or 60%. The figure .60 would go on line 6.

Calculating Child Support

Calculating child support begins by turning to page 137, which is part of the CHILD SUPPORT GUIDELINES in Appendix A of this book. You will see the heading "Washington State Child Support Schedule." Using the table in that section, you can determine the child support for your situation. Child support worksheets are also contained in that section.

Example:

You and your spouse have two children. One child is age 7 and the other child is age 13. Read down the left column until you come to your combined monthly net income amount. In this continuing example, you would use $5,000 per month (or the lower figure if your combined income falls between brackets). Reading across the table to the column titled "Two Children Family," you will see that the basic child support figure is $574 per month for the child age 7, and $708 per month for the child age 13. Adding these two figures creates a basic child support figure of $1,282 (line 5 of the worksheet).

Your share of this support obligation would be 40%, or $512.80 ($1,282 x .4). Your spouse's share would be 60%, or $769.20 per month. Therefore, if your two children primarily reside with you, your spouse would pay you $769.20 per month (line 7 of the worksheet). If your two children primarily reside with your spouse, you would pay $512.80 per month (line 7 of the worksheet).

Using the same income example, if you had two children who were both ages 0–11, the basic child support obligation would be $1,148 per month ($574 x 2). Your share of this support obligation would be 40%, or $459.20 per month. Your spouse's share would be 60%, or $688.80 per month.

If you had two children who were both ages 12–18, the basic support obligation would be $1,416 ($708 x 2). Your share would be 40%, or $566.40 per month; your spouse's share would be 60%, or $849.60 per month.

This works fine, except when one of the bases for deviation set forth on page 44 exists. If this is the case, seek the assistance of an attorney to properly calculate child support.

The law also requires that each parent pay his or her share of health insurance premiums for the children only, extraordinary uninsured medical and dental expenses, day care, educational expenses, and long-distance travel expenses. Health insurance premiums are normally included in the child support worksheets at lines 8a and 14a. The remaining expenses listed can either be included in the worksheets, paid separately to the provider of the service, or reimbursed to the other parent. Many parents also agree to proportionately split the cost of their children's extracurricular activities, although this is not required by law.

A word about health insurance and payment of extraordinary medical expenses. A parent is only required to provide health insurance for the children if it is available through the parent's employment or union affiliation and costs no more than 25% of his or her line 7 share of basic child support. With regard to extraordinary medical expenses, at line 8e of the worksheets, there will be a figure that is 5% of the line 5 basic support obligation. Each month, the parent receiving support is entirely responsible for extraordinary medical expenses up to that line 8e amount. All expenses beyond that threshold are then split proportionately between the parents.

SPOUSAL SUPPORT

Spousal support or *maintenance* (Washington's term for *alimony*) may be granted to either the husband or the wife. Unlike child support, there are no hard and fast rules or formulas that control the amount and duration of spousal maintenance in Washington. An award of maintenance must only be fair and equitable given the circumstances of the case. RCW 26.09.090 provides the following general factors to be considered:

❂ the time necessary for the spouse seeking maintenance to become employable either through on-the-job training or reeducation;

❂ the standard of living established during the marriage;

❂ the length of the marriage;

❂ the age, physical and emotional condition, and financial obligations of the spouse seeking maintenance;

❂ the ability of the spouse from whom maintenance is sought to meet his or her financial needs and financial obligations; and,

❂ the financial resources of the party seeking maintenance and the ability of that party to meet his or her financial needs. This includes looking at how the assets and liabilities are divided between the parties and whether child support is received.

As an alternative to maintenance, you may want to try to negotiate to receive a greater percentage of the property instead. This may be less of a hassle in the long run, but beware—it may change the tax consequences of your divorce. (See the section on "Taxes" in Chapter 12.)

WHICH PROCEDURE TO USE

There is technically only one divorce procedure in Washington. However, it is discussed here as if there were three types of divorce procedures. These are really divorces under different situations, with each situation calling for a different approach. These three situations are:

1.   consent divorce;

2.   uncontested divorce; and,

3.   contested divorce.

– Caution –

Before you can use any divorce procedure, you or your spouse must have lived in Washington for at least 180 days, and in the county where you file for at least ten days. (The one exception to this is if your spouse was born in, or is a citizen of, a foreign country, and you can convince the judge that your child is at risk of being taken out of the United States and kept in another country by your spouse.)

Chapter 6 of this book describes the consent divorce, Chapter 7 describes the uncontested divorce, and Chapter 8 describes the contested divorce. You should read this entire book once before you begin filling out any court forms.

Consent Divorce

A *consent* divorce is when you and your spouse agree on everything. To be eligible for the consent procedure, you and your spouse need to be in total agreement on the following matters:

- ✪ that you want a divorce;

- ✪ whether any maintenance will be paid, and if so, how much;

- ✪ how your property and debts will be divided;

- ✪ parenting arrangements for any children;

- ✪ how much child support will be paid by the obligor spouse; and,

- ✪ that you both are willing to sign an agreement about these matters, and any other papers required to get a divorce in the easiest and simplest manner.

If you are in agreement on all of these matters, you may use the procedure outlined in Chapter 6.

Uncontested Divorce

If you cannot qualify for the consent divorce procedure (because your spouse will not cooperate on one or more of the matters listed on this this page), you have to use the uncontested procedure or the contested procedure. The uncontested procedure is mainly designed for:

- ✪ when your spouse does not respond to your petition or

- ✪ when your spouse cannot be located.

To use the uncontested procedure, you will need to read both Chapter 6 and Chapter 7.

Contested Divorce

The contested procedure is necessary when you and your spouse are arguing over some matter and cannot resolve it. This may be the result of disagreement over the parenting of your children, the payment of child support or spousal maintenance, the division of your property, or any combination of these items. Chapter 8 of this book, dealing with the contested divorce, builds on the consent and uncontested procedure chapters. You first need to read Chapter 6 and Chapter 7 to get a basic understanding of the forms and procedures. Then, read Chapter 8 for additional instructions on handling the contested situation. Be sure to read through all three chapters before you start filling out any forms.

If your case becomes contested, it is also time to seriously consider getting a lawyer. If you do not think you can afford a lawyer, you may be able to require your spouse to pay for your lawyer. Find a lawyer who will give you a free or inexpensive initial consultation. He or she will explain your options regarding the lawyer's fees. (See Chapter 3 for more information about lawyers.)

General Procedures

This chapter includes general information that will be of use to you regardless of which divorce procedure you use. Some of this information will not be used until you have selected procedures and are preparing your forms. This is done to avoid unnecessarily repeating information. For example, in all cases, you will need to file forms with the court clerk and use certain forms to notify your spouse. Rather than repeat this information in the following chapter, you will simply be referred back to the appropriate section of this chapter.

AN INTRODUCTION TO LEGAL FORMS

Many of the forms in this book follow forms created by the Superior Court of Washington. An advantage to having such standard forms is that court clerks and judges will accept them. However, these official forms are changed frequently, with some forms being eliminated entirely. If you need additional forms or want to be sure you have the most recent forms, check with the clerk of the court in your county or visit **www.courts.wa.gov**.

The forms in Appendix C of this book are legally correct. However, you may encounter a clerk or judge who is very particular about how he or she wants the forms. If you have any problem with the forms being accepted, you can try one or more of the following.

✪ Ask the clerk or judge what is wrong with your form, then try to change it to suit the clerk or judge.

✪ Ask the clerk or judge if there is either a local form or another mandatory form available. If there is, find out where you can get it, and use it. The instructions in this book will still help you.

✪ Consult a lawyer.

You may tear the forms out of this book to file with the court. However, it is best to make photocopies of the forms and keep the originals blank to use in case you make mistakes. With all the forms also available on the CD-ROM, making changes and printing a clear, original form should be no problem. If you will be using the forms in the book instead of printing them from the CD-ROM, instructions in this book tell you to type in certain information. However, it may not be absolutely necessary to use a typewriter. Check with the clerk of the court or the county local rules to determine if typing is necessary.

Each form is referred to by both the title of the form and a form number. Be sure to check the form number because some of the forms have similar titles. The form number is found in the bottom left corner of the first page of each form. Also, a list of the forms, by both number and name, is found at the beginning of Appendix C.

Caption   You will notice that many of the forms in Appendix C of this book have similar headings. The top portion of these court forms will all be completed in the same manner. This portion of a court form is referred to as the *caption*. It contains three basic elements: the identity of the court by county, the names of the parties, and the case number.

To fill out the caption, do the following.

◈ Type in the name of the county in which the court is located.

◈ For the names of the parties, type your full name and your spouse's full name on the appropriate lines or boxes. Do not use nicknames or shortened versions of names. You should use the names as they appear on your marriage license, if possible.

◈   You will not be able to type in a case number until after you file your **PETITION FOR DISSOLUTION** with the court clerk. The clerk will assign a case number and will write it on your **PETITION FOR DISSOLUTION** and any other papers you file with it. You must type in the case number on all papers you file later. The format of the case number will vary from county to county. An example of a caption follows.

SUPERIOR COURT OF WASHINGTON
_____KING_____ COUNTY

RHETT BUTLER_____,
                    Plaintiff,

vs.   Case No._____05-3-12345-6_____

SCARLETT O'HARA BUTLER_____,
                    Defendant.

FILING WITH THE COURT CLERK

Once you have decided which forms you need and have them all prepared, it is time to file your case with the court clerk. The instructions for particular forms tell you how many copies you will need. You will usually need at least four—the original to leave with the clerk, a copy for yourself, a copy for your spouse, and it is probably a good idea to make an extra copy, just in case the clerk asks for more copies or you decide to hire an attorney later.

Filing is actually as simple as making a bank deposit, although the following information will help things go smoothly. First, call the court clerk's office. You can find the phone number under the county government section of your phone directory. Ask the clerk the following questions (along with any other questions that come to mind, such as where the clerk's office is located and what hours they are open, if you do not already know).

- ✪ How much is the filing fee for a divorce?

- ✪ Does the court have any special forms that need to be filed with the **PETITION FOR DISSOLUTION**? (If there are such special forms that do not appear in this book, you will need to go to the law library or clerk's office to get them.)

- ✪ How many copies of the **PETITION FOR DISSOLUTION** and other forms do you need to file with the clerk? (This will tell you if you need more than the recommended four copies.)

Next, take your **PETITION FOR DISSOLUTION** and any other forms you determine are necessary to the clerk's office. The clerk handles many different types of cases, so be sure to look for signs indicating to which office or window you should go. If it is too confusing, ask someone where to file a **PETITION FOR DISSOLUTION**.

Once you have found the right place, simply hand the papers to the clerk and say, "I would like to file this." The clerk will examine the papers, then do one of two things—accept it for filing (and either collect the filing fee or direct you to where to pay it), or tell you that something is not correct. If you are told something is wrong, ask the clerk to explain to you what is wrong and how to correct the problem.

Although clerks are not permitted to give legal advice, the minor problems they spot are items they can tell you how to correct. It is often possible to figure out how to correct the forms from their explanation.

Any papers you need to file after filing your **PETITION FOR DISSOLUTION** will be filed in the same manner, except you will not need to pay a filing fee.

NOTIFYING YOUR SPOUSE

If you are using the consent divorce procedure, you do not need to worry about the information in this section. In a consent divorce, your spouse will sign either an *Acceptance of Service* or a *Joinder* contained in the **PETITION FOR DISSOLUTION**, so it will be obvious that he or she knows about the divorce. (see form 2, p.163.) However, in all other cases, you are required to notify your spouse that you have filed for divorce. This gives your spouse a chance to respond to your **PETITION FOR DISSOLUTION**. (If you are unable to find your spouse, you will also need to read Chapter 10.)

Summons

The way to notify your spouse that you filed for a divorce is called *personal service*, which is when any adult person other than yourself personally delivers the papers to your spouse. There are also companies that will serve your spouse for a small fee. These companies are called *process servers*.

If you are having your spouse served, you will need to complete a **SUMMONS**. (form 1, p.161.) The **SUMMONS** should be filed with the court and served to your spouse at the same time as the **PETITION FOR DISSOLUTION**. Once service has been accomplished, the individual who serves your spouse will need to complete a **RETURN OF SERVICE** and file that document with the court. (See form 7, p.215.) One advantage of having a professional process server serve your spouse is that he or she will complete and file this form for you.

Proof of Mailing

Once your spouse has been served with the **SUMMONS** and **PETITION FOR DISSOLUTION**, you may simply mail him or her copies of any papers you file later (with the exception of certain temporary or restraining orders that are issued without the usual hearing and advance notice to your spouse). Different courts and judges will require different proof of mailing. Check with the clerk of the court in your county or the judge's bailiff to determine those requirements.

SETTING A COURT HEARING

In most larger counties, you can select your own hearing date subject to certain time constraints outlined by local rules. In other counties, you will need to contact the clerk of the court or the judge's bailiff.

Once you have set a date and time for the hearing, you will also need to know where the hearing will be. Ask the secretary for the location. You will need the street address of the courthouse, as well as the room number, floor, or other location within the building.

Notice of Hearing If you need to set a hearing date, you will need to notify your spouse of when the hearing will be. This is done by preparing a *Notice of Hearing* or *Note for Motion*. Different courts have different forms to set hearings. Check with the clerk of the court in your county to obtain the required local form.

COURTROOM MANNERS

There are certain rules of procedure that are used in a court. These are really rules of good conduct or manners, and are designed to keep things orderly. Many of the rules are written down, although some are unwritten customs that have developed over many years. They are not difficult and most of them make sense. Following these suggestions will make the judge respect your maturity and professional manner. It will also increase the likelihood that you will get the things you request.

Show Respect for the Judge To show respect for the judge, do not do anything to cause anger, such as arguing with him or her. Be polite and call the judge "Your Honor." Although many lawyers address judges as "Judge," this is not proper.

Many of the following rules also relate to showing respect for the court. This also means wearing appropriate clothing. Do not wear a hat, T-shirt, blue jeans, shorts, or revealing clothing.

When the Judge Talks, Listen When the judge talks, listen. Even if the judge interrupts you, stop talking immediately and listen. Never interrupt the judge when he or she is talking. If you have something to say, wait until the judge is finished, then ask, "Your Honor, may I respond?" This behavior exemplifies respect for the judge.

Only One Person can Talk at a Time Each person is allotted his or her own time to talk in court. The judge can only listen to one person at a time, so do not interrupt your spouse when it is his or her turn. As difficult as it may be, stop talking if your spouse interrupts you. (Let the judge tell your spouse to keep quiet and let you have your say.)

Talk to the Judge, not to Your Spouse

Many people get in front of a judge and argue with each other. They actually turn away from the judge, face each other, and argue as if they are in the room alone. This has several negative results. The judge cannot understand what either one is saying since they both start talking at once, they both look foolish for losing control, and the judge gets angry with both of them. Whenever you speak in a court-room, look only at the judge. Try to pretend that your spouse is not there. Remember, you are there to convince the judge that you should have certain things. You do not need to convince your spouse.

Talk Only When It is Your Turn

If you set the hearing, the usual procedure is for you to present your case first. When you are done speaking, your spouse will have a chance to talk. Let your spouse have his or her say. When he or she is finished, you will get another chance to respond to what has been said.

Stick to the Subject

Many people cannot resist the temptation to get off track and start telling the judge all the problems with their marriage over the past twenty years. This just wastes time and aggravates the judge. Stick to the subject and answer the judge's questions simply and to the point.

Keep Calm

Judges like things to go smoothly in their courtrooms. They do not like shouting, name-calling, crying, or other displays of emotion. Give your judge a pleasant surprise by keeping calm and focusing on the issues.

Show Respect for Your Spouse

Even if you do not respect your spouse, act like you do. Simply refer to your spouse as "Mr. Smith" or "Ms. Smith" (using his or her correct name, of course).

NEGOTIATING

It is beyond the scope of this book to present a comprehensive course in negotiation techniques. However, a few basic rules may help.

Ask for More Than You Want

Asking for more than you want always gives you some room to compromise and end up with close to what you really want. With property division, this means you will review your **Property Inventory** (worksheet 1) and decide what items you really want, would like to have, and do not care much about. Also, try to figure out what items your spouse really wants, would like to have, and does not care much about.

At the beginning, you will state your desired property. Your list will include:

- ✪ everything you really want;

- ✪ everything you would like to have;

- ✪ some of the things you do not care about; and,

- ✪ some of the things you think your spouse really wants or would like to have.

Once you find out what is on your spouse's list, you begin trading items. Generally, try to give your spouse things that he or she really wants and that you do not care about, in return for your spouse giving you the items you really care about and would like to have.

Parenting tends to be an issue that cannot be negotiated. It is often used as a threat by one of the parties in order to get something else, such as more of the property or lower child support. If the real issue is one of these other matters, do not be concerned by a threat of a custody fight. In these cases, the other party probably does not really want to be primary residential parent and will not fight for it. If the real issue is custody, you will not be able to negotiate for it and will have to let the judge decide anyway.

Child support is the one thing that usually cannot be negotiated. Absent certain specific circumstances, the court must set child support based on the calculations set forth in the child support worksheets.

Let Your Spouse Start the Bidding   For example, if you are negotiating the value of a piece of property, try to get your spouse to name the amount he or she thinks it should be first. If your spouse starts with a figure almost to what you had in mind, it will be much easier to get to your figure. If your spouse begins with a figure far from yours, you know how far in the other direction to begin your bid.

Give Your Spouse Time to Think and Worry

Your spouse is probably just as afraid as you are about the possibility of losing to the judge's decision, and would like to settle. Do not be afraid to state your final offer, then walk away. Give your spouse a day or two to think it over. He or she may call back and make a better offer. If not, you can always reconsider and make a different offer in a few days, but do not be too willing to do this, or your spouse may think you will give in even more.

Know Your Bottom Line

Before you begin negotiating, set a point that you will not go beyond. If you have decided that there are four items of property that you absolutely must have, and your spouse is only willing to agree to let you have three, it is time to end the bargaining session, go home, and let the court get involved.

By the time you have read this far, you should be aware of two things: 1) the judge will divide your property just about equally and 2) the judge *will* use the child support guidelines. This awareness should give you an idea of the outcome if the judge is asked to decide these issues, which should help you to set your bottom line.

Consent Divorce

The procedures described in this chapter may be used in the most simple cases. The following chapters build on this chapter, so be sure to read this chapter entirely—even if you need to use another procedure. In order to have a consent divorce, you must meet the following basic requirements.

- ✪ You or your spouse have resided in Washington for at least the past six months, and are residents of the county where the case will be filed.

- ✪ You and your spouse agree that you want a divorce, and are both willing to sign any papers and attend any court hearings necessary to obtain a divorce.

- ✪ You and your spouse agree as to how your property will be divided.

- ✪ You and your spouse agree on the subject of spousal maintenance (either that neither of you will pay maintenance or who will pay, how much, and for how long).

❉   If you have a child, you and your spouse agree on a **PARENTING PLAN** and how much child support will be paid.

If you do not meet all of these conditions, you do not have a consent divorce. You should still read this chapter, however, as it will help you understand divorce procedures better. If your disagreements are not major, you may want to try to work out a compromise. Read this chapter and have your spouse read it. Then, compare the consent divorce procedure to the procedures in Chapter 7 and Chapter 8 of this book. Once you see how much easier a consent divorce is, you may want to try harder to resolve your differences.

Basically, the procedure is as follows.

❉   You and your spouse complete all the necessary forms.

❉   You file those forms with the court clerk.

❉   You (and your spouse, if he or she wants) appear for a brief hearing with the judge.

The forms listed below are discussed in this chapter. There may be other forms needed, but the following can serve as a general checklist of the basic forms you may need for your consent divorce.

- ☐ **PETITION FOR DISSOLUTION** (form 2)

- ☐ **DECREE OF DISSOLUTION** (form 3)

- ☐ **FINDINGS OF FACT AND CONCLUSION OF LAW** (form 4)

- ☐ **PARENTING PLAN** (form 6)

- ☐ **ORDER OF CHILD SUPPORT** (form 5)

- ☐ **CHILD SUPPORT WORKSHEETS** (form 5)

PETITION FOR DISSOLUTION

The **PETITION FOR DISSOLUTION** is the paper (*pleading*) needed to open your case. (see form 2, p.163.) The **PETITION FOR DISSOLUTION** asks the judge to give you a divorce. Complete the **PETITION FOR DISSOLUTION** as follows.

◈ Complete the top portion according to the instructions in Chapter 5, page 57. Leave the file number blank for the clerk to fill in when you file.

◈ In paragraphs 1.1, 1.2, and 1.33, type in the information called for about you, your spouse, and your children.

◈ In paragraph 1.4, you request that your marriage be dissolved and allege that your marriage is irretrievably broken.

◈ In paragraph 1.5, fill in the date when and location (city and state) where you were married.

◈ In paragraph 1.6, allege whether you are not yet separated or the date of separation. For the purposes of the **PETITION FOR DISSOLUTION**, the date of separation will be the date that you believe your marriage was over. Usually, this is the date that one spouse moved out of the home. If you and your spouse are still living in your family home together, it can be the date you ceased marital counseling or, quite obviously, the date that you are filling out these forms.

◈ In paragraph 1.7, you will allege why the Washington court has jurisdiction (the legal power to make decisions) over your spouse. Usually, this is simply because your spouse is currently living in Washington. However, if your spouse is no longer living in Washington, the court can still have jurisdiction over him or her if you were married in and subsequently lived in Washington.

◈ In paragraphs 1.8 and 1.9, if you have a proposal about how you would like to divide your debts and assets, you can include that proposal here. Be careful, however, because if you later change your mind, your spouse can try to hold you to the proposal you set forth in these paragraphs. If you do not have a specific proposal, you can just ask the court make a determination of how your debts and assets should be divided at a later date. This does not mean that only a judge can later decide who is awarded which assets and liabilities. It merely leaves the door open for you and your spouse to come to an agreement, or if you cannot, gives the judge the power to decide for you.

◈ In paragraph 1.10, you will either state that spousal mainte- nance should not be paid or received by either party, or that one of you has a need for spousal maintenance. You should include a very brief narrative of why one party needs spousal maintenance and why the other party has the ability to pro- vide the same.

◈ In paragraph 1.11, you will allege whether or not a continu- ing restraining order is necessary for either you and/or your children.

◈ In paragraph 1.12, you will allege whether the wife is preg- nant, and if she is, who the father of the child is believed to be.

◈ In paragraph 1.13, if you have children, you will allege why the court has jurisdiction over those children. Usually, it is because the children have lived in Washington for at least the past six months.

◈ In paragraph 1.14, you will request that child support be set according to the Washington State Child Support Schedule (the Economic Table). You will also be given the option of attaching a proposed **PARENTING PLAN**, so that your spouse can see what type of parenting arrangements you are proposing at the same time as he or she receives the **PETITION FOR DISSOLUTION**. Regardless of whether you provide a proposed **PARENTING PLAN** at same time as the **PETITION FOR DISSOLUTION**, you will need to explain whether anyone other than you or your spouse has a claim to custody of or visitation rights to your children. You will also need to explain whether you have been involved in or are aware of any other legal proceedings concerning your children.

❖ In paragraph 1.15, you will provide a brief narrative of anything else you would like the court to do and why. You will likely leave this section blank.

❖ In the Section II, entitled "RELIEF REQUESTED," you will check the boxes that correspond with what you would like the court to grant you (or what you and your spouse have agreed to). For example, if in the **PETITION FOR DISSOLUTION** you alleged that spousal maintenance should be awarded, you should check the first box under Section II and the box that corresponds with which spouse this maintenance should be awarded to. If you have children, you will want to check the boxes that ask the court to approve your **PARENTING PLAN** (regardless of whether you file a proposed **PARENTING PLAN** with the **PETITION FOR DISSOLUTION**) and determine child support.

❖ Once you have completed the **PETITION FOR DISSOLUTION**, you will sign it and fill in the place (city and state) and date you signed. You are signing this pleading under *penalty of perjury*. This means that you are affirming that everything you have said in the petition is true and correct to the best your knowledge and belief. It is a crime to knowingly make a false statement.

Joinder   Under the consent divorce process—again, assuming that you and your spouse are in agreement on most, if not all, issues—your spouse can sign the *Joinder* portion of the **PETITION FOR DISSOLUTION**. This will alleviate the necessity of you having to prepare and file a **SUMMONS**, of having your spouse served, and of your spouse having to file a **RESPONSE** to the **PETITION FOR DISSOLUTION**.

FINALIZING

Once you have the **PETITION FOR DISSOLUTION** completed and signed by both you and your spouse, you will take it to the courthouse to file. Filing the **PETITION FOR DISSOLUTION** opens your case with the court. Once the **PETITION FOR DISSOLUTION** is filed, you must wait ninety days before your divorce can be finalized. In that intervening time, you and your spouse will need to complete the following documents discussed in the following sections to present to the judge.

DECREE OF DISSOLUTION

The **DECREE OF DISSOLUTION** is the paper the judge will sign at the final hearing to formally grant a divorce. (see form 3, p.173.) This document also sets forth the final division of debts and assets, the details of any award of maintenance, and orders the parents to comply with the **ORDER OF CHILD SUPPORT** and **PARENTING PLAN**. If you and your spouse have agreed to everything, you will prepare and sign the **DECREE OF DISSOLUTION** before the hearing and give it to the judge to sign at the end of the hearing.

Complete the **DECREE OF DISSOLUTION** as follows.

◈   Complete the top portion of the form according to the instructions in Chapter 5 on page 57. On the right side of the caption, check the "Decree of Dissolution" box.

◈   At paragraph 1.1, check the box that applies to your situation. If you and your spouse are not agreeing that a restraining order should be entered as part of the **DECREE OF DISSOLUTION**, check the "Does not apply" box. If you and your spouse are agreeing to a restraining order, check the "Restraining Order Summary" box. If you check the "Restraining Order Summary" box, immediately below that, write in the name of the person or persons who are restrained and the name of the person or persons who are protected. Keep in mind that a restraining order can only apply to you, your spouse, or your children. You cannot restrain or protect any other third parties. If the restraining order is to be mutual (you and your spouse are both the restrained and the protected parties), write both your names in both places.

◈   At paragraph 1.2, check the box that applies to your situation. Generally, real property means real estate. If you and your spouse do not own real property (either a house or vacant land), check the "Does not apply" box. If you and your spouse own real property, check the "Real Property Judgment Summary" box. If you checked this summary box, immediately below that, type in either the tax assessor's property tax parcel number or the legal description. The tax assessor's parcel number can be found on the property tax assessment form you may receive each year. The legal description can be found on the deed to the property. If you do not have either of these documents in your possession, you can obtain this information from the recorder's office of your county.

◈ At paragraph 1.3, check the box that applies to your situation. If either you or your spouse are going to be paying money to the other at any time after the entry of the **DECREE OF DISSOLUTION**, in order to complete the division of your assets (this does not include payment of child support or spousal maintenance), check the "Judgment Summary" box. Below that, at line A, type in the name of the person to receive the money and at line B, type the of the person paying the money. At line C, type in the amount of money to be paid. At line D, if you and your spouse have agreed that interest on the amount at line C would begin to accrue at some time prior to the entry of the **DECREE OF DISSOLUTION**, type the amount of accrued interest here. Leave lines E, F, and G blank. At line H, if you and your spouse have agreed that the amount at line C will accrue interest after the entry of the **DECREE OF DISSOLUTION**, fill in the agreed upon interest rate here. Leave lines I, J, K, and L blank. If there is no money to be paid after the entry of the **DECREE OF DISSOLUTION** (not including child support or spousal maintenance), check the "Does not apply" box.

◈ At paragraph 3.1, check the first box.

◈ At paragraph 3.2, if you do not have a prenuptial agreement, check the fourth box and type in all of the assets to be awarded to the Husband. Be as specific as you can. For example, if the Husband is to be awarded a vehicle, do not merely write "car." Write in the year, make, and model, as well as the license and VIN number of the vehicle to be awarded to the Husband. However, do not include full account numbers for bank accounts and the like. Divorces, like most civil actions, are public records, which means anyone can access and look at your file through the court. If you include account numbers, you could expose yourself to fraud and identity theft. If you need more space, you can attach an additional sheet to the **DECREE OF DISSOLUTION**. If you do so, be sure to write that additional assets awarded to the Husband are set forth on the attached EXHIBIT HP. At the top of the attached sheet, write "EXHIBIT HP." If you have a prenuptial agreement, you should consult with an attorney to evaluate the enforceability or unenforceability of the agreement.

◈ At paragraph 3.3, if you do not have a prenuptial agreement, check the fourth box and type in all of the assets to be awarded to the Wife. Follow the same instructions for paragraph 3.2 for describing the assets, except that any attached page showing the property awarded to the Wife would be called "EXHIBIT WP."

◈ At paragraph 3.4, if you do not have a prenuptial agreement, check the fourth box and type in all of the liabilities (debts) to be paid by the Husband. Be as specific as you can. For example, if the Husband is to pay a credit card, do not merely write "Visa bill." Write in the issuing bank (e.g., Bank of America Visa) and the balance owed. However, do not include full account numbers. Divorces, like most civil actions, are public records, which means anyone can access and look at your file through the court. If you include account numbers, you could expose yourself to fraud and identity theft. If you need more space, you can attach an additional sheet to the **DECREE OF DISSOLUTION**. If you do so, be sure to indicate that additional liabilities to be paid by the Husband are set forth on the attached as EXHIBIT HL. At the top of the attached sheet, write "EXHIBIT HL." If you have a prenuptial agreement, you should consult with an attorney to evaluate the enforceability or unenforceability of the agreement.

◈ At paragraph 3.5, if you do not have a prenuptial agreement, check the fourth box and type in all of the liabilities (debts) to be paid by the Wife. Follow the same instructions for paragraph 3.4 for describing the liabilities, except that any attached page showing debts awarded to the Wife would be called "EXHIBIT WL."

◈ Paragraph 3.6 contains an optional "Hold Harmless Provision." If you check the second box, you and your spouse have agreed that if your spouse fails to pay any debt awarded to him or her, and you end up having to pay it, you may sue your spouse for the amount of the debt you had to pay, plus any attorney's fees or costs you incurred in defending against the creditor's attempts to collect the amount due from you instead of your spouse. If you and your spouse agree to such a provision, check the second box. If you do not, check the first box. If you agree that such a provision will only apply to certain debts, check the third box and write in the debts to which it will apply.

✦ Paragraph 3.7 deals with spousal maintenance. If no spousal maintenance is to be paid by or to either spouse, check the first box. If spousal maintenance is to be paid by or to either spouse, check the fourth box. Then, check the box that corresponds to the party paying maintenance and fill in the amount. Then, check how often per month maintenance is to be paid. Be sure that if maintenance is to be paid more frequently than monthly, that you put the periodic amount, not the total amount in the preceding sentence. For example, if you and your spouse have agreed that you will pay $500 per month in spousal maintenance at a rate of $250 on the first of each month and $250 on the fifteenth of each month, be sure to write in the first sentence that you will pay "$250 maintenance" and then check the "semimonthly" box.

At the end of the third sentence of this fourth subparagraph, write in the date (day, month, and year) that the first maintenance payment is due. You should also write in the specific day(s) of the month maintenance is to be paid. After the sentence that starts "The obligation to pay future maintenance" and ends "unless specified below:" you will write in how long maintenance is to be paid, usually set forth in a term of months or years. If you and your spouse intend for spousal maintenance to continue even if the spouse receiving maintenance remarries, you must specifically say so, since, per statute, maintenance automatically terminates upon the remarriage of the receiving spouse. Below that, you will indicate to whom spousal maintenance payments are to be made. If maintenance payments are to be made directly to you, check the first box. If you want your spouse to pay them to the Washington State Child Support Registry along with his or her child support payment, check the second box.

◈   Paragraph 3.8 addresses *restraining orders*. If you and your spouse do not want a restraining order entered as part of the **DECREE OF DISSOLUTION**, check the first box. If you are both agreeing to a restraining order (whether against either of you or a mutual order), check the second box. If you check the second box, below that you will check all the boxes that apply to your situation and fill in the names of any children to be included in the restraining order. The restraining order then needs to be entered into the appropriate law enforcement database. Check the box next to the "CLERK'S ACTION" paragraph and write in the name of the police or sheriff's department where the protected person(s) lives. The clerk of the court will then forward the restraining order information to that agency. Under the "SERVICE" section, check the first box. Under the "EXPIRATION" section, enter in the date on which you and your spouse agree the restraining order will expire. If you do not want the order expire, leave this blank.

◈   At paragraph 3.9, if there were no children born of the marriage, check the first box. If there were children born of the marriage, check the second box.

◈   At paragraph 3.10, if there were no children born of the marriage, check the first box. If there were children born of the marriage, check the second box and write in "this date" at the end of the first sentence after the second box.

◈   At paragraph 3.11, if there were no children born of the marriage, check the first box. If there were children born of the marriage, check the second box and write in "this date" at the end of the first sentence after the second box.

◈   At paragraph 3.12, check the first box.

◈   At paragraph 3.13, if neither you nor your spouse want a name change, check the first box. If either you or your spouse wants a name change, check the appropriate box and write in the name that you or your spouse would like to have.

◈   Leave paragraph 3.14 blank.

◈ Below where the judge is to sign, the petitioner will check the "Presented by" box and the respondent will check the "Approved by" and the "Notice of Presentation Waived" box. Under the signature lines, the petitioner will write in his or her name under the first line and write "Pro Se" after the name. The respondent will do the same under the second line. Then you will each sign above your name.

◈ You will take this document to be signed by judge. It must be signed by the judge to make your divorce final before it is filed with the court.

FINDINGS OF FACT AND CONCLUSIONS OF LAW

Along with the **DECREE OF DISSOLUTION**, you will also need to prepare the **FINDINGS OF FACT AND CONCLUSIONS OF LAW**. (form 4, p.181.) The **FINDINGS OF FACT AND CONCLUSIONS OF LAW** is the document that explains the totality of the property you and your spouse own, the debts you owe, the reasons why maintenance is appropriate (or not), explains that you have children that need to be provided for, and directs the court to grant you a divorce by signing the **DECREE OF DISSOLUTION**. This pleading must be presented to and signed by the judge at the same time as the **DECREE OF DISSOLUTION**. Complete the **FINDINGS OF FACT AND CONCLUSIONS OF LAW** as follows.

◈ Complete the top portion of the form according to the instructions in Chapter 5, page 57.

◈ At "I. BASIS FOR FINDINGS," check the first box.

◈ At paragraph 2.1, check the first box.

◈ At paragraph 2.2, check the first box if your spouse signed a *Joinder*. If you had your spouse personally served, check the "personal service on" box and fill in the date. If you served your spouse by publication or mail (see Chapter 10), write that fact in here.

➔ At paragraph 2.3, check the second box. Below that, if your spouse lives in Washington, check the first box. If your spouse does not live in Washington but agreed to have the divorce go through in Washington, check the "Other" box and write in "Respondent has consented to personal jurisdiction in Washington."

➔ At paragraph 2.4, write in the date of your marriage and the place you were married. This will likely be a city and state (e.g., Seattle, Washington), but may be a city and country (e.g., Acapulco, Mexico) or just a country (e.g., the Island of Jamaica).

➔ At paragraph 2.5, check the first box and write in the date you and your spouse separated. This is generally considered to be the date you and your spouse agreed that the marriage was over. Often, this is the date one of you moved out of the family home.

➔ At paragraph 2.6, check the first box.

➔ At paragraph 2.7, check the box that applies to your situation. Usually, you will not have a prenuptial agreement, so you will check the first box. If you have a prenuptial agreement, you should consult with an attorney to evaluate the enforceability or unenforceability of the agreement.

➔ At paragraph 2.8, check the box that applies to your situation. If no assets were acquired during the marriage—either real property (generally real estate) or personal property (generally everything else including cars, boats, furniture, bank accounts, retirement accounts, etc.)—check the first box. If assets were acquired during the marriage, check the fourth box. Below that, describe the asset. Be as specific as you can. For example, if you and your spouse acquired a vehicle during the marriage, do not merely write "car." Write in the year, make, and model, as well as the license number and VIN of the vehicle. However, do not include full account numbers for bank accounts and the like. Divorces, like most civil actions, are public records, which means anyone can access and look at your file through the court. If you include account numbers, you could expose yourself to fraud and identity theft. If you need more space, you can attach an additional sheet to the **FINDINGS OF FACT AND CONCLUSIONS OF LAW**. If you do so, be sure to write that additional community property is set forth on the attached EXHIBIT CP. At the top of the attached sheet, write "EXHIBIT CP." If you have a prenuptial agreement, you should consult with an attorney to evaluate the enforceability or unenforceability of the agreement.

❖   At paragraph 2.9, check the box that applies to your situation. If no separate property exists (assets were acquired either before the marriage or after separation, or were acquired during the marriage as a gift or inheritance by one spouse), check the first box. If separate property exists, check the fourth box, and follow the same instructions for paragraph 2.8 for describing the assets, except that any attached page describing separate property would be called "EXHIBIT SP."

❖   At paragraph 2.10, check the box that applies to your situation. If no liabilities (debts) were acquired during the marriage, check the first box. If liabilities were acquired during the marriage, check the fourth box. Below that, describe the liability. Be as specific as you can. For example, if you and your spouse acquired credit card debt during the marriage, do not merely write "Visa bill." Write in the issuing bank (e.g., Bank of America Visa) and the balance owed. However, do not include full account numbers. Divorces, like most civil actions, are public records, which means anyone can access and look at your file through the court. If you include account numbers, you could expose yourself to fraud and identity theft. If you need more space, you can attach an additional sheet to the **FINDINGS OF FACT AND CONCLUSIONS OF LAW**. If you do so, be sure to write that additional community liabilities are set forth on the attached EXHIBIT CL. At the top of the attached sheet, write "EXHIBIT CL." If you have a prenuptial agreement, you should consult with an attorney to evaluate the enforceability or unenforceability of the agreement.

❖   At paragraph 2.11, check the box that applies to your situation. If no liabilities (debts) were incurred prior to marriage or after the date of separation, check the first box. If separate lia-

bilities were incurred, check the fourth box, and follow the same instructions for paragraph 2.10 for describing the liability except that any attached page describing separate debts would be called "EXHIBIT SL."

◆ Paragraph 2.12 applies to maintenance. If spousal maintenance is neither to be paid nor received, check the first box. If spousal maintenance is to be paid and received by either spouse, check the third box. In the space below, write "The paying spouse had the ability to pay maintenance and the receiving spouse has the need for maintenance." Then, explain any additional factors such as the receiving spouse has health problems or needs assistance to retrain to enter the workforce.

◆ Paragraph 2.13 applies to any restraining order that may be entered through the **Decree of Dissolution**. If no restraining order is to be entered, check the first box. If a restraining order is to be entered, check the second box. Then check the box that corresponds to the person being restrained. In the space below, briefly describe why a restraining order is necessary. This does not need to be more than "it is necessary to keep the peace between the parties."

◆ At paragraph 2.14, check the first box.

◆ At paragraph 2.15, check the box(es) that fit your situation.

◆ At paragraph 2.16, if neither you nor your spouse have any dependent children, including any children born to other relationships, check the first box. If either you or your spouse have any dependent children, including any children born to other relationships, check the second box. Below that, write in the name of the child, the child's age, and the full names of the parents of the child.

◆ At paragraph 2.17, if there were no children born of the marriage, and neither you nor your spouse has any dependent children, check the first box. If you or your spouse only have children from previous relationships, check the second box. If there are any children born of the marriage, check the third box. Then, check the second box below that corresponds to the sentence that begins, "This state is the home state of the child because." Beyond that, check either the first or second box as it applies to your situation. If you cannot check either of these boxes, you should consult an attorney, as you may have issues regarding jurisdiction that are too complicated to explain here.

◈ At paragraph 2.18, if there were no children born of the marriage, check the first box. If there were children born of the marriage, check the second and third boxes, and write "this date" in the blank space in the second sentence.

◈ At paragraph 2.19, if there were no children born of the marriage, check the first box. If there were children born of the marriage, check the second box and write "this date" in the blank space in the second sentence.

◈ Leave paragraph 2.20 blank.

◈ At paragraph 3.1, check the first box.

◈ At paragraph 3.2, check the first box.

◈ Paragraph 3.3 is a preprinted statement to the court that you should not alter.

◈ At paragraph 3.4, check the box that applies to your situation.

◈ At paragraph 3.5, check the first box.

◈ Leave paragraph 3.6 blank.

Below where the judge is to sign, the petitioner will write in his or her name under the first line and write "Pro Se" after the name. The respondent will do the same under the second line. You will each sign above your name.

You will take this document to be signed by judge along with the **DECREE OF DISSOLUTION**. It must be signed by the judge to make your divorce final before it is filed with the court.

ORDER OF CHILD SUPPORT

If children were born during the marriage, you will also need to prepare an **ORDER OF CHILD SUPPORT** (form 5, p.191) and **CHILD SUPPORT WORKSHEETS** (see Appendix A), and a **PARENTING PLAN**. (form 6, p.203.) You and your spouse will need to sign these documents and present them to the judge for him or her to sign, along with the **DECREE OF DISSOLUTION** and **FINDINGS OF FACT AND CONCLUSIONS OF LAW**.

Complete the **ORDER OF CHILD SUPPORT** as follows.

◈ Complete the top section of the form according to the instructions in Chapter 5, page 57.

◈ Under "I. JUDGMENT SUMMARY," if all child support has been paid in full to the date you are completing this form, check the "Does not apply" box. If back child support is owed, check the second box and complete the judgment summary (see the instructions for paragraph 1.3 of the **DECREE OF DISSOLUTION**).

◈ At paragraph 2.1, check the first box.

◈ Paragraph 2.2 is a statement to the court that you should not alter.

◈ Leave paragraph 2.3 blank.

◈ At paragraph 3.1, enter the name(s) and age(s) of your child(ren).

◈ At paragraph 3.2, fill in the name, address, and birth date of the person paying child support. If the net income of this parent is known, check the appropriate box and fill in the net income. If income is being *imputed* (see Chapter 4), check the appropriate box and fill in the amount of imputed income.

◈ At paragraph 3.3, fill in the name, address, and birth date of the person paying support. If the net income of this parent is known, check the appropriate box and fill in the net income. If income is being *imputed* (see Chapter 4), check the appropriate box and fill in the amount of imputed income.

❖ Paragraph 3.4 is a statement to the court that you should not alter.

❖ At paragraph 3.5, check the first box and fill in the amount of monthly support to be paid per child. Check any additional box(es) (if appropriate) and fill in any additional information necessary.

❖ At paragraph 3.6, fill in the total amount of child support shown on the worksheet at line 15.

❖ At paragraph 3.7, if the amounts shown in paragraphs 3.5 and 3.6 are the same, check the first box. If they are different, check the second box and any subsequent box(es) that apply. Where the form asks for the factual basis, include a brief narrative of why you and your spouse have agreed to deviate from the amount of child support at paragraph 3.6.

❖ At paragraph 3.8, check the first or second box as appropriate.

❖ At paragraph 3.9, fill in the requested information.

❖ At paragraph 3.10, check the first box.

❖ At paragraph 3.11, check the box that corresponds to how you would like child support to be paid. If you and your spouse have agreed that the *Division of Child Support* (DCS) will collect child support through garnishment or wage assignment (see paragraph 3.12), check the first box. If you and your spouse have agreed that DCS will merely process the payments your spouse voluntarily makes each month, check the second box. If you and your spouse have agreed that child support will be paid directly to you, check the third box and fill in the address to where you would like your spouse to mail his or her child support payment.

❖ At paragraph 3.12, if you have checked the first box under paragraph 3.11, do not check any of the boxes under paragraph 3.12. If you and your spouse have checked the second or third boxes under paragraph 3.11, check the first box under paragraph 3.12 and the appropriate box below that (you will usually check the first box).

◈ At paragraph 3.13, check the box that reflects your agreement with your spouse as to when child support will terminate. Usually, this will be the third box.

◈ At paragraph 3.14, check the box that reflects your agreement with your spouse regarding payment of college expenses. If you cannot or do not want to make a determination as to if and how much will be paid for college expenses, check the second box. This means that even though your divorce will be final, when it comes time for your child to go to college, you or your spouse can either agree to the payment of college expenses or you can file a motion asking the court to make a decision.

◈ At paragraph 3.15, you will check the box(es) that correspond to your situation. If all expenses (except medical—see paragraphs 3.18 and 3.19) are included in the basic transfer payment, check the first box. If there are expenses that are to be paid in addition to the basic transfer payment, check the appropriate boxes.

◈ At paragraph 3.16, check the first box. This does not mean that child support can never be adjusted later. You can always adjust child support as allowed by statute.

◈ At paragraph 3.17, check the second box and explain how the tax exemption(s) associated with your child(ren) will be allocated between you and your spouse. You should confer with an accountant to determine the best allocation of exemption(s).

◈ At paragraph 3.18, at paragraph (b), fill in the insurance premium cost thresholds as explained in that paragraph. Below that, if appropriate, check the box(es) that apply to your agreement with your spouse, primarily any agreement that one parent will provide insurance and the other will not, or that insurance will be provided even if exceeds the premium thresholds in paragraph (b).

➧ At paragraph 3.19, fill in the information as explained in that paragraph.

➧ At paragraph 3.20 and 3.21, check the box(es) appropriate to your situation.

➧ Leave paragraph 3.22 blank.

➧ Under the line where the judge signs the order, write "[your name], Pro Se" below the signature line in the "Presented by:" section, and write "[your spouse's name], Pro Se" below the signature line in the "Approved for entry:" section. You and your spouse will then sign accordingly.

Child Support Worksheets Complete the **CHILD SUPPORT WORKSHEETS** as instructed in Chapter 4 and Appendix A. Sign and date the worksheets as indicated and attach them to the **ORDER OF CHILD SUPPORT**.

PARENTING PLAN

When children are involved, a **PARENTING PLAN** is also necessary. The **PARENTING PLAN** sets out in detail the times and dates the children will reside with each parent. A **PARENTING PLAN** must be specific enough to be enforceable. It also provides for transportation arrangements (other than cost) and how certain basic decisions regarding the children will be made. In some counties, both parents must complete a parenting class before the judge will sign the **PARENTING PLAN**. Ask the clerk's office if your county has this requirement, and if so, the type of class that must be taken.

Complete the **PARENTING PLAN** as follows.

➧ Complete the top portion of the form according to the instructions in Chapter 5, page 57. Check the "Final Order" box in the right side of the caption.

➧ Directly below the caption, check the first box and write "this date" in the blank space.

➔ Under "I. GENERAL INFORMATION," fill in the name(s) and age(s) of the child(ren) born of your marriage.

➔ Under "II. BASIS FOR RESTRICTIONS," check any and all box(es) appropriate to your situation.

➔ At paragraphs 3.1 and 3.2, check the box(es) that reflect your agreement with your spouse. Be as specific as possible by including days of the week and times whenever possible. You *cannot* merely state "As the parents agree."

➔ At paragraphs 3.3, 3.4, and 3.5, check the appropriate boxes and explain how you and your spouse will share the children's winter break, spring break, and midwinter break, and summer, if applicable.

➔ At paragraph 3.6, check the "Does not apply" box if you and your spouse intend that all vacations will be taken during the school breaks or during the summer, if you included special summer arrangements. Otherwise, check the second box and explain when vacations will be taken.

➔ At paragraphs 3.7 and 3.8, for each holiday and special occasion, specify whether your child(ren) will be with the mother in odd years, in even years, or every year. Do the same for the father. Check any additional box(es) and add any additional holidays that may be important to you (for example, Easter or Chanukah).

➔ At paragraph 3.9, check the second box and allocate how conflicting residential provisions shall be resolved. For example, if a child's birthday falls on a holiday, which trumps the other.

➔ At paragraph 3.10, check the first box if you checked "Does not apply" at paragraph 2.1 and 2.2. If any boxes are checked at paragraph 2.1 and 2.2, check the second or third box and the box that corresponds to the restricted parent. Then, explain the restrictions or why there are no restrictions in the plan.

◈ At paragraph 3.11, explain the transportation arrangements you and your spouse have agreed to, other than how the cost of those arrangements will be allocated.

◈ At paragraph 3.12, check the appropriate box. This is the one place where the term "custodian" is still used, as certain other state and federal statutes (for example, federal child kidnapping statutes) require that one parent be designated as custodian. This is normally the parent with whom the child resides the majority of the time. This designation does not alter either parent's rights or responsibilities under the **PARENTING PLAN**.

◈ Leave paragraph 3.13 blank.

◈ Paragraph 3.14 must be included in every **PARENTING PLAN** and is explained further in Chapter 4.

◈ At paragraph 4.2, check the box(es) that correspond to how you and your spouse have agreed the decisions listed will be made. If you have additional decisions you and your spouse would like to specifically address, you can write them in here.

◈ At paragraph 4.3, check the first box if you checked "Does not apply" at paragraph 2.1 and 2.2. If any boxes are checked at paragraph 2.1 and 2.2, check the second or third box and the box that corresponds to the restricted parent. Then, explain the restrictions or why there are no restrictions in the plan.

◈ Under "V. DISPUTE RESOLUTION," check the appropriate box(es) that reflect your agreement with your spouse regarding dispute resolution. Every **PARENTING PLAN** must designate how you and your spouse will attempt to resolve disputes over the **PARENTING PLAN** before resorting to court action. If there are restrictions under paragraph 2.1 or 2.2, the box ordering only court action should be checked.

◈ Under "VI. OTHER PROVISIONS," you may write in any additional agreements regarding parenting that are not otherwise addressed in the **PARENTING PLAN**. For example, you and your spouse may have an agreement that he or she will call the children every Wednesday at 7:00 p.m. If you have no other provisions, check the first box.

✦ Under "VII. DECLARATION FOR PROPOSED PARENTING PLAN," check the first box.

✦ Under "VIII. ORDER BY THE COURT," write "[your name], Pro Se" below the signature line in the "Presented by:" section and write "[your spouse's name], Pro Se" below the signature line in the "Approved for entry:" section. You and your spouse will then sign accordingly.

When ninety days has elapsed, you will need to contact the court to arrange a date to appear in court and have the judge sign the pleadings. Since most counties differ in that procedure, contact the clerk of the court in your county to ask how this is accomplished. Many courts also have family law facilitators who will help you to do this. Information on the family law facilitators office in your county can be found at **www.courts.wa.gov**.

Uncontested Divorce

For purposes of this book, a *contested* case is one in which you and your spouse will be doing your arguing *in* court and leaving the decision up to the judge. An *uncontested* or consent case is one in which you will do your arguing and deciding *before* court, and the judge only needs to approve your decision. This chapter provides a general overview of the uncontested divorce procedure.

You probably will not know if you are going to have a contested case until you try the uncontested or consent route and fail. Therefore, the following sections are presented mostly to assist you in attempting the uncontested case. Chapter 8 specifically discusses the contested case, but builds on information in this chapter.

There are two ways that a case can be considered uncontested. One occurs when your spouse simply ignores the fact that you have filed for divorce. If your spouse is served and does not respond, you will need to file a certain set of forms, but will not have anything to fight about since your spouse is ignoring the situation. The other uncontested situation is when you cannot locate your spouse. In this situation, you will also need to file a certain set of forms, which are discussed more in Chapter 10.

The forms listed below are likely to be used in an uncontested procedure. There may be other forms needed, but they will be prepared and provided by the court. The following can serve as a checklist of the basic forms you may need for your uncontested divorce.

- ☐ **SUMMONS** (form 1)

- ☐ **PETITION FOR DISSOLUTION** (form 2)

- ☐ **MOTION AND DECLARATION FOR DEFAULT** (form 8)

- ☐ **ORDER FOR DEFAULT** (form 9)

- ☐ **DECREE OF DISSOLUTION** (form 3)

- ☐ **FINDINGS OF FACT AND CONCLUSIONS OF LAW** (form 4)

- ☐ **ORDER OF CHILD SUPPORT** (form 5)

- ☐ **PARENTING PLAN** (form 6)

Once all of the necessary forms have been filed, you will need to call the judge's secretary to arrange a hearing date for the final judgment. Tell the secretary that you need to schedule a *hearing to finalize a divorce*. Such a hearing should not usually take more than ten minutes. (See Chapter 9 for information on how to handle the final hearing.)

The following sections give instructions for when you need each form and how to complete it.

SUMMONS

The **SUMMONS** (form 1) notifies your spouse of his or her rights and obligations in responding to the **PETITION FOR DISSOLUTION**. (see form 2, p.163.) It is like a miniature road map to the dissolution process—it informs your spouse that you are seeking a divorce, and that he or she must respond in a certain way within a certain period of time. It further states that if your spouse does not follow those instructions, a **DECREE OF DISSOLUTION** containing the relief requested in the **PETITION FOR DISSOLUTION** may be signed by the court, whether he or she likes it or not.

Complete the **SUMMONS** as follows.

◈   Complete the top portion of the form according to the instructions in Chapter 5, page 57.

◈   At paragraph 1, check the first box.

◈   At the end of the form, fill in the date and type your name under the signature line with "Pro Se" afterwards. Then, sign above that line.

◈   Under that, on the left-hand side of the form under the "File Original" paragraph, type in the address of the court. On the right-hand side of the form, under the "Serve a Copy" paragraph, check the first box and type your address below.

PETITION FOR DISSOLUTION

The **PETITION FOR DISSOLUTION** is the paper needed to open your case. (see form 2, p.163.) The **PETITION FOR DISSOLUTION** asks the judge to give you a divorce. Complete the **PETITION FOR DISSOLUTION** as explained in Chapter 6.

MOTION AND DECLARATION OF DEFAULT

Your spouse has twenty-one days after being served with the **SUMMONS** and **PETITION FOR DISSOLUTION** (twenty-eight days if he or she was served in another state) to respond to the **PETITION FOR DISSOLUTION**. If your spouse fails to respond and is *not* in the military service, you will need to complete the **MOTION AND DECLARATION FOR DEFAULT** and the **ORDER FOR DEFAULT**. (see forms 8 and 9.)

The **MOTION AND DECLARATION OF DEFAULT** is the document that tells the court what you want (that you want you your **DECREE OF DISSOLUTION** to be entered by default) and why you want it (because your spouse was properly served but failed to respond). The **ORDER OF DEFAULT** is signed by the judge and actually declares that your spouse in default, and because of that, the relief you want in the **PETITION FOR DISSOLUTION** should be granted.

If your spouse *is* in the military service, you do not need to complete this form and should consult a lawyer. Federal laws designed to protect service personnel while overseas can create special problems in these situations. However, if your spouse is in the military and will cooperate by signing a *Joinder* or *Acceptance of Service* and all the necessary final pleadings (**Decree of Dissolution**, **Findings of Fact and Conclusions of Law**, and **Order of Child Support** and **Parenting Plan** if you have children), you can proceed without a lawyer.

Complete the **Motion and Declaration for Default** as follows.

◈ Complete the top portion of the form according to the instructions in Chapter 5, page 57.

◈ Under "I. MOTION," type your name in the blank in the first sentence. Then, fill in the date, check the "Signature of Petitioner" box, and sign above that.

◈ At paragraph 2.1, fill in the appropriate residency information.

◈ At paragraph 2.2, type "Respondent" in the first sentence. Then, check appropriate box below as it applies to your situation.

◈ At paragraph 2.3, type the names of the documents the respondent was served with and the date of service. Below that, check the box that applies to your situation and fill in any additional information as necessary.

◈ At paragraph 2.4, check the box that applies to your situation.

◈ At paragraph 2.5, if you have received absolutely no response from your spouse, check the first box. If your spouse has filed some sort of appearance but has not filed a "RESPONSE TO PETITION," check the second box.

◈ At paragraph 2.6, check the box that applies to your situation and fill in any additional information as necessary. If your spouse is on active duty in the military, consult an attorney.

◈ Leave paragraph 2.7 blank.

Once you have completed the **MOTION AND DECLARATION FOR DEFAULT**, you will sign it, and fill in the place (city and state) and date you signed. You are signing this pleading under penalty of perjury. This means that you are affirming that everything you have said in the petition is true and correct to the best your knowledge and belief. It is a crime to knowingly make any false statements.

ORDER OF DEFAULT

Complete the **ORDER FOR DEFAULT** (form 9, p.221) as follows.

◈   Under "I. BASIS," type your name in the blank.

◈   Paragraph 2.1 states that court has proper jurisdiction and venue. Do not change this line.

◈   At paragraph 2.2, type in the name of your spouse, the titles of the forms he or she was served with, and the date of service.

◈   At paragraph 2.3, check the box that applies to your situation.

◈   At paragraph 2.4, check the box that applies to your situation.

◈   Leave paragraph 2.5 blank.

◈   Below where the judge is to sign, write your name under the signature line and write "Pro Se" after your name. Then, sign above your name.

You will take the **MOTION AND DECLARATION FOR DEFAULT** and **ORDER FOR DEFAULT** with you to be reviewed and signed by the judge, along with the **DECREE OF DISSOLUTION**, **FINDINGS OF FACT AND CONCLUSIONS OF LAW**, and the **ORDER OF CHILD SUPPORT** with **CHILD SUPPORT WORKSHEETS**, and **PARENTING PLAN**, if you have children. (All of these forms are discussed in Chapter 6.)

Contested Divorce

This book cannot turn you into a trial lawyer. It can be very risky to try to handle a contested case yourself, but it has been done. Procedurally, there are several differences between contested cases and consent or uncontested cases. In a consent case, the judge will usually go along with whatever you and your spouse have worked out. In an uncontested case, the judge will usually go along with whatever you want (as long as it appears reasonable), because your spouse has not objected to what you are requesting. However, in a contested case, you need to prove your entitlement to what you are asking. This means you will need to prepare for a trial, as more preparation, documentation, and witness testimony are necessary. A trial is conducted in the same manner as what you see on television, except that it is not held before a jury, only in front of a judge. Trials are very time-consuming and very difficult. If you think your matter will have to be resolved by trial, you should seek the services of an attorney as early in the divorce process as possible.

You may also have to do extra work to get the evidence you need, such as by sending out subpoenas or even hiring a private investigator. Also, make sure that your spouse is properly notified of any court hearings and that he or she is sent copies of any papers you file with the court clerk.

FORMS

Some of the forms discussed in Chapter 7 will also be used in a contested case. In fact, a contested case will begin the same way as an uncontested case. You will begin by filing the following two documents.

☐ **SUMMONS** (form 1). (See Chapter 7 for information about how to complete form 1.)

☐ **PETITION FOR DISSOLUTION** (form 2). (See Chapter 6 for information about how to complete form 2.)

NOTE: *There may be other additional administrative documents you need to file that you can get from the clerk of the court.*

Other forms that will, or may, be necessary in a contested case are discussed later in this chapter.

The case will become contested within about twenty days, when your spouse files an **RESPONSE TO PETITION** that shows he or she is contesting at least one issue. When it becomes apparent that you have a contested divorce, it is probably time to consider hiring an attorney, especially if the issue of parenting or child custody is involved. If you are truly ready to go to war over a **PARENTING PLAN**, it shows that this is an extremely important matter for you, and you may want to get professional assistance. You can expect a contested case when your spouse is seriously threatening to fight you every inch of the way or when he or she hires an attorney.

Yet you should not assume that you need an attorney just because your spouse has hired one. It may be easier to deal with your spouse's attorney than with your spouse. The attorney is not as emotionally involved and may see your settlement proposal as reasonable. Try to work things out with the lawyer first—you can always hire your own lawyer if your spouse's is not reasonable.

– Caution –

Be very cautious about signing any papers until you are certain you understand what they mean. You may want to have an attorney review any papers prepared by your spouse's lawyer before you sign them.

PROPERTY AND DEBTS

Generally, the judge will look at your property and debts and try to divide them fairly. This does not necessarily mean they will be divided 50/50. You want to offer the judge a reasonable solution that looks fair. Adultery or other misconduct on the part of one party generally *cannot* be used by the other party to justify an unequal division of property and debts.

It is time to review the **PROPERTY INVENTORY** (worksheet 1) and the **DEBT INVENTORY** (worksheet 2) you prepared earlier. Make a list of what you want the judge to award to you and what you want the judge to award to your spouse, along with a brief explanation of why the judge should adopt your proposal for each item. It will help if you can convince the judge of one or more of the following.

- ✪ You are the one who primarily uses that item.

- ✪ You use the item in your employment, business, or hobby.

- ✪ You are willing to give up something else you really want in exchange for that item. (Of course, you will try to give up something from your *do not care* or *like to have* list.)

- ✪ The item is needed for your children.

- ✪ The item should be considered your separate property because you owned it prior to the marriage or it was a gift or inheritance to you alone (such as from one of your relatives), or was a court award for pain and suffering.

- ✪ You got the property by exchanging it for property you had before you got married, for property you received as a gift or through an inheritance, or purchased it with a court award for pain and suffering.

The best thing you can do is make up a list of how you think the property should be divided. Make a reasonably fair and equal list, regardless of how angry you are at your spouse. If the judge changes some of it to appear fair to your spouse, you will still get more of what you want than if you do not offer a suggestion.

NOTE: *This is not an exception to the negotiating rule that lets your spouse make the first offer, because you are no longer just negotiating with your spouse. You are now negotiating with the judge. You are trying to impress the judge with your fairness, not convincing your spouse.*

Additionally, you must have any papers that can support why you should get the item and the value of all property. Papers such as dated sales receipts, cancelled checks, loan documents, bank statements, credit card statements, income tax returns, certified copies of wills, probate court papers, or court judgments are useful.

CHILD CUSTODY AND VISITATION

Generally, the parent who has been the child's primary caretaker will be designated the primary residential parent. Review the guidelines the judge will use to decide that question (these can be found in Chapter 4). For each item listed in that section, write down an explanation of how it applies to you, forming your argument for your hearing with the judge.

Many parenting battles revolve around the *fitness* of one or both of the parents. If you become involved in this type of a fight, you should consult a lawyer. Charges of *unfitness* (such as illegal drug use, child abuse, immoral sexual conduct) can require long court hearings involving the testimony of many witnesses, as well as the possible employment of private investigators. For such a hearing, you will require the help of an attorney who knows the law, the questions to ask witnesses, and the rules of evidence.

If the only question is whether you or your spouse have been the main caretaker of the child, you can always have friends, neighbors, and relatives come into the hearing (if they are willing to help you out) to testify on your behalf. It may not be necessary for you to hire an attorney, but if you need to subpoena unwilling witnesses to testify, you should have one.

The judge's decision regarding parenting will have to be put into the **PARENTING PLAN**. (see form 6, p.203.)

CHILD SUPPORT

In Washington, as in most states, the question of child support is mostly a matter of a mathematical calculation. Getting the proper child support calculation depends upon the accuracy of the income information presented to the judge.

There usually will not be much room to argue about the amount of child support. If you claim your spouse has not provided accurate income information, it is up to you to prove this to the judge by showing the income information you obtained from your spouse's employer or other income source.

The only area open for argument is when special needs (such as day care and educational expense) are claimed by the party asking for child support, or if one party is requesting a deviation from the standard child support calculation. (see Chapter 4.) Once again, it is necessary for that party to provide proof of the cost of these special needs by producing billing statements, receipts, or other papers to show the amount of these needs or the basis for the deviation.

The judge's decision regarding child support will have to be put into the **ORDER OF CHILD SUPPORT** and **CHILD SUPPORT WORKSHEETS**. (see form 5, p.191 and Appendix A.)

SPOUSAL SUPPORT

A dispute over maintenance may require a lawyer. Such a claim may require the testimony of expert witnesses (such as doctors, accountants, and actuaries), which requires the special skills of an attorney.

If maintenance has been requested, look at the section of the **PETITION FOR DISSOLUTION** or *Response to Petition* asking for alimony. The reasons given will be the subject of the trial. You should determine what information (including papers and the testimony of witnesses) you will need to present to the judge to either support or refute the reasons maintenance was requested.

The most common reason is that the person needs help until he or she can get training to enter the work force. The questions that will need to be answered include the following.

- What has the person been trained for in the past?

- What type of training is needed before the person can again be employable in that field?

- How long will this training take?

- What amount of income can be expected upon employment?

- How much money is required for the training?

IF YOU REACH A SETTLEMENT

In the event that you and your spouse manage to reach an agreement before your trial on any or all issues, you should inform the court prior to trial. It is to your advantage to agree on as many matters as possible, because it will reduce the amount of time you need to spend preparing for and attending the trial, and the amount of money you will need to spend on an attorney if you have hired one.

The Trial

One of your first steps in preparing for a trial is to get a trial date scheduled. The procedure for this varies from county to county. Your hearing may take place in a large courtroom like those you see on TV or in a small hearing room.

You will need to formally notify your spouse of the date of the trial. Even if you can call your spouse on the phone, you still need to send a formal notice.

You must have copies of all documents (*exhibits*) you want the court to consider at the trial. You will likely need to furnish these documents for your spouse, or your spouse's attorney, and the court in advance of the trial. You will also likely need to tell your spouse, or your spouse's attorney, and the court who will testify and what those individuals will testify to. Finally, you should file a short statement with the court (called a *Trial Brief*) outlining the issues in your case and your proposed resolution. Also, check with your county's local rules to determine if there are additional county-specific documents required.

GENERAL PROCEDURES

Plan to arrive at the hearing room at least ten minutes before the scheduled trial time. Have your witnesses (if any) with you and be ready to present your case.

Usually there will be someone for you to check-in with inside the court room. This may be the judge's clerk or secretary. Be careful not to interrupt or disturb any hearing that may be in progress.

When it is your turn to present your case, begin by stating your name, that you are representing yourself, and what you are asking the judge to do. You can use your *Trial Brief* as an outline. You will then be given an opportunity to present any evidence you may have to support your request.

It is impossible for this book to turn you into a lawyer. However, the following will give you some general guidance in presenting your case to the judge.

NOTE: *In addition to the information provided here, be sure to read the section in Chapter 5 on "Courtroom Manners."*

Testimony of Witnesses

You are entitled to have witnesses testify. Regarding such testimony, you need to be aware of a rule of evidence known as the *hearsay rule*. To put it very simply, the hearsay rule is that a witness cannot testify to what another person told the witness. For example, it would violate the hearsay rule for your friend Jane to testify that, "John Doe told me he saw Mr. Smith hit little Billy with a leather belt." Instead, you should have John Doe testify to what he saw. Law students spend many hours in the classroom studying the hearsay rule and its many exceptions, so there is no way it can be fully explained here. Just try to use witnesses who have first-hand knowledge of what they are testifying about.

You may be a witness on your own behalf. You may even be your only witness. When you testify, simply tell the judge what you want him or her to know. After you are finished, your spouse (or his or her attorney) may ask you questions. Also, the judge may ask you questions.

When you have another person testify on your behalf, you need to ask the witness questions. You should begin by having the witness identify him- or herself and telling how he or she knows you or your family.

Example:

Question: *Please state your name.*

Answer: *John Smith.*

Question: *How do you know my family?*

Answer: *I have worked with you for six years, and have been with you and your family on numerous social occasions.*

After this type of introduction, you need to ask questions that will allow your witness to tell the judge what happened. Your questions should be fairly simple. Do not ask more than one question at a time. Ask one question and wait for the witness to answer it before you ask another. Also, be very careful not to put words in the witness's mouth.

Example:

Correct:

Question: *Where were you on July 4th of this year?*

Answer: *At your house for a Fourth of July barbeque.*

Question: *Did you observe anything unusual that day?*

Answer: *Yes. I observed Mrs. Smith spanking your son.*

Question: *Please describe exactly what you saw.*

Incorrect:

Question: *You saw my wife spank my son last Fourth of July, did you not?*

Incorrect:

Question: *This past Fourth of July my wife spanked my son with a ruler because he spilled mustard on his shirt, and you were over at my house for a barbecue...*

In the correct example, the witness is being allowed to tell the story. In the first incorrect example, the person asking the question is the one telling what happened, not the witness. In the second incorrect example, the person asking the questions is not only telling what happened, but is not even asking a question.

After you have finished, your spouse (or your spouse's attorney) will have an opportunity to ask questions. The judge may also ask questions. If the questioning by these people raises any matters that you believe need clarification, you may ask more questions. Once everyone is finished with your witness, he or she will be excused and you can then call your next witness.

If you do not have any more witnesses, and have presented all of your documents, you can simply say "That is all I have" or "I rest."

Expert Witness

An expert witness is a witness who is being called to testify because he or she has some type of special training, education, or expertise. In divorce cases, the most common expert witnesses are psychologists, psychiatrists, and counselors, or those who testify about the value of an asset, such as a real estate appraiser. If there are charges of physical abuse, you may also have a physician testify as an expert witness. Whereas a regular witness usually only testifies about what he or she observed, an expert witness also gives opinions and interprets what was observed. For example, a regular witness will usually not be allowed to give an opinion as to whether a person he or she observed was in a state of shock because this witness does not have the proper expertise to determine whether a person is in a state of shock. A physician would be able to give such an opinion, because he or she has the proper education to make such a determination.

When questioning an expert witness, you must first have the judge determine that the witness qualifies as an expert. To do this, ask the witness questions about his or her education and training, any licenses held, and experience working in the field for which he or she is to be qualified as an expert. Once the witness has given this testimony, you say to the judge, "I move that this witness be qualified as an expert witness."

Your spouse (or your spouse's attorney) may ask the witness questions or object to the witness being qualified as an expert. Further questioning, by you or the judge, may resolve whatever objection is raised. If the judge agrees the witness is not qualified, then the witness will not be allowed to testify as an expert, but may still testify as a regular witness. Once the witness is qualified as an expert, you may ask questions so the information you want is presented.

Documents as evidence. Introducing a document into evidence is a three-step procedure.

1. *Mark the document as an exhibit.* For example, the plaintiff would do this with his or her first document by saying: "Your Honor, may I have this marked as Petitioner's Exhibit A?" (If you are the defendant, it will be marked as a respondent's exhibit.)

   NOTE: *In dissolution cases, the plaintiff is often referred to as the petitioner and the defendant as the respondent.*

   To help avoid any confusion, it is common to have one party's documents identified by a number (i.e., 1, 2, 3, etc.), and the other party's documents identified by a letter (i.e., A, B, C, etc.). There are several ways in which a document may be marked. The identification number or letter may be written on the document or a sticker with the designation affixed to the document. Marking may be done by you, by the judge's clerk, or by the court reporter.

2. *Have the document identified by a witness.* The plaintiff would wait until the document is marked, then would hand it to the witness and say: "I am showing you what has been marked as Petitioner's Exhibit A. Can you identify this?" The witness should then tell what the document is, and how he or she knows what it is. The purpose at this point is only to determine what the document is, not to discuss what information it contains or what it means.

   If you are the one introducing the document, then you will need to state what the document is.

Example:
"Your Honor, this is a copy of the W-2 form I received from my employer last week."

---

3. *Ask the judge to admit the document into evidence.* The plaintiff would say to the judge: "Your Honor, I move that Petitioner's Exhibit A be admitted into evidence." At this point, your spouse (or your spouse's attorney) will have an opportunity to object. If there is no objection, or if the objection is overruled by the judge, the judge will admit the document into evidence by saying something like "So admitted," or "Petitioner's Exhibit A is admitted."

If there is an objection, you may need to ask the witness more questions to overcome the objection.

Example:

If the witness stated that the document is "a letter I received from Mr. Smith, and it is dated January 27, 2006," your spouse's attorney may respond, "I object. How do we know it is really from Mr. Smith?" The plaintiff should then ask the witness, "How do you know the letter is from Mr. Smith?" The witness might state, "The envelope it came in had Mr. Smith's correct return address, and I have known Mr. Smith for twelve years and recognize the signature as Mr. Smith's."

Once the document is admitted into evidence, ask the witness any questions you have about the content or significance of the document.

Questioning Your Spouse's Witnesses

If you are the petitioner, you will present your case first. After you finish, your spouse will present his or her case. You will have the opportunity to question (or *cross-examine*) the witnesses who testify for your spouse. When cross-examining a witness, keep in mind one of the most basic rules followed by most lawyers—never ask a question unless you know what the answer will be.

If you do not obey this rule, asking the question may allow the witness to give an answer that strengthens your spouse's case. Many people feel that if they have an opportunity to question a witness, then they must do so. There is nothing wrong with saying "I have no questions," and let the witness go before he or she can do any more damage to your case.

PREPARING THE FINAL PLEADINGS

Once the hearing is finished and the judge announces his or her decision on the issues, the plaintiff must prepare the necessary final pleadings. These documents include the **DECREE OF DISSOLUTION**, **FINDINGS OF FACT AND CONCLUSIONS OF LAW**, **ORDER OF CHILD SUPPORT**, **CHILD SUPPORT WORKSHEETS**, and **PARENTING PLAN**. (Refer to Chapter 6 for specific instructions on how to prepare these documents.)

Usually, your spouse will also need to review and sign the final pleadings you have prepared. Obviously, it is unlikely that this will occur all in one day, so you may have to go back before your trial judge to have him or her sign the final pleadings or clarify any disputes you and your spouse may have about the way you have drafted the pleadings. If there is a dispute, the judge will only consider whether you have drafted the pleadings according to the way he or she ruled. The judge will not consider arguments about whether he or she made the right decision on an issue.

Getting Help

Again, going to trial is very time consuming and technically difficult. However, once trial begins, if you feel you are in over your head, it is unlikely that the judge will stop the trial to allow you to obtain an attorney. Also, the closer you are to the trial date, the harder it may be to obtain an attorney, because trials are so time and labor intensive. If you are sure your case is heading to trial, the sooner you seek legal counsel, the better.

chapter 10

When You Cannot Find Your Spouse

Your spouse has run off and you have no idea of where he or she might be. How do you have the sheriff deliver a copy of your legal form **SUMMONS** (form 1) and **PETITION FOR DISSOLUTION** (form 2) to your spouse? The answer is, you cannot have him or her personally served. Instead of personal service, you will give notice through *service by publication*. This is one of the more complicated procedures in the legal system. Carefully follow the steps listed in this chapter.

THE DILIGENT SEARCH

The court will only permit publication if you cannot locate your spouse. You must establish that you cannot locate your spouse by informing the court of what you have done to try to find him or her. In making this search, you should try the following.

- ✪ Check the phone book and directory assistance in the area where you live.

- ✪ Check directory assistance in the area where you last knew your spouse to be, or in the any area where you have reason to think your spouse may be living.

✪ Ask friends and relatives who might know where your spouse may be.

✪ Check with the post office where your spouse last lived to see if there is a forwarding address. (You can write to the post office and request this information by mail if it is too far away.)

✪ Check property tax records in the county of your spouse's last known address to see if your spouse owns property. You can also check other counties if you have reason to think he or she may own property there.

✪ Check with the Washington Secretary of State to see if your spouse has a current driver's license or any car registrations.

✪ Check with any other sources you know that may lead you to a current address (such as landlords, prior employers, etc.).

If you do come up with a current address, go back to personal service, but if not, continue with this procedure.

YOU KNOW WHERE YOUR SPOUSE LIVES

If you think you know where your spouse lives, but he or she is avoiding being personally served or lives out of state, you will need to complete a **MOTION AND DECLARATION TO SERVE BY MAIL** (form 10, p.223), an **ORDER ALLOWING SERVICE BY MAIL** (form 11, p.225), and a **SUMMONS BY MAIL** (form 12, p.227).

Motion and Declaration to Serve by Mail

Complete the **MOTION AND DECLARATION TO SERVE BY MAIL** as follows.

◈ Complete the top portion of the form according to the instructions in Chapter 5, page 57.

◈ Under "I. MOTION," type your name in the blank in the first sentence. Then, fill in the date, write your name under the signature line and "Pro Se" after your name, and sign above that.

◈ At paragraph 2.1, check either box one or box two if it applies to you, and fill in your spouse's name. If none of these options apply, leave this section blank.

◈ At paragraph 2.2, check either box one or box two if it applies to you. If neither of these options apply, leave this section blank.

◈ At paragraphs 2.3 and 2.4, write in a brief description of why you believe your spouse is avoiding service and what you have done to locate him or her.

◈ Paragraph 2.5 is statement to the court that you should not alter.

◈ At paragraph 2.6, fill in the address where you believe your spouse would be most likely to receive his or her mail.

◈ At paragraph 2.7, check the box that applies to your situation and fill in any additional information as necessary.

◈ Leave paragraph 2.8 blank.

Once you have completed the **MOTION AND DECLARATION TO SERVE BY MAIL**, you will sign it and fill in the place (city and state) and date you signed. You are signing this pleading under penalty of perjury. This means that you are affirming that everything you have said in the petition is true and correct to the best your knowledge and belief. It is a crime to knowingly make any false statements.

Order Allowing Service by Mail

An **ORDER ALLOWING SERVICE BY MAIL** permits you to mail the **PETITION FOR DISSOLUTION** and **SUMMONS** to your spouse's last known address instead of having him or her personally served. If your are attempting to get such an order because your spouse is avoiding personal service, you will need to explain to the court how hard you have tried to have him or her served, and why you believe he or she is purposely avoiding you. For example, you might say that the process server has been to your spouse's house five times and a car was in the driveway, the lights were on, but no one would answer the door. If you think your spouse will be difficult to serve, it will be more advantageous for you to try to have him or her served by a professional process server, since if service cannot be accomplished, the process server will prepare a form for you called an *Affidavit of Attempts*. You can present this form to the court outlining all the steps that were taken to accomplish service. Complete the **ORDER ALLOWING SERVICE BY MAIL** as follows.

◈ Fill in the top portion of the form as instructed in Chapter 5, p.57.

◈ Under "I. BASIS" and "II. FINDINGS," type your spouse's name in the blank spaces.

◈ At paragraph 3.3, fill in the address you typed in paragraph 2.6 of the **MOTION** and **DECLARATION TO SERVE BY PUBLICATION.**

◈ At paragraph 3.4, check the box that applies to your situation and fill in any additional information as necessary.

◈ Below where the judge is to sign, write your name under the signature line and write "Pro Se" after your name. Then, sign above your name.

Summons by Mail

Complete the **SUMMONS BY MAIL** as follows.

◈ At paragraph 1, check the first box.

◈ At the end of the document, write your name under the signature line and write "Pro Se" after your name. Then, sign above your name. Under the section below that, check the first box and fill in the date you mail the **SUMMONS BY MAIL** and the **PETITION FOR DISSOLUTION** where indicated. You will usually mail the **SUMMONS** and **PETITION FOR DISSOLUTION** on the same day that they are filed.

You will need to obtain the **ORDER ALLOWING SERVICE BY MAIL** before you file the **SUMMONS BY MAIL** and the **PETITION FOR DISSOLUTION.** Contact the clerk of the court or the judge's bailiff to obtain a date for you to appear before the judge to do this. Sometimes you will not know that your spouse is avoiding service until you have already filed a regular **SUMMONS** along the **PETITION FOR DISSOLUTION.** In such a case, you will follow the same procedure described, and then file this second **SUMMONS BY MAIL** and mail it to your spouse along with the **PETITION FOR DISSOLUTION.** Make sure you precisely follow the mailing instructions contained in the **ORDER ALLOWING SERVICE BY MAIL.**

YOU DO NOT KNOW
WHERE YOUR SPOUSE LIVES

If you have no idea where your spouse lives, have no last known address for your spouse, and do not know where any of his or her family lives, you will need to prepare a **MOTION AND DECLARATION FOR SERVICE OF SUMMONS BY PUBLICATION** (form 13, p.229), **ORDER FOR SERVICE OF SUMMONS BY PUBLICATION** (form 14, p.231), and **SUMMONS BY PUBLICATION** (form 15, p.233).

Motion and Declaration for Service of Summons by Publication

Complete the **MOTION AND DECLARATION FOR SERVICE OF SUMMONS BY PUBLICATION** as follows.

◈ Complete the top portion of the form according to Chapter 5, page 57.

◈ Under "I. MOTION," fill in the date, write your name under the signature line and "Pro Se" after your name, and sign above that.

◈ At paragraph 2.1, check the box as it applies to your situation.

◈ At paragraphs 2.2 and 2.3, write in a brief description of why you believe your spouse is avoiding service and what you have done to locate him or her.

◈ At paragraph 2.4, check the second box.

Once you have completed the **MOTION AND DECLARATION FOR SERVICE OF SUMMONS BY PUBLICATION**, you will sign it and fill in the place (city and state) and date you signed. You are signing this pleading under penalty of perjury. This means that you are affirming that everything you have said in the petition is true and correct to the best your knowledge and belief. It is a crime to knowingly make any false statements.

Order for Service of Summons by Publication

An **ORDER FOR SUMMONS BY PUBLICATION** authorizes a copy of the **SUMMONS** to be printed in a local newspaper in lieu of personal service. The idea is that your spouse will receive notice by reading about it in the paper. This is highly unlikely, of course, but you need not be troubled with such realities in this case. If the court deems publication proper notice, then that is all you need. Complete the **Order for Service of Summons by Publication** as follows.

 ◈ Complete the top portion of the form according to the instructions in Chapter 5, p.57.

 ◈ Below where the judge is to sign, write your name under the signature line and write "Pro Se" after your name. Then, sign above your name.

Summons by Publication

Complete the **Summons by Publication** as follows.

 ◈ Complete the top portion of the form according to the instructions in Chapter 5, p.57.

 ◈ At paragraphs 1 and 2, check the boxes that apply to your situation.

 ◈ At paragraph 3, fill in the date that you anticipate will be date of the first publication of the summons.

 ◈ At the end of the document, write your name under the signature line and write "Pro Se" after your name. Then, sign above your name. Under the section below that, check the first box.

You will need to obtain the **Order for Service of Summons by Publication** before you file the **Summons by Publication** and the **Petition for Dissolution**. Contact the clerk of the court or the judge's bailiff to obtain a date for you to appear before the judge to do this. Sometimes you will not know that your spouse is avoiding service until you have already filed a regular **Summons** along the **Petition for Dissolution**. In such a case, you will follow the same procedures described, then file this second **Summons by Mail**, and then provide the **Summons by Publication** to the newspaper in which it will be published. If your spouse fails to respond to pleadings you have either mailed or had published within the time requirements contained in the **Summons**, you may obtain an **Order of Default**. (see form 9, p.221.)

Temporary Orders

In many divorce cases, it becomes necessary to have a judge issue temporary orders on the matters of child support, parenting, visitation, and spousal support. Such temporary orders may be desirable for any number of reasons. It may also be necessary to change such orders from time to time.

Example 1:

Your spouse has left you with the children, the mortgage, and monthly bills, and is not helping you out financially. You may want to ask the court to order your spouse to pay support for you and the children during the divorce process. Of course, if you were the only person bringing in income, do not expect to get any temporary support.

Example 2:

You and your spouse have separated, but have gotten into arguments over where the children will live until the divorce is final. Every time you allow the children to visit the other parent, you have a difficult time getting them back. You may want to ask the judge to enter a temporary **PARENTING PLAN**.

Example 3:

You are concerned for your safety or that your spouse may dissipate assets. You may want to ask the judge for an emergency (*ex parte*) order.

Example 4:

You already have a temporary order, but things are not working out or the circumstances have changed. You may want to ask the judge to change the temporary order.

TYPES OF FORMS

There are mandatory forms for obtaining temporary orders. All types of relief (child support, parenting, spousal maintenance, temporary use of property, or payment of debts) can be addressed using the same forms. This chapter discusses the following types of forms you will use in temporary hearing procedures:

- ✪ motions;

- ✪ orders; and,

- ✪ notices.

Motions   A *motion* is the basic form used to request the judge to either issue an initial order on a particular matter or to change an existing order. These include:

- ✪ **MOTION AND DECLARATION FOR TEMPORARY ORDER** (form 16) and

- ✪ *Motion and Declaration for Ex Parte Restraining Order and for Order to Show Cause.*

Orders   An *order* is the form the judge signs to resolve the issues brought up in the motion and response. These include:

- ✪ **TEMPORARY ORDER** (form 17);

- ✪ **TEMPORARY ORDER OF CHILD SUPPORT ORDER** (form 5);

✪   **Temporary Parenting Plan** (form 6); and,

✪   *Ex Parte Restraining Order / Order to Show Cause.*

Notices   A *notice* is a form used by one party to notify the other party that something is about to take place. This enables the other party to take appropriate action to protect his or her rights. The most common notice is a *notice of hearing*, which informs the other party of the date, time, and place of a court hearing, so they may submit forms and documents and attend the hearing. Most counties have a specific notice form that must be used. Check with the clerk of the court in your county for the form to notice a family law motion.

General Motion Procedures   The general procedure regarding motions for temporary custody, child support, visitation, and spousal support is as follows.

Prepare and file the motion. The person seeking the temporary order prepares and files the motion. There is no filing fee.

Notify other parties. The person seeking the temporary order notifies the other party. This is done by mailing the other party a copy of the motion and all other documents filed with the motion. Most counties have specific requirements of how far in advance the other party must be notified of the hearing. Check with the clerk of the court or the local court rules for the requirement for family law motions in your county.

Other party files a response. The spouse not seeking the order may file a response.

Attend the hearing. Both parties must attend the hearing with the judge. After hearing the oral arguments of the parties, the judge will then enter an order, which is prepared by the person seeking the order.

TEMPORARY ORDERS

Sometimes it will take you and your spouse a while to come to a final decision on parenting, child support, and spousal maintenance. In such a case, you may want to have temporary orders governing these issues, as well as payment of certain debts and use of certain assets, while final arrangements are being negotiated. If you and your spouse cannot agree to these temporary arrangements, you will need to prepare a **MOTION AND DECLARATION FOR TEMPORARY ORDER** (form 16, p.237) and **TEMPORARY ORDER** (form 17, p.241).

Complete the **MOTION AND DECLARATION FOR TEMPORARY ORDER** as follows.

◈ Complete the top portion of the form according to the instruction in Chapter 5, page 57.

◈ Under "I. MOTION," check all the boxes that correspond with all the issues you want the court to address.

◈ Under the signature line, type your name and "Pro Se" after that. Then, sign on the line above.

◈ Under "II. DECLARATION," you will need to provide a brief background history to the court and explain why the court should grant you the relief you are requesting. You will likely also need to attach exhibits that support your position. If you are requesting any sort of financial relief (child support, spousal maintenance, or payment of certain debts on your behalf), you will likely need to complete a **FINANCIAL DECLARATION** (form 18, p.245) and submit income information. Income information should *not* be attached to your motion. It should only be submitted to the court using the **SEALED FINANCIAL SOURCE DOCUMENTS COVER SHEET**. (see form 19, p.251.) Check with the local rules of your county to determine what financial documentation needs to be submitted.

Example:

If you are requesting spousal maintenance and child support, your declaration may read something like this:

My husband and I have been married for fifteen years. We have one child, Bobby, who is 13. From when Bobby was born until two years ago, I did not work outside the home. I now work part-time as a cashier at a local flower shop. I earn $1,000 net per month. My pay stubs are provided with the **SEALED FINANCIAL**

Source Documents Cover Sheet. *I only have a high school educa-tion, so my employment options at this time are limited. My husband is an executive at the Johnson Company, where he has worked throughout our marriage. He earns $6,000 net per month. He moved out of the house last month and Bobby lives primarily with me. As the court can see from my* **Financial Declaration,** *the monthly household expenses for Bobby and me total $3,500 per month. Based on our net incomes, I calculate child support to be $1,047.48 per month. Combined with my income, I need an additional $1,500 per month to meet our monthly household expenses. I am therefore asking my husband to pay $1,500 per month in spousal maintenance.*

At the end of your declaration, you will sign and fill in the place (city and state) and date you signed. You are signing this pleading under penalty of perjury. This means that you are affirming that everything you have said in the petition is true and correct to the best your knowledge and belief. It is a crime to knowingly make any false statements.

Sealed Financial Source Documents Cover Sheet

As previously mentioned, whenever financial information is filed with the court, it must be attached to a **Sealed Financial Source Documents Cover Sheet.** (see form 19, p.251.) Complete the **Sealed Financial Source Documents Cover Sheet** as follows.

◈ Complete the top portion of the form according to the instruc-tions in Chapter 5, page 57.

◈ Below that, check off the box(es) that correspond with the doc-uments you are attaching and fill in the date ranges of the documents.

◈ Sign and print your name under "Submitted by."

If you are requesting any kind of financial relief (child support, spousal maintenance, payment of debts), check with the local county rules or the family law facilitator in your county to determine what sort of financial information is required to be submitted and whether any additional doc-uments need to be prepared, such as a **Financial Declaration.**

Temporary Order

Once you have completed the **MOTION AND DECLARATION FOR TEMPORARY ORDERS**, you will also need to prepare a proposed **TEMPORARY ORDER** (form 17.) If your request includes child support or a **PARENTING PLAN**, you will need to prepare a proposed **ORDER OF CHILD SUPPORT** and **CHILD SUPPORT WORKSHEETS** and/or a proposed **PARENTING PLAN**. Instructions for preparing the proposed **ORDER OF CHILD SUPPORT**, **CHILD SUPPORT WORKSHEETS**, and **PARENTING PLAN** are contained in Chapter 6. The only difference of preparing proposed orders is that you will check the box indicating that fact instead of the box indicating they are final orders.

Complete the proposed **TEMPORARY ORDER** as follows.

◈ Complete the top portion of the form according to the instructions in Chapter 5, page 57.

◈ At paragraph 1.1, check the box that applies to your situation. If you are not seeking a restraining order, check the "Does not apply" box. If you are seeking a restraining order, check the "Restraining Order Summary" box. If you check that box, immediately below that write in the name of the person or persons who are restrained, and the name of the person or persons who are protected. Keep in mind that a restraining order can only apply to you, your spouse, or your children. You cannot restrain or protect any other third parties.

◈ At paragraph 1.2, check the box that applies to your situation. If you are asking that your spouse immediately pay you a certain sum, check the "Judgment Summary" box. Quite frankly, there will be very few situations where you will request a judgment at this stage.

◈ Paragraph 3.1 addresses "Restraining Orders." If you are not requesting a restraining order, check the first box. If you are requesting a restraining order, check the second box. If you check the second box, below that you will check all the boxes that apply to your situation and fill in the names of any children to be included in the restraining order. The restraining order then needs to be entered into the appropriate law enforcement database. Check the box next to the "CLERK'S ACTION" paragraph and write in the name of the police or sheriff's department where the protected person(s) live. The clerk of the court will then forward the restraining order information to that agency. Under the "SERVICE" section, check the first box. Under the "EXPIRATION DATE" section, enter in the date on which you and your spouse agree the restraining order will expire. If you do not want the order to expire, leave this blank.

◈   At paragraph 3.2, you will check the box(es) that correspond to the relief you want the court to grant, and fill in any additional information as necessary. You are completing this proposed **TEMPORARY ORDER** as if this was the order you wanted the judge to sign without any additions or changes.

◈   At paragraph 3.3, check the second box.

◈   Leave paragraph 3.4 blank.

◈   Below where the judge is to sign, write your name and "Pro Se" under the signature line that corresponds to the "Petitioner" or "Respondent," whichever party you are, and then sign.

Once you have completed the **MOTION AND DECLARATION FOR TEMPORARY ORDERS**, proposed **TEMPORARY ORDER**, and, if necessary, any additional pleadings, such as the **FINANCIAL DECLARATION**, **SEALED FINANCIAL SOURCE DOCUMENTS COVER SHEET**, **ORDER OF CHILD SUPPORT**, **CHILD SUPPORT WORKSHEETS**, or **PARENTING PLAN**, you will need to obtain a hearing date and fill out a **NOTE FOR MOTION**. The requirement for scheduling a motion and the **NOTE FOR MOTION** itself varies from county to county. Consult the county local rules, the clerk of the court, or the family law facilitator in your county for this information.

Now you are ready to serve your spouse with the motion, and any and all of the other pleadings you have prepared. Be sure to check with the local rules, the court clerk, the judge's secretary, or the family law facilitator to determine how far in advance of the hearing your spouse must be served, as this can vary from county to county. Unlike the **SUMMONS** and **PETITION FOR DISSOLUTION**, you can mail the motion to your spouse or give it to him or her directly. If you mail the motion, you will need to add three additional days to the time window for service set forth in the court rules. You will also need to file all original documents with the court and provide copies to the judge.

Most courts also require that your call the judge a few days before the hearing to confirm that the motion is still needed (i.e., that you and your spouse have not already reached an agreement). If confirmation of the hearing is required, it is very important that you do so. If you do not, the judge will not hear your motion and you will have to start the scheduling process all over again and notify your spouse of the new hearing date. Consult the county local rules, the clerk of the court, or the family law facilitator in your county for this information.

After your spouse has been served, he or she will have an opportunity to respond to the motion in writing. It is required that you receive a copy of the response and any proposed orders or additional pleadings your spouse files. You then get a chance to file a written reply with the court. Just as with the initial motion, this statement must have the case caption and the language that you are signing the statement under penalty of perjury. There is a template *Declaration* form available at **www.courts.wa.gov** that you can use.

Attending the Hearing

You will need to appear in person at the hearing and bring copies of all the pleadings you have prepared with you. Review the chapter on courtroom etiquette beforehand. In family law, all **MOTIONS FOR TEMPORARY ORDERS** are heard on the basis of the written materials you and your spouse submit. Other than the parties' oral arguments based on the declarations and other documents you have both submitted for the hearing, no other witnesses will testify at the hearing.

Challenging a Motion

If you are served with a **MOTION AND DECLARATION FOR TEMPORARY ORDERS** and other pleadings, and do not agree with what he or she is asking for, you will need to file a written response. You cannot just appear at the hearing and argue why your spouse should not get the relief he or she is seeking. You will need to prepare and file a **DECLARATION**. (form 16, p. 237.) Review the section above on filing a **MOTION AND DECLARATION FOR TEMPORARY ORDERS** on how to do this. If the **MOTION AND DECLARATION FOR TEMPORARY ORDERS** requests financial relief, you will likely also need to prepare a **FINANCIAL DECLARATION** and provide income information through the **SEALED FINANCIAL SOURCE DOCUMENTS COVER SHEET**. Check with the local county rules, the clerk of the court, the judge's bailiff, or the family law facilitator to determine what income information is needed, when the original of the response must be filed with the court, and when copies must be given to the judge and your spouse.

Like your spouse, you must also appear in person at the hearing. In family law, all **MOTIONS FOR TEMPORARY ORDERS** are heard on the basis of the written materials you and your spouse submit. So, other than the oral arguments of you and spouse at the hearing based on your declarations and the other documents you have both submitted for the hearing, no other witnesses will testify, although you may submit declarations from third parties who have information relevant to your case.

EX PARTE ORDERS

An *ex parte* order is entered with only one party being involved in the process. They are usually only used in an emergency situation, when there is a good reason for not waiting until the other party is notified of the motion and given an opportunity to respond before an order is entered.

Protecting Your Property

If you genuinely fear that your spouse will try to remove money from bank accounts, try to hide important papers showing what property you own, or hide items of property, you may want to take this same action before your spouse can. However, you can make a great deal of trouble for yourself with the judge if you do this to try to get these assets for yourself. So, make a complete list of any property you do take, and be sure to include these items in any financial statement you prepare or for anything else connected with your divorce case.

You may need to convince the judge that you only took these items temporarily, in order to preserve them until a **DECREE OF DISSOLUTION** is entered. Do not spend any cash you take from a bank account, or sell or give away any items of property. Any cash should be placed in a separate bank account, without your spouse's name on it, and kept separate from any other cash you have. (Of course, you may use funds to pay for necessary living expenses, such as rent, utility bills, food, medical bills, etc.)

Any papers such as deeds, car titles, stock or bond certificates, etc., should be placed in a safe-deposit box, without your spouse's name on them. The idea is not to take these things for yourself, but to get them in a safe place so your spouse cannot hide them and deny they ever existed.

Ex Parte Restraining Order

One other thing you can do to try to protect your property is seek an immediate **Ex Parte Restraining Order**. This type of order can also be used to obtain a personal restraining order and to prevent your spouse from removing the children from the State of Washington. However, if you are truly concerned about the latter two issues, you will either want to obtain an *Order for Protection* or seek the immediate advice of any attorney.

The general process for obtaining an *Ex Parte Restraining Order* is to complete the *Motion/Declaration for Ex Parte Restraining Order and for Order to Show Cause* and *Ex Parte Restraining Order/Order to Show Cause*. These forms can be obtained online at **www.courts.wa.gov**. There is generally someone at the courthouse available to assist you with these forms. Ask the clerk or the family law facilitator who to see.

In your Motion, you can both ask for immediate relief preventing your spouse from doing a certain act, and you can ask the court to award additional relief at a subsequent hearing. You will then appear before a judge who may or may not grant you the immediate relief you want. Assuming that relief is granted, a hearing will be held shortly thereafter to determine if the immediate relief granted should stay in place and whether any additional relief should be granted.

You will take the *Motion/Declaration for Ex Parte Restraining Order and for Order to Show Cause* and *Ex Parte Restraining Order/Order to Show Cause* to the judge to sign before you file the original and serve a copy to your spouse. You will also need to provide a copy of your motion for the judge for the second hearing. Check with the clerk of the court or the judge's bailiff on how to do this.

Unlike a **Motion and Declaration for Temporary Orders**, you will need to personally serve your spouse with all pleadings. You must serve your spouse with a copy of the *Ex Parte Restraining Order/Order to Show Cause* that shows the judge has signed it. See the section in this chapter concerning a **Motion and Declaration for Temporary Orders** for additional documentary requirements if you are seeking other temporary relief (for example child support and

PARENTING PLAN) in your *Motion/Declaration for Ex Parte Restraining Order and for Order to Show Cause*. Always check with the local rules, clerk of the court, the judge's bailiff, or the family law facilitator to see if there are additional documents that need to be prepared or served with your motion, as this may vary from county to county.

If your spouse obtained an ex parte order, you will probably first know about it when you receive a copy of the order. You may receive it in the mail, or be served by a sheriff deputy or other process server. A hearing will soon be had to determine if the relief granted in the ex parte order will stay in effect while the divorce is in progress. You will need to respond to this motion in the same way you would respond for a **MOTION FOR TEMPORARY ORDER**.

ENTERING ORDERS

Basically, a court order is *entered* when it is signed by the judge. If you and your spouse agree, and both of you sign the order, the order can simply be mailed or delivered to the judge. The judge will see both of your signatures and will know there is no argument. No hearing is required, and the judge will sign the order and mail copies back to you, or the judge's clerk will make copies for you at the courthouse.

If there has been a hearing on the motion, there are three ways to get the order signed by the judge. First, if the order can be quickly prepared at the hearing, it can be handed to the judge for his or her signature at that time. Second, the order can be prepared shortly after the hearing, and then mailed or delivered to the judge. Third, the order can be presented to the judge at a subsequent hearing.

Usually, a subsequent hearing is not necessary unless there is a dispute over what was ordered at the hearing on the motion, and whether what was ordered is accurately reflected in the proposed order. The accuracy of the proposed order can be questioned either by the judge or by your spouse (or by you if your spouse has prepared the order and you do not think it is accurate).

If you did not get your order prepared and signed by the judge at the hearing and there is a dispute over the order, you will need to contact the judge's clerk to determine how and when the judge would like to handle the subsequent hearing. One of two things will happen. Either the judge will end up signing your original proposed order or the judge will give you instructions about how he or she wants a new order prepared. If a new order is required, you will need to prepare the new order and submit it to the judge as soon as possible. (Be sure to read Chapter 9 regarding preparing for and presenting your case at the hearing.)

chapter 12

Special Circumstances

There are exceptions to every rule and every way of doing things. The divorce procedures discussed thus far have been explained with the caveat that the procedure is straightforward with no real extenuating factors. However, that is not always the case. This chapter explores some of the special circumstances that must be considered by some parties.

WHEN YOU CANNOT AFFORD COURT COSTS

If you cannot afford to pay the filing fee and other costs associated with the divorce, you can ask the court to waive the filing fees. In order to qualify for a waiver of the filing fee, you must be *indigent*. If you are indigent, your income is probably low enough for you to qualify for public assistance (welfare). Check with the family court facilitator in your county to determine if you qualify for a waiver, and obtain the forms to do so.

– Caution –

If you seek a waiver, you must prove that you meet the requirements for being declared indigent, and therefore, eligible to have the filing and service fees waived. Be aware that you can be held in contempt of court for giving false information.

PROTECTING YOURSELF AND YOUR CHILDREN

Some people have special concerns when getting prepared to file for a divorce. Two such concerns can be fear of physical attack by their spouse, and fear that their spouse will take the children and run away, go into hiding, or even take them out of the country. There are additional actions you can take if you are concerned about either or both of these situations.

If your spouse is determined and resourceful, there is no guaranteed way to prevent the things discussed in this section from happening. All you can do is put as many obstacles as possible in your spouse's way.

To protect yourself and your children from harm, you can seek an **ORDER FOR PROTECTION**. Your spouse must either have actually done something, threatened to do something, or you must have a reasonable fear of imminent physical harm. An **ORDER FOR PROTECTION** will subject your spouse to arrest for violating the requirements of the order. If you think you need an **ORDER FOR PROTECTION**, many county courts have domestic violence advocates who work for the court and can assist you with completing the forms.

Keep a copy of any personal protection order issued by the judge. If your spouse does anything that you believe violates the order, call the police. Show them the order when they arrive.

Kidnapping Prevention

If you are worried that your spouse may try to kidnap your children, you should make sure that the day care center, baby-sitter, relative, or whomever you leave the children with at any time is aware that you are in the process of a divorce, and that the children are only to be released to you personally (not to your spouse or to any other relative, friend, etc.).

To prevent your spouse from taking the children out of the United States, you can apply for a passport for each child. Once a passport is issued, the government will not issue another. So get their passports and lock up the passports in a safe-deposit box or other safe place where you are absolutely sure your spouse cannot get them. You can also file a motion to prevent the removal of the children from the state.

If you are genuinely worried that your spouse may try to take your child(ren) out of the country, it would be a good idea for you to consult a lawyer. This is too serious of a matter for you to try to handle yourself.

TAXES

As you are no doubt aware, the United States' income tax code is complicated and ever-changing. It is impossible to give detailed legal advice with respect to taxes in a book such as this. Therefore, it is strongly recommended that you consult your accountant, lawyer, or whomever prepares your tax return about the tax consequences of a divorce. A few general concerns are discussed in this chapter to give you an idea of some of the tax questions that can arise.

Taxes and Property Division

You and your spouse may be exchanging title to property as a result of your divorce. Generally, there will not be any tax to pay as the result of such a transfer. However, whomever gets a piece of property will be responsible to pay any tax that may become due upon sale.

The *Internal Revenue Service* (IRS) has issued numerous rulings about how property is to be treated in divorce situations. You need to be especially careful if you are transferring any tax shelters or other complicated financial arrangements, in which case you should consult a tax expert.

Taxes and Spousal Maintenance

Maintenance can cause the most tax problems of any aspect of divorce. The IRS is always making new rulings on whether an agreement is really maintenance or is really property division. The basic rule is that alimony is treated as income to the person receiving it and as a deduction for the person paying it.

In order to manipulate the tax consequences, many couples try to show something as part of the property settlement instead of as maintenance, or the reverse. As the IRS becomes aware of these *tax games*, it issues rulings on how it will view a certain arrangement.

If you are simply talking about the regular, periodic payment of cash, the IRS will probably not question that it is maintenance. The important thing is to consult a tax expert if you are considering any unusual or creative property settlement or alimony arrangements.

Taxes and Child Support

There are three fairly simple tax rules regarding child support.

1. Whoever has primary care gets to claim the children on his or her tax return unless both parents file an IRS form 8832 agreeing to a different arrangement each year. (Go to **www.irs.gov** to obtain the form or call the IRS at 800-839-1040 for more information.)

2. The parent receiving child support does not need to report it as income.

3. The parent paying child support cannot deduct it.

PENSION PLANS

The pension plans (retirement plans, IRAs, 401(k)s) of you and your spouse are marital assets. They may be very valuable assets. If you and your spouse are young and have not been working very long, you may not have pension plans worth worrying about. Also, if you have both worked and have similar pensions plans, it may be best just to include a provision in your settlement agreement that *each party shall keep his or her own pension plan*. But if you have been married a long time and your spouse worked while you stayed home to raise the children, your spouse's pension plan may be worth a lot of money. That plan may be necessary to see you through retirement.

If you and your spouse cannot agree on how to divide your pension plans, you should see an attorney about obtaining a *Qualified Domestic Relations Order* (QDRO, which is commonly pronounced *qwá-drow* by lawyers and judges). This document tells the pension plan manager how to divide payments. The valuation and division of pension plans are complicated matters that you should not attempt by yourself.

RELOCATION

Washington has special laws regarding a parent moving with the children once a **PARENTING PLAN** is in place. Absent the agreement of the parents to allow the move and the filing of a new **PARENTING PLAN**, the spouse who seeks to move with the children must obtain a court order authorizing the move. This requires notice of the move to the non-moving party and an opportunity for that party to object to the move.

This procedure need only be followed if a parent (normally, the primarily residential parent) seeks to relocate the children. The court cannot prevent an adult from relocating on his or her own.

Per statute, there is a rebuttable presumption that the intended relocation of a child will be allowed by the court. The nonmoving party may attempt to rebut that presumption based on the following factors.

- The relative strength, nature, quality, extent of involvement, and stability of the child's relationship with each parent, siblings, and other significant persons in the child's life.

- Prior agreements of the parties.

- Whether disrupting the contact between the child and the person with whom the child resides the majority of the time would be more detrimental to the child than disrupting contact between the child and the person objecting to the relocation.

- Whether either parent or a person entitled to residential time with the child is subject to limitations under RCW 26.09.191.

- The reasons of each person for seeking or opposing the relocation, and the good faith of each of the parties requesting or opposing the relocation.

- The age, developmental stage, and needs of the child, and the likely impact the relocation or its prevention will have on the child's physical, educational, and emotional development, taking into consideration any special needs of the child.

✪   The quality of life, resources, and opportunities available to the child and to the relocating party in the current and proposed geographic locations.

✪   The availability of alternative arrangements to foster and continue the child's relationship with and access to the other parent.

✪   The alternatives to relocation, and whether it is feasible and desirable for the other party to relocate also.

✪   The financial impact and logistics of the relocations or its prevention.

Notice of Intended Relocation of Children

Initially, the moving spouse is required to prepare a *Notice of Intended Relocation of Children*. This form must be filed with the court and served on the nonmoving parent at least sixty days prior to the move or no later than five days after learning of the need to move if sixty-days' notice cannot be given (for example, a spouse learns that her employer wants her to transfer out-of-state in thirty days). A *Notice of Intended Relocation of Children* is required any time a parent seeks to move a child outside of his or her current school district.

If the nonmoving spouse wants to object to the move or the proposed **Parenting Plan**, a separate set of forms must be completed within thirty days of receiving the *Notice of Intended Relocation*.

Contested relocation cases can be long and involved, and often require the assistance of an expert such as a *guardian ad litem*. You should seek the advice of any attorney in any contested relocation matter.

Glossary

A

acknowledgment. A statement, written or oral, made before a person authorized by law to administer oaths (such as a notary public).

adult. In most states, a person 18 years of age or older.

affiant. The legal term for the person who signs an affidavit.

affidavit. A person's written statement of facts, signed under oath before a person authorized to administer oaths (such as a notary public or court clerk).

alimony. *See spousal maintenance.*

annulment. A legal procedure by which a marriage is declared invalid.

answer. *See response.*

C

counterpetition. A response to a petition, which seeks some relief from the court rather than merely admitting or denying the allegations in the petition.

creditor. A person or institution to whom money is owed.

D

debtor. A person or institution who owes money.

decree. The final pleading that ends the marriage, divides property and debts of the marriage, and awards spousal maintenance.

deposition. The posing of verbal questions to one party, who is required to answer verbally under oath, usually before a court reporter.

E

equitable distribution. A way to divide marital property, the goal of which is to treat the parties fairly under the circumstances.

execute. To sign a legal document in the legally required manner (e.g., before witnesses or a notary public), thereby making it effective.

F

final judgment. The order of the court at the end of a trial or pursuant to a settlement agreement.

H

homestead. Real estate that is a person's primary place of residence. The homestead is given special treatment for property tax purposes and is exempt from the claims of creditors (other than a creditor holding a mortgage on the homestead property).

I

institution. As used in this book, any type of business entity (e.g., corporation, partnership, limited liability company), organization, or other entity other than an individual person.

instrument. A legal term for a document.

interrogatories. Written questions sent by one party to the other that must be answered in writing under oath.

irretrievably broken. A legal way of saying that a marriage is broken and cannot be repaired.

J

joint custody. A situation in which both parents share the responsibility of making decisions regarding their child.

joint tenancy. A way for two or more people to own property, so that when one owner dies, his or her interest in the property passes automatically to the remaining owner or owners.

M

maintenance. *See spousal maintenance.*

marital assets. Assets that are considered the property of both parties to a marriage.

motion. A party's written or oral request that the judge take certain action.

N

nonmarital assets. Assets that are considered the separate property of only one party to a marriage. Generally, these are assets that were acquired before the marriage, or acquired by one party as a separate gift or inheritance.

notary public. A person who is legally authorized by the state to acknowledge signatures on legal documents.

O

order of child support. The order that sets forth which parent pays (obligor) and which parent receives (obligee) child support.

P

parenting plan. The order that sets forth with which parent the children reside and when.

pay-on-death account. A financial account, such as a bank account or certificate of deposit, that is payable to a certain person upon the death of the account holder.

personal property. All property other than land and things permanently attached to the land (such as buildings).

petition. The title of the legal pleading that begins a divorce case.

pleading. Generally, any type of document that is filed with the court.

R

recording. The process of filing a deed, mortgage, or other legal document affecting title to land with the court clerk's office.

response. The title of a legal pleading that responds to a petition, usually by either admitting or denying the allegations in the petition.

S

spousal maintenance. Money paid by one spouse to help support the other spouse.

subpoena. An order from a court that a person appear before the court or at a deposition, and give testimony.

subpoena *duces tecum*. A particular type of subpoena that requires the person to bring certain, specified documents, records, or other items to the court or deposition.

T

tenancy by the entirety. This is essentially the same as joint tenancy, but it can only occur between a husband and wife. Upon the death of one spouse, the property automatically passes to the surviving spouse. In states that do not have a tenancy by the entirety, spouses typically hold property as joint tenants with rights of survivorship.

tenancy in common. A way for two or more people to own property, whereby if one of the owners dies, his or her interest in the property passes to his or her heirs (not to the other co-owners).

third party. As used in this book, a party who is neither a principal nor an agent under a power of attorney.

title. A document that proves ownership of property.

Washington Child Support Guidelines

The information in this appendix is taken from the official child support guidelines. If you would like to read the full text of these guidelines, check with your local law library for a copy of the *Revised Code of Washington 26.19*.

You may review these guidelines at:
www1.dshs.wa.gov/pdf/esa/dcs/schedule2000.pdf
or
www.courts.wa.gov/forms/?fa=forms.static&staticID=14
(Listed under "Domestic Relations Forms")

See "Legal Research" in Chapter 2 for more sources of information about all aspects of divorce in Washington. Also, be sure to read Chapter 4 for more information about calculating child support.

The basic procedure used to arrive at the total support obligation is as follows.

1. Each parent's monthly net income is calculated. This involves adding up the gross income from all sources, then applying allowed deductions to arrive at net income.

2. The parents' net incomes are added together to arrive at the total family income.

3. The base support amount is determined by using the tables in the section titled "Washington State Child Support Schedule Economic Table."

4. Amounts for extraordinary health care expenses, health care insurance, and child care expenses are added to the base support amount to arrive at the total support amount.

5. The total support amount is allocated between the parents based on their respective percentage of the total family income.

WASHINGTON STATE
CHILD SUPPORT SCHEDULE

Including:

- Definitions and Standards
- Instructions
- Economic Table
- Worksheets

Effective Dates:

Definitions & Standards	September 1, 2000
Instructions	September 1, 2000
Economic Table	September 1, 2000
Worksheets	September 1, 2000

WASHINGTON
COURTS
ADMINISTRATIVE OFFICE OF THE COURTS

Administrative Office of the Courts
State of Washington
1206 Quince Street SE
P.O. Box 41174
Olympia, WA 98504-1174

Order forms--voice mail telephone number	**(360) 705-5328**
Internet--download forms:	http://www.courts.wa.gov/
Questions about the Instructions or Worksheets?	Contact: Merrie Gough
Tel. (360) 357-2128	Fax (360) 357-2127
E-mail merrie.gough@courts.wa.gov *or*	webmaster@courts.wa.gov

Child Support Hotline, State DSHS, 1 (800) 442-KIDS

WASHINGTON STATE CHILD SUPPORT SCHEDULE
DEFINITIONS AND STANDARDS

DEFINITIONS

Unless the context clearly requires otherwise, these definitions apply to the standards following this section.

Basic child support obligation: means the monthly child support obligation determined from the economic table based on the parties' combined monthly net income and the number of children for whom support is owed.

Child support schedule: means the standards, economic table, worksheets and instructions, as defined in chapter 26.19 RCW.

Court: means a superior court judge, court commissioner and presiding and reviewing officers who administratively determine or enforce child support orders.

Deviation: means a child support amount that differs from the standard calculation.

Economic table: means the child support table for the basic support obligation provided in RCW 26.19.020.

Instructions: means the instructions developed by the Office of the Administrator for the Courts pursuant to RCW 26.19.050 for use in completing the worksheets.

Standards: means the standards for determination of child support as provided in chapter 26.19 RCW.

Standard calculation: means the presumptive amount of child support owed as determined from the child support schedule before the court considers any reasons for deviation.

Support transfer payment: means the amount of money the court orders one parent to pay to another parent or custodian for child support after determination of the standard calculation and deviations. If certain expenses or credits are expected to fluctuate and the order states a formula or percentage to determine the additional amount or credit on an ongoing basis, the term "support transfer payment" does not mean the additional amount or credit.

Worksheets: means the forms developed by the Office of the Administrator for the Courts pursuant to RCW 26.19.050 for use in determining the amount of child support.

APPLICATION STANDARDS

1. Application of the support schedule: The child support schedule shall be applied:
    a. in each county of the state;
    b. in judicial and administrative proceedings under titles 13, 26 and 74 RCW;
    c. in all proceedings in which child support is determined or modified;
    d. in setting temporary and permanent support;
    e. in automatic modification provisions or decrees entered pursuant to RCW 26.09.100; and
    f. in addition to proceedings in which child support is

determined for minors, to adult children who are dependent on their parents and for whom support is ordered pursuant to RCW 26.09.100.

The provisions of RCW 26.19 for determining child support and reasons for deviation from the standard calculation shall be applied in the same manner by the court, presiding officers and reviewing officers.

2. Written findings of fact supported by the evidence: An order for child support shall be supported by written findings of fact upon which the support determination is based and shall include reasons for any deviation from the standard calculation and reasons for denial of a party's request for deviation from the standard calculation. RCW 26.19.035(2)

3. Completion of worksheets: Worksheets in the form developed by the Office of the Administrator for the Courts shall be completed under penalty of perjury and filed in every proceeding in which child support is determined. The court shall not accept incomplete worksheets or worksheets that vary from the worksheets developed by the Office of the Administrator for the Courts.

4. Court review of the worksheets and order: The court shall review the worksheets and the order setting child support for the adequacy of the reasons set forth for any deviation or denial of any request for deviation and for the adequacy of the amount of support ordered. Each order shall state the amount of child support calculated using the standard calculation and the amount of child support actually ordered. Worksheets shall be attached to the decree or order or if filed separately shall be initialed or signed by the judge and filed with the order.

INCOME STANDARDS

1. Consideration of all income: All income and resources of each parent's household shall be disclosed and considered by the court when the court determines the child support obligation of each parent. Only the income of the parents of the children whose support is at issue shall be calculated for purposes of calculating the basic support obligation. Income and resources of any other person shall not be included in calculating the basic support obligation.

2. Verification of income: Tax returns for the preceding two years and current paystubs shall be provided to verify income and deductions. Other sufficient verification shall be required for income and deductions which do not appear on tax returns or paystubs.

3. Income sources included in gross monthly income: Monthly gross income shall include income from any source, including: salaries; wages; commissions; deferred compensation; overtime; contract-related benefits; income from second jobs; dividends; interest; trust income; severance pay; annuities; capital gains; pension retirement benefits; workers' compensation; unemployment benefits; spousal maintenance actually received; bonuses; social security benefits and disability insurance benefits.

Veterans' disability pensions: Veterans' disability pensions or regular compensation for disability incurred in or aggravated by service in the United States armed forces paid by the Veterans' Administration shall be disclosed to the court. The court may consider either type of compensation as disposable income for purposes of calculating the child support obligation.

4. Income sources excluded from gross monthly income: The following income and resources shall be disclosed but shall not be included in gross income: income of a new spouse or income of other adults in the household; child support received from other relationships; gifts and prizes; temporary assistance for needy families; Supplemental Security Income; general assistance and food stamps. Receipt of income and resources from temporary assistance for needy families, Supplemental Security Income, general assistance and food stamps shall not be a reason to deviate from the standard calculation.

VA aid and attendant care: Aid and attendant care payments to prevent hospitalization paid by the Veterans Administration solely to provide physical home care for a disabled veteran, and special compensation paid under 38 U.S.C. Sec. 314(k) through (r) to provide either special care or special aids, or both to assist with routine daily functions shall be disclosed. The court may not include either aid or attendant care or special medical compensation payments in gross income for purposes of calculating the child support obligation or for purposes of deviating from the standard calculation.

Other aid and attendant care: Payments from any source, other than veterans' aid and attendance allowance or special medical compensation paid under 38 U.S.C. Sec. 314(k) through (r) for services provided by an attendant in case of a disability when the disability necessitates the hiring of the services or an attendant shall be disclosed but shall not be included in gross income and shall not be a reason to deviate from the standard calculation.

5. Determination of net income: The following expenses shall be disclosed and deducted from gross monthly income to calculate net monthly income: federal and state income taxes (see the following paragraph); federal insurance contributions act deductions (FICA); mandatory pension plan payments; mandatory union or professional dues; state industrial insurance premiums; court-ordered spousal maintenance to the extent actually paid; up to two thousand dollars per year in voluntary pension payments actually made if the contributions were made for the two tax years preceding the earlier of the tax year in which the parties separated with intent to live separate and apart or the tax year in which the parties filed for dissolution; and normal business expenses and self-employment taxes for self-employed persons. Justification shall be required for any business expense deduction about which there is a disagreement. Items deducted from gross income shall not be a reason to deviate from the standard calculation.

Allocation of tax exemptions: The parties may agree which parent is entitled to claim the child or children as dependents for federal income tax exemptions. The court may award the exemption or exemptions and order a party to sign the federal income tax dependency exemption waiver. The court may divide the exemptions between the parties, alternate the exemptions between the parties or both.

6. Imputation of income: The court shall impute income to a parent when the parent is voluntarily unemployed or voluntarily underemployed. The court shall determine whether the parent is voluntarily underemployed or voluntarily unemployed based upon that parent's work history, education, health and age or any other relevant factors. A court shall not impute income to a parent who is gainfully employed on a full-time basis, unless the court finds that the parent is voluntarily underemployed and finds that the parent is purposely underemployed to reduce the parent's child support obligation. Income shall not be imputed for an unemployable parent. Income shall not be imputed to a parent to the extent the parent is unemployed or significantly underemployed due to the parent's efforts to comply with court-ordered reunification efforts under chapter 13.34 RCW or under a voluntary placement agreement with an agency supervising the child. In the absence of information to the contrary, a parent's imputed income shall be based on the median income of year-round full-time workers as derived from the United States Bureau of Census, current population reports, or such replacement report as published by the Bureau of Census. (See "Approximate Median Net Monthly Income" chart on page 5.)

ALLOCATION STANDARDS

1. Basic child support: The basic child support obligation derived from the economic table shall be allocated between the parents based on each parent's share of the combined monthly net income.

2. Health care expenses: Ordinary health care expenses are included in the economic table. Monthly health care expenses that exceed 5 percent of the basic support obligation shall be considered extraordinary health care expenses. Extraordinary health care expenses shall be shared by the parents in the same proportion as the basic support obligation.

3. Day care and special child rearing expenses: Day care and special child rearing expenses, such as tuition and long distance transportation costs to and from the parents for visitation purposes, are not included in the economic table. These expenses shall be shared by the parents in the same proportion as the basic child support obligation. RCW 26.19.080

4. The court may exercise its discretion to determine the necessity for and the reasonableness of all amounts ordered in excess of the basic child support obligation.

LIMITATIONS STANDARDS

1. Limit at 45 percent of a parent's net income:
Neither parent's total child support obligation may exceed 45 percent of net income except for good cause shown. Good cause includes but is not limited to possession of substantial wealth, children with day care expenses, special medical need, educational need, psychological need and larger families.

2. Income below six hundred dollars: When combined monthly net income is less than six hundred dollars, a support order of not less than twenty-five dollars per child per month shall be entered for each parent unless the obligor parent establishes that it would be unjust or inappropriate to do so in that particular case. The decision whether there is a sufficient basis to go below the

presumptive minimum payment must take into consideration the best interests of the child and circumstances of each parent. Such circumstances can include comparative hardship to the affected households, assets or liabilities, and earning capacity.

Basic subsistence limitation: A parent's support obligation shall not reduce his or her net income below the need standard for one person established pursuant to RCW 74.04.770, except for the presumptive minimum payment of twenty-five dollars per child per month or in cases where the court finds reasons for deviation. This section shall not be construed to require monthly substantiation of income. (See www.nwjustice.org for the "Washington State Need Standard Chart.")

3.   Income above five thousand and seven thousand dollars: In general setting support under this paragraph does not constitute a deviation. The economic table is presumptive for combined monthly net incomes up to and including five thousand dollars. When combined monthly net income exceeds five thousand dollars, support shall not be set at an amount lower than the presumptive amount of support set for combined monthly net incomes of five thousand dollars unless the court finds a reason to deviate below that amount. The economic table is advisory but not presumptive for combined monthly net income that exceeds five thousand dollars. When combined monthly net income exceeds seven thousand dollars, the court may set support at an advisory amount of support set for combined monthly net incomes between five thousand and seven thousand dollars or the court may exceed the advisory amount of support for combined monthly net income of seven thousand dollars upon written findings of fact.

DEVIATION STANDARDS

1.   Reasons for deviation from the standard calculation include but are not limited to the following:

a.   Sources of income and tax planning: The court may deviate from the standard calculation after consideration of the following:
i.   Income of a new spouse if the parent who is married to the new spouse is asking for a deviation based on any other reason. Income of a new spouse is not, by itself, a sufficient reason for deviation;
ii.   Income of other adults in the household if the parent who is living with the other adult is asking for a deviation based on any other reason. Income of the other adults in the household is not, by itself, a sufficient reason for deviation;
iii.   Child support actually received from other relationships;
iv.   Gifts;
v.   Prizes;
vi.   Possession of wealth, including but not limited to savings, investments, real estate holdings and business interests, vehicles, boats, pensions, bank accounts, insurance plans or other assets;
vii.   Extraordinary income of a child; or
viii.   Tax planning considerations. A deviation for tax planning may be granted only if the child would not receive a lesser economic benefit due to the tax planning.

b.   Nonrecurring income: The court may deviate from the standard calculation based on a finding that a particular source of income included in the calculation of the basic support obligation is not a recurring source of income. Depending on the circumstances, nonrecurring income may include overtime, contract-related benefits, bonuses or income from second jobs. Deviations for nonrecurring income shall be based on a review of the nonrecurring income received in the previous two calendar years.

c.   Debt and high expenses: The court may deviate from the standard calculation after consideration of the following expenses:
i.   Extraordinary debt not voluntarily incurred;
ii.   A significant disparity in the living costs of the parents due to conditions beyond their control;
iii.   Special needs of disabled children; or
iv.   Special medical, educational or psychological needs of the children.
v.   Costs anticipated to be incurred by the parents in compliance with court-ordered reunification efforts under chapter 13.34 RCW or under a voluntary placement agreement with an agency supervising the child.

d.   Residential schedule: The court may deviate from the standard calculation if the child spends a significant amount of time with the parent who is obligated to make a support transfer payment. The court may not deviate on that basis if the deviation will result in insufficient funds in the household receiving the support to meet the basic needs of the child or if the child is receiving temporary assistance for needy families. When determining the amount of the deviation, the court shall consider evidence concerning the increased expenses to a parent making support transfer payments resulting from the significant amount of time spent with that parent and shall consider the decreased expenses, if any, to the party receiving the support resulting from the significant amount of time the child spends with the parent making the support transfer payment.

e.   Children from other relationships: The court may deviate from the standard calculation when either or both of the parents before the court have children from other relationships to whom the parent owes a duty of support.
i.   The child support schedule shall be applied to the mother, father and children of the family before the court to determine the presumptive amount of support.
ii.   Children from other relationships shall not be counted in the number of children for purposes of determining the basic support obligation and the standard calculation.
iii.   When considering a deviation from the standard calculation for children from other relationships, the court may consider only other children to whom the parent owes a duty of support. The court may consider court-ordered payments of child support for children from other relationships only to the extent that the support is actually paid.

iv. When the court has determined that either or both parents have children from other relationships, deviations under this section shall be based on consideration of the total circumstances of both households.   All child support obligations paid, received and owed for all children shall be disclosed and considered.

2.   All income and resources of the parties before the court, new spouses, and other adults in the household shall be disclosed and considered as provided.   The presumptive amount of support shall be determined according to the child support schedule. Unless specific reasons for deviation are set forth in the written findings of fact and are supported by the evidence, the court shall order each parent to pay the amount of support determined by using the standard calculation.

3.   The court shall enter findings that specify reasons for any deviation or any denial of a party's request for any deviation from the standard calculation made by the court. The court shall not consider reasons for deviation until the court determines the standard calculation for each parent.

4.   When reasons exist for deviation, the court shall exercise discretion in considering the extent to which the factors would affect the support obligation.

5.   Agreement of the parties is not by itself adequate reason for any deviations from the standard calculations.

POST-SECONDARY EDUCATION STANDARDS

1.   The child support schedule shall be advisory and not mandatory for post-secondary educational support.

2.   When considering whether to order support for post-secondary educational expenses, the court shall determine whether the child is in fact dependent and is relying upon the parents for the reasonable necessities of life. The court shall exercise its discretion when determining whether and for how long to award post-secondary educational support based upon consideration of factors that include but are not limited to the following: age of the child; the child's needs; the expectations of the parties for their children when the parents were together; the child's prospects, desires, aptitudes, abilities or disabilities; the nature of the post-secondary education sought and the parent's level of education, standard of living and current and future resources. Also to be considered are the amount and type of support that the child would have been afforded if the parents had stayed together.

3.   The child must enroll in an accredited academic or vocational school, must be actively pursuing a course of study commensurate with the child's vocational goals and must be in good academic standing as defined by the institution. The court-ordered post-secondary educational support shall be automatically suspended during the period or periods the child fails to comply with these conditions.

4.   The child shall also make available all academic records and grades to both parents as a condition of receiving post-secondary educational support.   Each parent shall have full and equal access to the post-secondary education records as provided by statute (RCW 26.09.225).

5.   The court shall not order the payment of post-secondary educational expenses beyond the child's twenty-third birthday, except for exceptional circumstances, such as mental, physical or emotional disabilities.

6.   The court shall direct that either or both parents' payments for post-secondary educational expenses are made directly to the educational institution if feasible. If direct payments are not feasible, then the court in its discretion may order that either or both parents' payments are made directly to the child if the child does not reside with either parent. If the child resides with one of the parents, the court may direct that the parent making the support transfer payments make the payments to the child or to the parent who has been receiving the support transfer payments.

WASHINGTON STATE CHILD SUPPORT SCHEDULE
INSTRUCTIONS FOR WORKSHEETS

Fill in the names and ages of only those children whose support is at issue.

PART I: BASIC CHILD SUPPORT OBLIGATION

Pursuant to INCOME STANDARD #1: Consideration of all income, "only the income of the parents of the children whose support is at issue shall be calculated for purposes of calculating the basic support obligation." (See page 1.)

Pursuant to INCOME STANDARD #2: Verification of income, "tax returns for the preceding two years and current paystubs are required for income verification purposes. Other sufficient verification shall be required for income and deductions which do not appear on tax returns or paystubs." (See page 1.)

GROSS MONTHLY INCOME

Gross monthly income is defined under INCOME STANDARD #3: Income sources included in gross monthly income. (See page 1.)

Income exclusions are defined under INCOME STANDARD #4: Income sources excluded from gross monthly income. (See page 2.) Excluded income must be disclosed and listed in Part VI of the worksheets.

Monthly Average of Income:
- If income varies during the year, divide the annual total of the income by 12.
- If paid weekly, multiply the weekly income by 52 and divide by 12.
- If paid every other week, multiply the two-week income by 26 and divide by 12.
- If paid twice a month (bi-monthly), multiply the bi-monthly income by 24 and divide by 12.

If a parent is unemployed, underemployed or the income of a parent is unknown, refer to "INCOME STANDARD #6: Imputation of income." (See page 2.)

In the absence of information to the contrary, a parent's imputed income shall be based on the following table.

Approximate Median Net Monthly Income

MALE	age	FEMALE
$1,363	15-24	$1,222
$2,154	25-34	$1,807
$2,610	35-44	$1,957
$2,846	45-54	$2,051
$2,880	55-64	$1,904
$2,828	65 +	$1,940

U.S. Bureau of the Census, Money Income in the United States: 1998, Current Population Reports, Median Income of People by Selected Characteristics: 1998, Full-Time, Year-Round Workers, Table 7.

[Net income has been determined by subtracting FICA (7.65 percent) and the tax liability for a single person (one withholding allowance).]

LINE 1a, Wages and Salaries: Enter the average monthly total of all salaries, wages, contract-related benefits, income from second jobs and bonuses.

LINE 1b, Interest and Dividend Income: Enter the average monthly total of dividends and interest income.

LINE 1c, Business Income: Enter the average monthly income from self-employment.

LINE 1d, Spousal Maintenance Received: Enter the monthly amount of spousal maintenance actually received.

LINE 1e, Other Income: Enter the average monthly total of other income. (Other income includes, but is not limited to: trust income, severance pay, annuities, capital gains, pension retirement benefits, workers compensation, unemployment benefits, social security benefits and disability insurance benefits.)

LINE 1f, Total Gross Monthly Income: Add the monthly income amounts for each parent (lines 1a through 1e) and enter the totals on line 1f.

MONTHLY DEDUCTIONS FROM GROSS INCOME

Allowable monthly deductions from gross income are defined under INCOME STANDARD #5: Determination of net income. (See page 2.)

Monthly Average of Deductions: If a deduction is annual or varies during the year, divide the annual total of the deduction by 12 to determine a monthly amount.

LINE 2a, Income Taxes: Enter the monthly amount actually owed for state and federal income taxes. (The amount of income tax withheld on a paycheck may not be the actual amount of income tax owed due to tax refund, etc. It is appropriate to consider tax returns from prior years as indicating the actual amount of income tax owed if income has not changed.)

LINE 2b, FICA/Self Employment Taxes: Enter the total monthly amount of FICA, Social Security, Medicare and Self-employment taxes owed.

LINE 2c, State Industrial Insurance Deductions: Enter the monthly amount of state industrial insurance deductions.

LINE 2d, Mandatory Union/Professional Dues: Enter the monthly cost of mandatory union or professional dues.

LINE 2e, Pension Plan Payments: Enter the monthly cost of pension plan payments. (For information regarding limitations on the allowable deduction of voluntary pension plan payments, refer to INCOME STANDARD #5: Determination of net income. See page 2.)

LINE 2f, Spousal Maintenance Paid: Enter the monthly amount of spousal maintenance actually paid pursuant to a court order.

LINE 2g, Normal Business Expenses: If self-employed, enter the amount of normal business expenses. (Pursuant to INCOME STANDARD #5: Determination of net income, "justification shall be required for any business expense deduction about which there is a disagreement." See page 2.)

LINE 2h, Total Deductions From Gross Income: Add the monthly deductions for each parent (lines 2a through 2g) and enter the totals on line 2h.

LINE 3, Monthly Net Income: For each parent subtract total deductions (line 2h) from total gross monthly income (line 1f) and enter these amounts on line 3.

LINE 4, Combined Monthly Net Income: Add the parents' monthly net incomes (line 3) and enter the total on line 4.

If the combined income on line 4 is less than $600, skip to line 7.

LINE 5, Basic Child Support Obligation: In the work area provided on line 5, enter the basic support obligation amounts determined for each child. Add these amounts together and enter the total in the box on line 5. (To determine a per child basic support obligation, see the following economic table instructions.)-

ECONOMIC TABLE INSTRUCTIONS

To use the Economic Table to determine an individual support amount for each child:

- **Locate in the left-hand column the combined monthly net income amount closest to the amount entered on line 4 of Worksheet** (round up when the combined monthly net income falls halfway between the two amounts in the left-hand column);

- **locate on the top row the family size for the number of children for whom child support is being determined** (when determining family size for the required worksheets, do not include children from other relationships); and

- **circle the two numbers in the columns listed below the family size that are across from the net income amount. The amount in the "A" column is the basic support amount for a child up to age 11. The amount in the "B" column is the basic support amount for a child 12 years of age or older.**

LINE 6, Proportional Share of Income: Divide the monthly net income for each parent (line 3) by the combined monthly net income (line 4) and enter these amounts on line 6. (The entries on line 6 when added together should equal 1.00.)

LINE 7, Each Parent's Basic Child Support Obligation: Multiply the total basic child support obligation (amount in box on line 5) by the income share proportion for each parent (line 6) and enter these amounts on line 7. (The amounts entered on line 7 added together should equal the amount entered on line 5.)

If the combined monthly net income on line 4 is less than $600, enter on line 7 each parent's support obligation, which is the presumptive minimum amount of $25 multiplied by the number of children. Then skip to line 15(a) and enter the same amount.

PART II: HEALTH CARE, DAY CARE, AND SPECIAL CHILD REARING EXPENSES

Pursuant to ALLOCATION STANDARD #4: "the court may exercise its discretion to determine the necessity for and the reasonableness of all amounts ordered in excess of the basic child support obligation." (See page 2.)

Pursuant to ALLOCATION STANDARD #2: Health care expenses and #3: Day care and special child rearing expenses, extraordinary health care, day care and special child rearing expenses shall be shared by the parents in the same proportion as the basic support obligation. (See page 2.)   NOTE: The court order should reflect that extraordinary health care, day care and special child rearing expenses not listed should be apportioned by the same percentage as the basic child support obligation.

Monthly Average of Expenses: If a health care, day care, or special child rearing expense is annual or varies during the year, divide the annual total of the expense by 12 to determine a monthly amount.

HEALTH CARE EXPENSES

LINE 8a, Monthly Health Insurance Premiums Paid For Child(ren): List the monthly amount paid by each parent for health care insurance for the child(ren) of the relationship. (When determining an insurance premium amount, do not include the portion of the premium paid by an employer or other third party and/or the portion of the premium that covers the parent or other household members.)

LINE 8b, Uninsured Monthly Health Care Expenses Paid For Child(ren): List the monthly amount paid by each parent for the child(ren)'s health care expenses not reimbursed by insurance.

LINE 8c, Total Monthly Health Care Expenses: For each parent add the health insurance premium payments (line 8a) to the uninsured health care payments (line 8b) and enter these amounts on line 8c.

LINE 8d, Combined Monthly Health Care Expenses: Add the parents' total health care payments (line 8c) and enter this amount on line 8d.

LINE 8e, Maximum Ordinary Monthly Health Care: Multiply the basic support obligation (line 5) times .05.

LINE 8f, Extraordinary Monthly Health Care Expenses: Subtract the maximum monthly health care deduction (line 8e) from the combined monthly health care payments (line 8d) and enter this amount on line 8f. (If the resulting answer is "0" or a negative number, enter a "0".)

DAY CARE AND SPECIAL CHILD REARING EXPENSES

LINE 9a, Day Care Expenses: Enter average monthly day care costs.

LINE 9b, Education Expenses: Enter the average monthly costs of tuition and other related educational expenses.

LINE 9c, Long Distance Transportation Expenses: Enter the average monthly costs of long distance travel incurred pursuant to the residential or visitation schedule.

LINE 9d, Other Special Expenses: Identify any other special expenses and enter the average monthly cost of each.

LINE 9e, Total Day Care and Special Expenses: Add the monthly expenses for each parent (lines 9a through 9d) and enter these totals on line 9e.

LINE 10, Combined Monthly Total of Day Care and Special Expenses: Add the parents' total expenses (line 9e) and enter this total on line 10.

LINE 11, Total Extraordinary Health Care, Day Care and Special Expenses: Add the extraordinary health care payments (line 8f) to the combined monthly total of day care and special expenses (line 10) and enter this amount on line 11.

LINE 12, Each Parent's Obligation For Extraordinary Health Care, Day Care And Special Expenses: Multiply the total extraordinary health care, day care, and special expense amount (line 11) by the income proportion for each parent (line 6) and enter these amounts on line 12.

PART III: GROSS CHILD SUPPORT OBLIGATION

LINE 13, Gross Child Support Obligation: For each parent add the basic child support obligation (line 7) to the obligation for extraordinary health care, day care and special expenses (line 12). Enter these amounts on line 13.

PART IV: CHILD SUPPORT CREDITS

Child support credits are provided in cases where parents make direct payments to third parties for the cost of goods and services which are included in the standard calculation support obligation (e.g., payments to an insurance company or a day care provider).

LINE 14a, <u>Monthly Health Care Expenses Credit</u>: Enter the total monthly health care expenses amounts from line 8c for each parent.

LINE 14b, <u>Day Care And Special Expenses Credit</u>: Enter the total day care and special expenses amounts from line 9e for each parent.

LINE 14c, <u>Other Ordinary Expense Credit</u>: If approval of another ordinary expense credit is being requested, in the space provided, specify the expense and enter the average monthly cost in the column of the parent to receive the credit. (It is generally assumed that ordinary expenses are paid in accordance with the child's residence. If payment of a specific ordinary expense does not follow this assumption, the parent paying for this expense may request approval of an ordinary expense credit. This credit is discretionary with the court.)

LINE 14d, <u>Total Support Credits</u>: For each parent, add the entries on lines 14 a through c and enter the totals on line 14d.

PART V: STANDARD CALCULATION/ PRESUMPTIVE TRANSFER PAYMENT

LINE 15a, if combined monthly income on line 4 is below $600, for each parent enter the amount from line 7 on line 15a. If the court does not deviate from the standard calculation, the transfer payment should equal the amount in the paying person's column. Skip to Part VI.

LINE 15b, if combined income on line 4 is $600 or more, for each parent subtract the total support credits (line 14d) from the gross child support obligation (line 13) and enter the resulting amounts on line 15b.

LINE 15c, Multiply line 3 by .45. If that amount is less than 15(b) enter that amount on line 15(c). If the amount is equal to or greater than line 15(b) leave line 15(c) blank. You do not qualify for the 45% net income limitation standard.

LINE 15d, Subtract the standard need amount (page 3, Basic subsistence limitation) from the amount on Line 3 for each parent. If that amount is less than Line 15(b) enter that amount or $25 per child, whichever is greater, on line 15(d). If that amount is equal to or greater than line 15(b) leave line 15(d) blank. You do not qualify for a need standard limitation.

LINE 15e, Enter the lowest amount from lines 15(b), 15(c) and 15(d) on line 15(e). If the court does not deviate from the standard calculation, the transfer payment should

equal the amount in the paying person's column.

PART VI: ADDITIONAL FACTORS FOR CONSIDERATION

Pursuant to INCOME STANDARD #1: <u>Consideration of all income</u>, "all income and resources of each parent's household shall be disclosed and considered by the court when the court determines the child support obligation of each parent." (See page 1.)

LINE 16 a-h, <u>Household Assets</u>: Enter the estimated present value of assets of the household.

LINE 17, <u>Household Debt</u>: Describe and enter the amount of liens against assets owned by the household and/or any extraordinary debt.

OTHER HOUSEHOLD INCOME

LINE 18a, <u>Income of Current Spouse</u>: If a parent is currently married to someone other than the parent of the child(ren) for whom support is being determined, list the name and enter the income of the present spouse.

LINE 18b, <u>Income of Other Adults In The Household</u>: List the names and enter the incomes of other adults residing in the household.

LINE 18c, <u>Income of Children</u>: If the amount is considered to be extraordinary, list the name and enter the income of children residing in the home.

LINE 18d, <u>Income from Child Support</u>: List the name of the child(ren) for whom support is received and enter the amount of the support income.

LINE 18e, <u>Income from Assistance Programs</u>: List the program and enter the amount of any income received from assistance programs. (Assistance programs include, but are not limited to: temporary assistance for needy families, SSI, general assistance, food stamps and aid and attendance allowances.)

LINE 18f, <u>Other Income</u>: Describe and enter the amount of any other income of the household. (Include income from gifts and prizes on this line.)

LINE 19, <u>Nonrecurring Income</u>: Describe and enter the amount of any income included in the calculation of gross income (LINE 1f) which is nonrecurring. (Pursuant to

DEVIATION STANDARD #1b: Nonrecurring income,"
depending on the circumstances, nonrecurring income may
include overtime, contract-related benefits, bonuses or income
from second jobs". See page 3.)

**LINE 20, <u>Child Support Paid for Other Children</u>: List
the names and ages and enter the amount of child support
paid for other children.**

**LINE 21, <u>Other Children Living in Each Household</u>: List
the names and ages of children, other than those for whom
support is being determined, who are living in each
household.**

**LINE 22, <u>Other Factors For Consideration</u>: In the space
provided list any other factors that should be considered
in determining the child support obligation.** (For
information regarding other factors for consideration, refer to
DEVIATION STANDARDS. See page 3.)

Nonparental Custody Cases: When the children do not reside
with either parent, the household income and resources of the
children's custodian(s) should be listed on line 22.

WASHINGTON STATE CHILD SUPPORT SCHEDULE
ECONOMIC TABLE
MONTHLY BASIC SUPPORT OBLIGATION <u>PER CHILD</u>
(KEY: A = AGE 0-11 B = AGE 12-18)

Combined Monthly Net Income	One Child Family A	B	Two Children Family A	B	Three Children Family A	B	Four Children Family A	B	Five Children Family A	B
For income less than $600, the obligation is based upon the resources and living expenses of each household. Minimum support shall not be less than $25 per child per month except when allowed by RCW 26.19.065(2).										
600	133	164	103	127	86	106	73	90	63	78
700	155	191	120	148	100	124	85	105	74	91
800	177	218	137	170	115	142	97	120	84	104
900	199	246	154	191	129	159	109	135	95	118
1000	220	272	171	211	143	177	121	149	105	130
1100	242	299	188	232	157	194	133	164	116	143
1200	264	326	205	253	171	211	144	179	126	156
1300	285	352	221	274	185	228	156	193	136	168
1400	307	379	238	294	199	246	168	208	147	181
1500	327	404	254	313	212	262	179	221	156	193
1600	347	428	269	333	225	278	190	235	166	205
1700	367	453	285	352	238	294	201	248	175	217
1800	387	478	300	371	251	310	212	262	185	228
1900	407	503	316	390	264	326	223	275	194	240
2000	427	527	331	409	277	342	234	289	204	252
2100	447	552	347	429	289	358	245	303	213	264
2200	467	577	362	448	302	374	256	316	223	276
2300	487	601	378	467	315	390	267	330	233	288
2400	506	626	393	486	328	406	278	343	242	299
2500	526	650	408	505	341	421	288	356	251	311
2600	534	661	416	513	346	428	293	362	256	316
2700	542	670	421	520	351	435	298	368	259	321
2800	549	679	427	527	356	440	301	372	262	324
2900	556	686	431	533	360	445	305	376	266	328
3000	561	693	436	538	364	449	308	380	268	331
3100	566	699	439	543	367	453	310	383	270	334
3200	569	704	442	546	369	457	312	386	272	336
3300	573	708	445	549	371	459	314	388	273	339
3400	574	710	446	551	372	460	315	389	274	340
3500	575	711	447	552	373	461	316	390	275	341
3600	577	712	448	553	374	462	317	391	276	342
3700	578	713	449	554	375	463	318	392	277	343
3800	581	719	452	558	377	466	319	394	278	344
3900	596	736	463	572	386	477	326	404	284	352
4000	609	753	473	584	395	488	334	413	291	360
4100	623	770	484	598	404	500	341	422	298	368
4200	638	788	495	611	413	511	350	431	305	377
4300	651	805	506	625	422	522	357	441	311	385
4400	664	821	516	637	431	532	364	449	317	392
4500	677	836	525	649	438	542	371	458	323	400
4600	689	851	535	661	446	552	377	467	329	407
4700	701	866	545	673	455	562	384	475	335	414
4800	713	882	554	685	463	572	391	483	341	422
4900	726	897	564	697	470	581	398	491	347	429
5000	738	912	574	708	479	592	404	500	353	437
5100	751	928	584	720	487	602	411	509	359	443
5200	763	943	593	732	494	611	418	517	365	451
5300	776	959	602	744	503	621	425	525	371	458
5400	788	974	612	756	511	632	432	533	377	466
5500	800	989	622	768	518	641	439	542	383	473
5600	812	1004	632	779	527	651	446	551	389	480
5700	825	1019	641	791	535	661	452	559	395	488
5800	837	1035	650	803	543	671	459	567	401	495
5900	850	1050	660	815	551	681	466	575	407	502
6000	862	1065	670	827	559	691	473	584	413	509
6100	875	1081	680	839	567	701	479	593	418	517
6200	887	1096	689	851	575	710	486	601	424	524
6300	899	1112	699	863	583	721	493	609	430	532
6400	911	1127	709	875	591	731	500	617	436	539
6500	924	1142	718	887	599	740	506	626	442	546
6600	936	1157	728	899	607	750	513	635	448	554
6700	949	1172	737	911	615	761	520	643	454	561
6800	961	1188	747	923	623	770	527	651	460	568
6900	974	1203	757	935	631	780	533	659	466	575
7000	986	1218	767	946	639	790	540	668	472	583

In general setting support under this paragraph does not constitute a deviation. The economic table is presumptive for combined monthly net incomes up to and including five thousand dollars. When combined monthly net income exceeds five thousand dollars, support shall not be set at an amount lower than the presumptive amount of support set for combined monthly net income of five thousand dollars unless the court finds a reason to deviate below that amount. The economic table is advisory but not presumptive for combined monthly net income that exceeds five thousand dollars. When combined monthly net income exceeds seven thousand dollars, the court may set support at an advisory amount of support set for combined monthly net incomes between five thousand and seven thousand dollars or the court may exceed the advisory amount of support set for combined monthly net incomes of seven thousand dollars upon written findings of fact.

WSCSS-Economic Table 9/2001

Washington State Child Support Schedule
Worksheets **(CSW)**

Mother   **Father**

County   **Superior Court Case Number**

Children and Ages:		
Part I: Basic Child Support Obligation (See Instructions, Page 5)		
1. Gross Monthly Income	**Father**	**Mother**
a. Wages and Salaries	$	$
b. Interest and Dividend Income	$	$
c. Business Income	$	$
d. Spousal Maintenance Received	$	$
e. Other Income	$	$
f. Total Gross Monthly Income (add lines 1a through 1e)	$	$
2. Monthly Deductions from Gross Income		
a. Income Taxes (Federal and State)	$	$
b. FICA (Soc.Sec.+Medicare)/Self-Employment Taxes	$	$
c. State Industrial Insurance Deductions	$	$
d. Mandatory Union/Professional Dues	$	$
e. Pension Plan Payments	$	$
f. Spousal Maintenance Paid	$	$
g. Normal Business Expenses	$	$
h. Total Deductions from Gross Income (add lines 2a through 2g)	$	$
3. Monthly Net Income (line 1f minus 2h)	$	$
4. Combined Monthly Net Income (add father's and mother's monthly net incomes from line 3) (If combined monthly net income is less than $600, skip to line 7.)	$	
5. Basic Child Support Obligation (enter total amount in box →) Child #1 Child #3 / Child #2 Child #4	$	

	Father	Mother
6. Proportional Share of Income (each parent's net income from line 3 divided by line 4)		
7. Each Parent's Basic Child Support Obligation (multiply each number on line 6 by line 5) (If combined net monthly income on line 4 is less than $600, enter each parent's support obligation of $25 per child. Number of children: _____ . Skip to line 15a and enter this amount.)	$	$
Part II: Health Care, Day Care, and Special Child Rearing Expenses (See Instructions, Page 7)		
8. Health Care Expenses		
a. Monthly Health Insurance Premiums Paid for Child(ren)	$	$
b. Uninsured Monthly Health Care Expenses Paid for Child(ren)	$	$
c. Total Monthly Health Care Expenses (line 8a plus line 8b)	$	$
d. Combined Monthly Health Care Expenses (add father's and mother's totals from line 8c)	$	
e. Maximum Ordinary Monthly Health Care (multiply line 5 times .05)	$	
f. Extraordinary Monthly Health Care Expenses (line 8d minus line 8e., if "0" or negative, enter "0")	$	
9. Day Care and Special Child Rearing Expenses		
a. Day Care Expenses	$	$
b. Education Expenses	$	$
c. Long Distance Transportation Expenses	$	$
d. Other Special Expenses (describe)	$	$
	$	$
	$	$
e. Total Day Care and Special Expenses (Add lines 9a through 9d)	$	$
10. Combined Monthly Total Day Care and Special Expenses (add father's and mother's day care and special expenses from line 9e)	$	
11. Total Extraordinary Health Care, Day Care, and Special Expenses (line 8f plus line 10)	$	
12. Each Parent's Obligation for Extraordinary Health Care, Day Care and Special Expenses (multiply each number on line 6 by line 11)	$	$
Part III: Gross Child Support Obligation		
13. Gross Child Support Obligation (line 7 plus line 12)	$	$
Part IV: Child Support Credits (See Instructions, Page 7)		
14. Child Support Credits		
a. Monthly Health Care Expenses Credit	$	$
b. Day Care and Special Expenses Credit	$	$
c. Other Ordinary Expenses Credit (describe)	$	$
d. Total Support Credits (add lines 14a through 14c)	$	$

WSCSS-Worksheets (CSW) 9/2000 Page 2 of 5   Continued to Next Page

Part V: **Standard Calculation/Presumptive Transfer Payment** (See Instructions, Page 8)		
15. Standard Calculation	**Father**	**Mother**
a. Amount from line 7 if line 4 is below $600. Skip to Part VI.	$	$
b. Line 13 minus line 14d, if line 4 is over $600 (see below if appl.)	$	$
Limitation standards adjustments		
c. Amount on line 15b adjusted to meet 45% net income limitation	$	$
d. Amount on line 15b adjusted to meet need standard limitation	$	$
e. Enter the lowest amount of lines 15b, 15c or 15d:	$	$
Part VI: **Additional Factors for Consideration** (See Instructions, Page 8)		
16. Household Assets (List the estimated present value of all major household assets.)	Father's Household	Mother's Household
a. Real Estate	$	$
b. Stocks and Bonds	$	$
c. Vehicles	$	$
d. Boats	$	$
e. Pensions/IRAs/Bank Accounts	$	$
f. Cash	$	$
g. Insurance Plans	$	$
h. Other (describe)	$	$
	$	$
	$	$
17. Household Debt (List liens against household assets, extraordinary debt.)		
	$	$
	$	$
	$	$
	$	$
	$	$
18. Other Household Income		
a. Income Of Current Spouse (if not the other parent of this action)		
Name	$	$
Name	$	$
b. Income Of Other Adults In Household		
Name	$	$
Name	$	$
c. Income Of Children (if considered extraordinary)		
Name	$	$
Name	$	$
d. Income From Child Support		
Name	$	$
Name	$	$

WSCSS-Worksheets (CSW) 9/2000 Page 3 of 5   Continued to Next Page

Other Household Income (continued)	Father's Household	Mother's Household
e. Income From Assistance Programs		
Program	$	$
Program	$	$
f. Other Income (describe)		
	$	$
	$	$
19. Non-Recurring Income (describe)		
	$	$
	$	$
20. Child Support Paid For Other Children		
Name/age:	$	$
Name/age:	$	$
Name/age:	$	$
21. Other Children Living In Each Household		
(First names and ages)		
22. Other Factors For Consideration		

Other factors for consideration (continued)

Signature and Dates

I declare, under penalty of perjury under the laws of the State of Washington, the information contained in these Worksheets is complete, true, and correct.

_____
Mother's Signature

_____
Father's Signature

_____ _____
Date   City

_____ _____
Date   City

_____
Judge/Reviewing Officer

_____
Date

This worksheet has been certified by the State of Washington Administrative Office of the Courts. Photocopying of the worksheet is permitted.

Worksheets

This appendix contains worksheets to help you evaluate your situation and collect information you will need.

WORKSHEET 1: PROPERTY INVENTORY 156
WORKSHEET 2: DEBT INVENTORY. 157

Property Inventory

(1) S	(2) Description	(3) ID#	(4) Value	(5) Balance	(6) Equity Owed	(7) Owner H-W-J	(8) H	(9) W

Debt Inventory

(1) S	(2) Creditor	(3) Account No.	(4) Notes	(5) Monthly Payment	(6) Balance Owed	(7) Date	(8) Owner H-W-J	(9) H	(10) W

Blank Forms

Be sure to read Chapter 6 before you begin using the forms in this appendix. Each form in this appendix may be identified by its title as well as by the form number, which is found in the upper right corner of the first page of each form. Instructions for completing these forms are found throughout this book. The instructions for a particular form may be found by looking for the form number under the heading "legal forms" in the index. You will not need to use all of the forms in this appendix.

It is suggested that you make photocopies of the forms in this Appendix and keep the originals blank to make additional copies in the event you make mistakes or need additional copies. You can also use the CD-ROM to fill in the forms or print blank copies as needed. (see "How to Use the CD-ROM" on p.ix.) Also, the forms may change at any time. To be sure you have the most recent version of a form, check the Washington Courts website at **www.courts.wa.gov**.

TABLE OF FORMS

FORM 1: SUMMONS 161

FORM 2: PETITION FOR DISSOLUTION OF MARRIAGE...................163

FORM 3: DECREE OF DISSOLUTION 173

FORM 4: FINDINGS OF FACT AND CONCLUSIONS OF LAW 181

FORM 5: ORDER OF CHILD SUPPORT 191

FORM 6: PARENTING PLAN......................................203

FORM 7: RETURN OF SERVICE 215

FORM 8: MOTION AND DECLARATION FOR DEFAULT 217

FORM 9: ORDER OF DEFAULT 221

FORM 10: MOTION AND DECLARATION TO SERVE BY MAIL.............223

FORM 11: ORDER ALLOWING SERVICE BY MAIL......................225

FORM 12: SUMMONS BY MAIL....................................227

FORM 13: MOTION AND DECLARATION FOR SERVICE OF SUMMONS
         BY PUBLICATION.......................................229

FORM 14: ORDER FOR SERVICE OF SUMMONS BY PUBLICATION 231

FORM 15: SUMMONS BY PUBLICATION 233

FORM 16: MOTION AND DECLARATION FOR TEMPORARY ORDER.........237

FORM 17: TEMPORARY ORDER 241

FORM 18: FINANCIAL DECLARATION 245

FORM 19: SEALED FINANCIAL SOURCE DOCUMENTS 251

SUPERIOR COURT OF WASHINGTON
COUNTY OF

In re the Marriage of:

	NO.
Petitioner,	
and	SUMMONS
	(SM)
Respondent.	

TO THE RESPONDENT:

1.   The petitioner has started an action in the above court requesting:

      [ ]   that your marriage be dissolved.
      [ ]   a legal separation.
      [ ]   that the validity of your marriage be determined.

      Additional requests, if any, are stated in the petition, a copy of which is attached to this summons.

2.   You must respond to this summons and petition by serving a copy of your written response on the person signing this summons and by filing the original with the clerk of the court. If you do not serve your written response within 20 days (or 60 days if you are served outside of the state of Washington) after the date this summons was served on you, exclusive of the day of service, the court may enter an order of default against you, and the court may, without further notice to you, enter a decree and approve or provide for the relief requested in the petition. In the case of a dissolution of marriage, the court will not enter the final decree until at least 90 days after filing and service. If you serve a notice of appearance on the undersigned person, you are entitled to notice before an order of default or a decree may be entered.

3.   Your written response to the summons and petition must be on form WPF DR 01.0300, Response to Petition (Domestic Relations). This form may be obtained by contacting the clerk of the court at the address below, by contacting the Administrative Office of the Courts at (360) 705-5328, or from the Internet at the Washington State Courts homepage:

http://www.courts.wa.gov/forms

4.   If this action has not been filed with the court, you may demand that the petitioner file this action with the court. If you do so, the demand must be in writing and must be served upon the person signing this summons. Within 14 days after you serve the demand, the petitioner must file this action with the court, or the service on you of this summons and petition will be void.

5.   If you wish to seek the advice of an attorney in this matter, you should do so promptly so that your written response, if any, may be served on time.

6.   One method of serving a copy of your response on the petitioner is to send it by certified mail with return receipt requested.

This summons is issued pursuant to Superior Court Civil Rule 4.1 of the state of Washington.

Dated: _____   _____

                                                   Signature of Lawyer or Petitioner

                                                   Print or Type Name

FILE ORIGINAL OF YOUR RESPONSE WITH THE CLERK OF THE COURT AT:

SERVE A COPY OF YOUR RESPONSE ON:

[ ] Petitioner [You may list an address that is not your residential address where you agree to accept legal documents.]

[ ] Petitioner's Lawyer

[Name of Court]

[Name]

[Address]

[Address]

SUPERIOR COURT OF WASHINGTON
COUNTY OF

In re the Marriage of:

                                            Petitioner,

and

                                            Respondent.

NO.

**PETITION FOR DISSOLUTION
OF MARRIAGE
(PTDSS)**

I. BASIS

1.1   IDENTIFICATION OF PETITIONER.

Name (first/last)   , Birth date

Last known residence   (county and state).

1.2   IDENTIFICATION OF RESPONDENT.

Name (first/last)   , Birth date

Last known residence   (county and state).

1.3   CHILDREN OF THE MARRIAGE DEPENDENT UPON EITHER OR BOTH SPOUSES.

The husband and wife are both the parents of the following dependent children:

Name (first/last)   Age

Name (first/last)   Age

Name (first/last)   Age

Name (first/last)   Age

Name (first/last)   Age

Name (first/last)   Age

The husband is and the wife is not the parent of the following dependent children:

Name (first/last)   Age

Name (first/last)   Age

The wife is and the husband is not the parent of the following dependent children:

Name (first/last)   Age

Name (first/last)   Age

1.4   ALLEGATION REGARDING MARRIAGE.

This marriage is irretrievably broken.

1.5   DATE AND PLACE OF MARRIAGE.

The parties were married on   at

                          [Date]   [City and State]

1.6   SEPARATION.

[ ]   Husband and wife are not separated.

[ ]   Husband and wife separated on   [Date].

1.7   JURISDICTION.

This court has jurisdiction over the marriage.

[ ]   This court has jurisdiction over the respondent because:

       [ ]   the respondent is presently residing in Washington.

       [ ]   the petitioner and respondent lived in Washington during their marriage and the petitioner continues to reside, or be a member of the armed forces stationed, in this state.

       [ ]   the petitioner and respondent may have conceived a child while within Washington.

       [ ]   Other:

[ ]   This court does not have jurisdiction over the respondent.

1.8   PROPERTY.

There is community or separate property owned by the parties. The court should make a fair and equitable division of all the property.

[ ]   The division of property should be determined by the court at a later date.
[ ]   The petitioner's recommendation for the division of property is set forth below.

   [ ]   The petitioner should be awarded the parties' interest in the following property:

   [ ]   The respondent should be awarded the parties' interest in the following property:

   [ ]   Other:

1.9   DEBTS AND LIABILITIES.

[ ]   The parties have no debts and liabilities.
[ ]   The parties have debts and liabilities. The court should make a fair and equitable
        division of all debts and liabilities.
        [ ]   The division of debts and liabilities should be determined by the court at a later
                date.
        [ ]   The petitioner's recommendation for the division of debts and liabilities is set
                forth below.

                [ ]   The petitioner should be ordered to pay the following debts and liabilities
                        to the following creditors:

                [ ]   The respondent should be ordered to pay the following debts and
                        liabilities to the following creditors:

        [ ]   Each party should pay their debts incurred since separation.
        [ ]   Other:

1.10   SPOUSAL MAINTENANCE.

[ ]   Spousal maintenance should not be ordered.
[ ]   There is a need for spousal maintenance as follows:

[ ]   Other:

1.11 CONTINUING RESTRAINING ORDER.

[ ]   Does not apply.

[ ]   A continuing restraining order should be entered which restrains or enjoins the respondent from assaulting, harassing, molesting or disturbing the peace of the petitioner.

[ ]   A continuing restraining order should be entered which restrains or enjoins the respondent from going onto the grounds of or entering the home, work place or school of the petitioner or the day care or school of the following children:

[ ]   A continuing restraining order should be entered which restrains or enjoins the respondent from knowingly coming within or knowingly remaining within   (distance) of the home, work place or school of the petitioner or the day care or school of these children:
Other:

[ ]   Other:

1.12 PREGNANCY.

[ ]   The wife is not pregnant.

[ ]   The wife is pregnant. The father of the unborn child is [ ] the husband [ ] not the husband [ ] unknown.

1.13 JURISDICTION OVER THE CHILDREN.

[ ]   Does not apply because there are no dependent children.

[ ]   This court has jurisdiction over the children for the reasons set forth below:

[ ]   This court has exclusive continuing jurisdiction. The court has previously made a child custody, parenting plan, residential schedule or visitation determination in this matter and retains jurisdiction under RCW 26.27.211.

[ ]   This state is the home state of the children because

    [ ]   the children lived in Washington with a parent or a person acting as a parent for at least six consecutive months immediately preceding the commencement of this proceeding.

    [ ]   the children are less than six months old and have lived in Washington with a parent or a person acting as parent since birth.

    [ ]   any absences from Washington have been only temporary.

    [ ]   Washington was the home state of the children within six months before the commencement of this proceeding and the children are absent from the state but a parent or person acting as a parent continued to live in this state.

[ ]   The children and the parents or the children and at least one parent or person acting as a parent, have significant connection with the state other than mere physical presence; and substantial evidence is available in this state concerning the children's care, protection, training and personal relationships; and

        [ ]   the children have no home state elsewhere.
        [ ]   the children's home state has declined to exercise jurisdiction on the ground that this state is the more appropriate forum under RCW 26.27.261 or .271.

[ ]   All courts in the children's home state have declined to exercise jurisdiction on the ground that a court of this state is the more appropriate forum to determine the custody of the children under RCW 26.27.261 or .271.

[ ]   No other state has jurisdiction.

[ ]   This court has temporary emergency jurisdiction over this proceeding because the children are present in this state and the children have been abandoned or it is necessary in an emergency to protect the children because the children, or a sibling or parent of the children is subjected to or threatened with abuse. RCW 26.27.231.

[ ]   Other:

1.14   CHILD SUPPORT AND PARENTING PLAN FOR DEPENDENT CHILDREN.

[ ]   The parties have no dependent children.
[ ]   Support for the dependent children listed below, should be set pursuant to the Washington State Child Support Schedule.

Name of Child	Mother's Name	Father's Name

The petitioner's proposed parenting plan for the children listed above:

[ ]   is attached and is incorporated by reference as part of this Petition.
[ ]   will be filed and served at a later date pursuant to RCW 26.09.181.

(The following information is required only for those children who are included in the petitioner's proposed parenting plan.)

During the last five years, the children have lived:

[ ]   in no place other than the state of Washington and with no person other than the petitioner or the respondent.

[ ]   in the following places with the following persons (list each place the children lived, including the state of Washington, the dates the children lived there and the names of the persons with whom the children lived. The present addresses of those persons must be listed in the required Confidential Information Form):

Claims to custody or visitation:

[ ]   The petitioner does not know of any person other than the respondent who has physical custody of, or claims to have custody or visitation rights to, the children.

[ ]   The following persons have physical custody of, or claim to have custody or visitation rights to the children (list their names and the children concerned below and list their present addresses in the Confidential Information Form. Do not list the responding party):

Involvement in any other proceeding concerning the children:

[ ]   The petitioner has not been involved in any other proceeding regarding the children.

[ ]   The petitioner has been involved in the following proceedings regarding the children (list the court, the case number, and the date of the judgment or order):

Other legal proceedings concerning the children:

[ ]   The petitioner does not know of any other legal proceedings concerning the children.

[ ]   The petitioner knows of the following legal proceedings which concern the children (list the children concerned, the court, the case number, and the kind of proceeding):

1.15   OTHER.

II. RELIEF REQUESTED

The petitioner REQUESTS the court to enter a decree of dissolution and to grant the relief below.

[ ]   Provide reasonable maintenance for the [ ] husband [ ] wife.
[ ]   Approve the petitioner's proposed parenting plan for the dependent children listed in paragraph 1.14.
[ ]   Determine support for the dependent children listed in paragraph 1.14 pursuant to the Washington State Child Support Schedule.
[ ]   Approve the separation contract or prenuptial agreement.
[ ]   Divide the property and liabilities.
[ ]   Change name of wife to (first, middle, last):   .
[ ]   Change name of husband to (first, middle, last):   .
[ ]   Enter a continuing restraining order.
[ ]   Order payment of day care expenses for the children listed in paragraph 1.14
[ ]   Award the tax exemptions for the dependent children listed in paragraph 1.14 as follows:

[ ]   Order payment of attorney's fees, other professional fees and costs.
[ ]   Other:

Dated: _____   _____
                                               Signature of Petitioner or Lawyer/WSBA No.

                                               Print or Type Name

I declare under penalty of perjury under the laws of the state of Washington that the foregoing is true and correct.

Signed at _____, [City] _____ [State] on_____ [Date].

_____   _____
Signature of Petitioner   Print or Type Name

[ ]   JOINDER.

The respondent joins in the petition. By joining in the petition, the respondent agrees to the entry of a decree in accordance with the petition, without further notice.

Dated: _____   _____

                                            Signature of Respondent

                                            Print or Type Name

This page intentionally blank.

SUPERIOR COURT OF WASHINGTON
COUNTY OF

In re the Marriage of:
 	
Petitioner,
 	
and
 	
Respondent.
	NO.
	
	[ ] DECREE OF DISSOLUTION **(DCD)**
	[ ] DECREE OF LEGAL SEPARATION
	       (DCLGSP)
	[ ] DECLARATION CONCERNING
	       VALIDITY **(DCINMG)**
	
	[ ]Clerk's action required

I. JUDGMENT/ORDER SUMMARIES

1.1   RESTRAINING ORDER SUMMARY:
    [ ] Does not apply.   [ ] Restraining Order Summary is set forth below:

Name of person(s) restrained: _____. Name of person(s)
protected:._____. **See paragraph 3.8.**

VIOLATION OF A RESTRAINING ORDER IN PARAGRAPH 3.8 BELOW WITH ACTUAL KNOWLEDGE OF ITS TERMS IS A CRIMINAL OFFENSE UNDER CHAPTER 26.50 RCW AND WILL SUBJECT THE VIOLATOR TO ARREST. RCW 26.09.050.

1.2   REAL PROPERTY JUDGMENT SUMMARY:
    [ ] Does not apply.   [ ] Real Property Judgment Summary is set forth below:

Assessor's property tax parcel or account number:
    Or

Legal description of the property awarded (including lot, block, plat, or section, township, range, county and state):

	See Page _____ for full legal description

1.3   MONEY JUDGMENT SUMMARY:
    [ ] Does not apply.   [ ]   Judgment Summary is set forth below.

A. Judgment creditor   _____
B. Judgment debtor   _____
C. Principal judgment amount $ _____
D. Interest to date of judgment $ _____
E. Attorney's fees $ _____

F. Costs $ _____

G. Other recovery amount $ _____

H. Principal judgment shall bear interest at _____ % per annum

I.   Attorney's fees, costs and other recovery amounts shall bear interest at _____ % per annum

J. Attorney for judgment creditor   _____

K. Attorney for judgment debtor   _____

L. Other:

END OF SUMMARIES

II. BASIS

Findings of Fact and Conclusions of Law have been entered in this case.

III. DECREE

IT IS DECREED that:

3.1   STATUS OF THE MARRIAGE.

    [ ]   The marriage of the parties is dissolved.

    [ ]   The husband and wife are legally separated.

    [ ]   The marriage of the parties is invalid.

    [ ]   The marriage of the parties is valid.

3.2   PROPERTY TO BE AWARDED THE HUSBAND.

    [ ]   Does not apply.

    [ ]   The husband is awarded as his separate property the property set forth in Exhibit _____. This exhibit is attached or filed and incorporated by reference as part of this decree.

    [ ]   The husband is awarded as his separate property the property set forth in the separation contract or prenuptial agreement executed by the parties on _____ [date]. The separation contract or prenuptial agreement is incorporated by reference as part of this Decree. The prenuptial agreement or, pursuant to RCW 26.09.070(5), the separation contract [ ] is [ ] is not filed with the court.

    [ ]   The husband is awarded as his separate property the following property (list real estate, furniture, vehicles, pensions, insurance, bank accounts, etc.):

    [ ]   Other:

DECREE (DCD) (DCLSP) (DCINMG) - Page 2 of 7
WPF DR 04.0400 (6/2004) - RCW 26.09.030; .040; .070 (3)

3.3   PROPERTY TO BE AWARDED TO THE WIFE.

   [ ]   Does not apply.
   [ ]   The wife is awarded as her separate property the property set forth in Exhibit _____. This
            exhibit is attached or filed and incorporated by reference as part of this decree.
   [ ]   The wife is awarded as her separate property the property set forth in the separation
            contract or prenuptial agreement referenced above.
   [ ]   The wife is awarded as her separate property the following property (list real estate,
            furniture, vehicles, pensions, insurance, bank accounts, etc.):

   [ ]   Other:

3.4   LIABILITIES TO BE PAID BY THE HUSBAND.

   [ ]   Does not apply.
   [ ]   The husband shall pay the community or separate liabilities set forth in Exhibit _____.
            This exhibit is attached or filed and incorporated by reference as part of this decree.
   [ ]   The husband shall pay the community or separate liabilities as set forth in the separation
            contract or prenuptial agreement referenced above.
   [ ]   The husband shall pay the following community or separate liabilities:

                        Creditor   Amount

   [ ]   Other:

Unless otherwise provided herein, the husband shall pay all liabilities incurred by him since the date of separation.

3.5   LIABILITIES TO BE PAID BY THE WIFE.

[ ]   Does not apply.
[ ]   The wife shall pay the community or separate liabilities set forth in Exhibit _____. This exhibit is attached or filed and incorporated by reference as part of this decree.
[ ]   The wife shall pay the community or separate liabilities as set forth in the separation contract or prenuptial agreement referenced above.
[ ]   The wife shall pay the following community or separate liabilities:

<u>Creditor</u>   <u>Amount</u>

[ ]   Other:

Unless otherwise provided herein, the wife shall pay all liabilities incurred by her since the date of separation.

3.6   HOLD HARMLESS PROVISION.

[ ]   Does not apply.
[ ]   Each party shall hold the other party harmless from any collection action relating to separate or community liabilities set forth above, including reasonable attorney's fees and costs incurred in defending against any attempts to collect an obligation of the other party.
[ ]   Other:

3.7   SPOUSAL MAINTENANCE.

[ ]   Does not apply.
[ ]   The [ ] husband [ ] wife shall pay maintenance as set forth in Exhibit _____. This exhibit is attached or filed and incorporated by reference as part of this decree.
[ ]   Spousal maintenance shall be paid as set forth in the separation contract or prenuptial agreement referenced above.
[ ]   The [ ] husband [ ] wife shall pay $ _____ maintenance. Maintenance shall be paid [ ] weekly [ ] semi-monthly [ ] monthly.
         The first maintenance payment shall be due on _____ [Date].

DECREE (DCD) (DCLSP) (DCINMG) - Page 4 of 7
WPF DR 04.0400 (6/2004) - RCW 26.09.030; .040; .070 (3)

The obligation to pay future maintenance is terminated upon the death of either party or the remarriage of the party receiving maintenance unless otherwise specified below:

Payments shall be made:

[ ] directly to the other spouse.

[ ] to the Washington State Child Support Registry (only available if child support is ordered).

[ ] to the clerk of this court as trustee for remittance to the other spouse (only available if there are no dependent children).

[ ] If a spousal maintenance payment is more than 15 days past due and the total of such past due payments is equal to or greater than $100, or if the obligor requests a withdrawal of accumulated contributions from the Department of Retirement Systems, the obligee may seek a mandatory benefits assignment order under Chapter 41.50 RCW without prior notice to the obligor.

[ ] The Department of Retirement Systems may make a direct payment of all or part of a withdrawal of accumulated contributions pursuant to RCW 41.50.550(3).

[ ] Other:

3.8 CONTINUING RESTRAINING ORDER.

[ ] Does not apply.

[ ] A continuing restraining order is entered as follows:

[ ] The [ ] husband [ ] wife is restrained and enjoined from assaulting, harassing, molesting or disturbing the peace of the other party.

[ ] The [ ] husband [ ] wife is restrained and enjoined from going onto the grounds of or entering the home, work place or school of the other party, or the day care or school of the following named children: _____

_____

[ ] The [ ] husband [ ] wife is restrained and enjoined from knowingly coming within or knowingly remaining within _____(distance) of the home, work place or school of the other party, or the day care or school of these children: _____.

Other:_____.

[ ] Other:

VIOLATION OF A RESTRAINING ORDER IN PARAGRAPH 3.8 WITH ACTUAL KNOWLEDGE OF ITS TERMS IS A CRIMINAL OFFENSE UNDER CHAPTER 26.50 RCW AND WILL SUBJECT THE VIOLATOR TO ARREST. RCW 26.09.060.

[ ] CLERK'S ACTION. The clerk of the court shall forward a copy of this order, on or before the next judicial day, to: _____ law

---

> enforcement agency which shall enter this order into any computer-based criminal intelligence system available in this state used by law enforcement agencies to list outstanding warrants. (**A law enforcement information sheet must be completed by the party or the party's attorney and provided with this order before this order will be entered into the law enforcement computer system**.)
>
> SERVICE:
>
> [ ]   The restrained party or attorney appeared in court or signed this order; service of this order is not required.
>
> [ ]   The restrained party or attorney did not appear in court; service of this order is required.
>
> EXPIRATION.
>
>   This restraining order expires on: _____ (month/day/year).
>   This restraining order supersedes all previous temporary restraining orders in this cause number.

3.9   JURISDICTION OVER THE CHILDREN.

[ ]   Does not apply because there are no dependent children.
[ ]   The court has jurisdiction over the children as set forth in the Findings of Fact and Conclusions of Law.

3.10   PARENTING PLAN.

[ ]   Does not apply.
[ ]   The parties shall comply with the Parenting Plan signed by the court on _____ [Date]. The Parenting Plan signed by the court is approved and incorporated as part of this decree.

3.11   CHILD SUPPORT.

[ ]   Does not apply.
[ ]   Child support shall be paid in accordance with the order of child support signed by the court on _____ [Date]. This order is incorporated as part of this decree.

3.12   ATTORNEY'S FEES, OTHER PROFESSIONAL FEES AND COSTS.

[ ]   Does not apply.
[ ]   Attorney's fees, other professional fees and costs shall be paid as set forth in the separation contract or prenuptial agreement referenced above.
[ ]   Attorney's fees, other professional fees and costs shall be paid as follows:

3.13   NAME CHANGES.

      [ ]   Does not apply.

      [ ]   The wife's name shall be changed to _____ [First, Middle, Last Name].

      [ ]   The husband's name shall be changed to _____ [First, Middle, Last Name].

3.14   OTHER.

Dated: _____

                                                               _____
                                                               JUDGE/COMMISSIONER

Petitioner or petitioner's attorney:	Respondent or respondent's attorney:
A signature below is actual notice of this order.	A signature below is actual notice of this order.
[ ] Presented by:	[ ] Presented by:
[ ] Approved for entry:	[ ] Approved for entry:
[ ] Notice for presentation waived:	[ ] Notice for presentation waived:

_____   _____

Signature   WSBA No.   Signature   WSBA No.

_____   _____

Print or Type Name   Print or Type Name

This page intentionally blank.

SUPERIOR COURT OF WASHINGTON
COUNTY OF

In re the Marriage of:

Petitioner,	NO.
and	FINDINGS OF FACT AND CONCLUSIONS OF LAW (FNFCL)
Respondent.	

I. BASIS FOR FINDINGS

The findings are based on:

[ ]   agreement.
[ ]   an order of default entered on   [Date].
[ ]   trial. The following people attended:

    [ ]   Petitioner.
    [ ]   Petitioner's Lawyer.
    [ ]   Respondent.
    [ ]   Respondent's Lawyer.
    [ ]   Other:

II. FINDINGS OF FACT

Upon the basis of the court record, the court FINDS:

2.1   RESIDENCY OF PETITIONER.

The petitioner

    [ ]   is a resident of the state of Washington.
    [ ]   is not a resident of the state of Washington.
    [ ]   is a member of the armed forces and has been stationed in this state for at least 90 days.

2.2   NOTICE TO THE RESPONDENT.

The respondent

[ ]   appeared, responded or joined in the petition.
[ ]   was served in the following manner:

2.3   BASIS OF PERSONAL JURISDICTION OVER THE RESPONDENT.

[ ]   There are no facts to establish personal jurisdiction over the respondent.
[ ]   The facts below establish personal jurisdiction over the respondent.

[ ]   The respondent is presently residing in Washington.
[ ]   The parties lived in Washington during their marriage and the petitioner continues to reside, or be a member of the armed forces stationed, in this state.
[ ]   The parties may have conceived a child while within Washington.
[ ]   Other:

2.4   DATE AND PLACE OF MARRIAGE.

The parties were married on   [Date] at
                                                           [City and State].

2.5   STATUS OF THE PARTIES.

[ ]   Husband and wife separated on   [Date].
[ ]   Husband and wife are not separated.

2.6   STATUS OF THE MARRIAGE.

[ ]   The marriage is irretrievably broken and at least 90 days have elapsed since the date the petition was filed and since the date the summons was served or the respondent joined.
[ ]   The petitioner wishes to be legally separated.
[ ]   The petitioner is petitioning for a declaration concerning the invalidity of the marriage. The court FINDS the following facts concerning the validity of the marriage:

2.7   SEPARATION CONTRACT OR PRENUPTIAL AGREEMENT.

[ ]   There is no written separation contract or prenuptial agreement.
[ ]   A written separation contract or prenuptial agreement was executed on
                    [Date] and is incorporated herein.

        [ ]   The separation contract or prenuptial agreement should be approved.
        [ ]   The separation contract or prenuptial agreement should not be approved because:

[ ]   Other:

2.8   COMMUNITY PROPERTY.

[ ]   The parties do not have real or personal community property.
[ ]   The parties have real or personal community property as set forth in Exhibit   . This
        exhibit is attached or filed and incorporated by reference as part of these findings.
[ ]   The parties have real or personal community property as set forth in the separation contract
        or prenuptial agreement referenced above.
[ ]   The parties have the following real or personal community property:

[ ]   Other:

2.9   SEPARATE PROPERTY.

[ ]   The husband has no real or personal separate property.
[ ]   The wife has no real or personal separate property.
[ ]   The parties have separate property as set forth in the separation contract or prenuptial
        agreement referenced above.
[ ]   The husband has real or personal separate property as set forth in Exhibit   . This
        exhibit is attached or filed and incorporated by reference as part of these findings.
[ ]   The wife has real or personal separate property as set forth in Exhibit   . This exhibit is
        attached or filed and incorporated by reference as part of these findings.

[ ]   The husband has the following real or personal separate property:

[ ]   The wife has the following real or personal separate property:

[ ]   Other:

2.10   COMMUNITY LIABILITIES.

[ ]   There are no known community liabilities.
[ ]   The parties have incurred community liabilities as set forth in Exhibit   . This exhibit is attached or filed and incorporated by reference as part of these findings.
[ ]   The parties have community liabilities as set forth in the separation contract or prenuptial agreement referenced above.
[ ]   The parties have incurred the following community liabilities:

Creditor	Amount

[ ]   Other:

2.11   SEPARATE LIABILITIES.

[ ]   The husband has no known separate liabilities.
[ ]   The wife has no known separate liabilities.
[ ]   The husband has incurred separate liabilities as set forth in Exhibit   . This exhibit is attached or filed and incorporated by reference as part of these findings.
[ ]   The parties have separate liabilities as set forth in the separation contract or prenuptial agreement referenced above.
[ ]   The wife has incurred separate liabilities as set forth in Exhibit   . This exhibit is attached or filed and incorporated by reference as part of these findings.

[ ] The husband has incurred the following separate liabilities:

<u>Creditor</u>   <u>Amount</u>

[ ] The wife has incurred the following separate liabilities:

<u>Creditor</u>   <u>Amount</u>

[ ] Other:

2.12 MAINTENANCE.

[ ] Maintenance was not requested.
[ ] Maintenance shall be paid as set forth in the separation contract or prenuptial agreement referenced above.
[ ] Maintenance should not be ordered because:

[ ] Maintenance should be ordered because:

[ ] Other:

2.13 CONTINUING RESTRAINING ORDER.

[ ] Does not apply.
[ ] A continuing restraining order against the [ ] husband [ ] wife [ ] both parties is necessary because:

[ ] Other:

2.14   FEES AND COSTS.

[ ]   There is no award of fees or costs.
[ ]   Attorney's fees, other professional fees and costs shall be paid as set forth in the separation contract or prenuptial agreement referenced above.
[ ]   The [ ] husband [ ] wife has the need for the payment of fees and costs and the other spouse has the ability to pay these fees and costs. The [ ] husband [ ] wife has incurred reasonable attorney's fees and costs in the amount of $.
[ ]   Other:

2.15   PREGNANCY.

[ ]   The wife is not pregnant.
[ ]   The wife is pregnant. The father of the unborn child is [ ] the husband [ ] not the husband [ ] undetermined.
[ ]   Other:

2.16   DEPENDENT CHILDREN.

[ ]   The parties have no dependent children of this marriage.
[ ]   The children listed below are dependent upon either or both spouses.

Name of Child	Age	Mother's Name	Father's Name

[ ]   Other:

2.17   JURISDICTION OVER THE CHILDREN.

[ ]   Does not apply because there are no dependent children.
[ ]   This court does not have jurisdiction over the children.
[ ]   This court has jurisdiction over the children for the reasons set forth below.

[ ]   This court has exclusive continuing jurisdiction. The court has previously made a child custody, parenting plan, residential schedule or visitation determination in this matter and retains jurisdiction under RCW 26.27.211.

[ ]   This state is the home state of the children because:

         [ ]   the children lived in Washington with a parent or a person acting as a parent for at least six consecutive months immediately preceding the commencement of this proceeding.

         [ ]   the children are less than six months old and have lived in Washington with a parent or a person acting as parent since birth.

         [ ]   any absences from Washington have been only temporary.

         [ ]   Washington was the home state of the children within six months before the commencement of this proceeding and the children are absent from the state but a parent or person acting as a parent continued to live in this state.

[ ]   The children and the parents or the children and at least one parent or person acting as a parent, have significant connection with the state other than mere physical presence; and substantial evidence is available in this state concerning the children's care, protection, training and personal relationships; and

         [ ]   the children have no home state elsewhere.

         [ ]   the children's home state has declined to exercise jurisdiction on the ground that this state is the more appropriate forum under RCW 26.27.261 or .271.

[ ]   All courts in the children's home state have declined to exercise jurisdiction on the ground that a court of this state is the more appropriate forum to determine the custody of the children under RCW 26.27.261 or .271.

[ ]   No other state has jurisdiction.

[ ]   This court has temporary emergency jurisdiction over this proceeding because the children are present in this state and the children have been abandoned or it is necessary in an emergency to protect the children because the children, or a sibling or parent of the children is subjected to or threatened with abuse. RCW 26.27.231.

[ ]   Other:

2.18   PARENTING PLAN.

[ ]   Does not apply.

[ ]   The parenting plan signed by the court on   [Date] is approved and incorporated as part of these findings.

         [ ]   This parenting plan is the result of an agreement of the parties.

         [ ]   Other:

2.19   CHILD SUPPORT.

      [ ]   Does not apply.
      [ ]   There are children in need of support and child support should be set pursuant to the
              Washington State Child Support Schedule. The Order of Child Support signed by the court
              on   [Date] and the child support worksheet, which has
              been approved by the court, are incorporated by reference in these findings.
      [ ]   Other:

2.20   OTHER.

III. CONCLUSIONS OF LAW

The court makes the following conclusions of law from the foregoing findings of fact:

3.1   JURISDICTION.

      [ ]   The court has jurisdiction to enter a decree in this matter.
      [ ]   Other:

3.2   GRANTING OF A DECREE.

      [ ]   The parties should be granted a decree.
      [ ]   Other:

3.3   DISPOSITION.

The court should determine the marital status of the parties, make provision for a parenting plan for any minor children of the marriage, make provision for the support of any minor child of the marriage entitled to support, consider or approve provision for the maintenance of either spouse, make provision for the disposition of property and liabilities of the parties, make provision for the allocation of the children as federal tax exemptions, make provision for any necessary continuing restraining orders, and make provision for the change of name of any party. The distribution of property and liabilities as set forth in the decree is fair and equitable.

3.4   CONTINUING RESTRAINING ORDER.

    [ ]   Does not apply.
    [ ]   A continuing restraining order should be entered.

3.5   ATTORNEY'S FEES AND COSTS.

    [ ]   Does not apply.
    [ ]   Attorney's fees, other professional fees and costs should be paid.

3.6   OTHER.

Dated: _____   _____
                                                   Judge/Commissioner

Presented by: Approved for entry:
                                      Notice of presentation waived:

_____   _____
Signature   Signature

Print or Type Name   Print or Type Name

This page intentionally blank.

SUPERIOR COURT OF WASHINGTON
COUNTY OF

In re the Marriage of:
 	
                               Petitioner,
 	
and
 	
                         Respondent.
	NO.
	
	ORDER OF CHILD SUPPORT
	
	[ ] Temporary **(TMORS)**
	[ ] Final Order **(ORS)**
	
	Clerk's Action Required

I. JUDGMENT SUMMARY

[ ]   Does not apply because no attorney's fees or back child support has been ordered.

[ ]   The judgment summary:

A.   Judgment creditor   _____

B.   Judgment debtor   _____

C.   Principal judgment amount (back child support) $ _____

       from _____ [Date] to _____ [Date]

D.   Interest to date of judgment $ _____

E.   Attorney's fees $ _____

F.   Costs $ _____

G.   Other recovery amount $ _____

H.   Principal judgment shall bear interest at _____ % per annum

I.   Attorney's fees, costs and other recovery amounts shall bear interest at _____ % per annum

J.   Attorney for judgment creditor   _____

K.   Attorney for judgment debtor   _____

L.   Other:

II. BASIS

2.1   TYPE OF PROCEEDING.

This order is entered pursuant to:
[ ]   a decree of dissolution, legal separation or a declaration of invalidity.
[ ]   an order determining parentage.
[ ]   an order for modification of child support.
[ ]   a hearing for temporary child support.
[ ]   an order of adjustment.
[ ]   an order for modification of a custody decree or parenting plan.
[ ]   other:

2.2   CHILD SUPPORT WORKSHEET.

The child support worksheet which has been approved by the court is attached to this order and is incorporated by reference or has been initialed and filed separately and is incorporated by reference.

2.3   OTHER:

III. FINDINGS AND ORDER

IT IS ORDERED that:

3.1   CHILDREN FOR WHOM SUPPORT IS REQUIRED.

        Name (first/last)   Age

3.2   PERSON PAYING SUPPORT (OBLIGOR).

        Name (first/last):
        Birth date:
        Service Address: [You may list an address that is not your residential address where you agree to accept legal documents.]

THE OBLIGOR PARENT MUST IMMEDIATELY FILE WITH THE COURT AND THE WASHINGTON STATE CHILD SUPPORT REGISTRY, AND UPDATE AS NECESSARY, THE CONFIDENTIAL INFORMATION FORM REQUIRED BY RCW 26.23.050.

THE OBLIGOR PARENT SHALL UPDATE THE INFORMATION REQUIRED BY PARAGRAPH 3.2 PROMPTLY AFTER ANY CHANGE IN THE INFORMATION. THE

DUTY TO UPDATE THE INFORMATION CONTINUES AS LONG AS ANY MONTHLY SUPPORT REMAINS DUE OR ANY UNPAID SUPPORT DEBT REMAINS DUE UNDER THIS ORDER.

[ ]   Monthly Net Income: $ _____
[ ]   The income of the obligor is imputed at $ _____ because:
     [ ]   the obligor's income is unknown.
     [ ]   the obligor is voluntarily unemployed.
     [ ]   the obligor is voluntarily underemployed.
     [ ]   other:

3.3   PERSON RECEIVING SUPPORT (OBLIGEE):

Name (first/last):
Birth date:
Service Address: [You may list an address that is not your residential address where you agree to accept legal documents.]

THE OBLIGEE MUST IMMEDIATELY FILE WITH THE COURT AND THE WASHINGTON STATE CHILD SUPPORT REGISTRY AND UPDATE AS NECESSARY THE CONFIDENTIAL INFORMATION FORM REQUIRED BY RCW 26.23.050.

THE OBLIGEE SHALL UPDATE THE INFORMATION REQUIRED BY PARAGRAPH 3.3 PROMPTLY AFTER ANY CHANGE IN THE INFORMATION. THE DUTY TO UPDATE THE INFORMATION CONTINUES AS LONG AS ANY MONTHLY SUPPORT REMAINS DUE OR ANY UNPAID SUPPORT DEBT REMAINS DUE UNDER THIS ORDER.

[ ]   Monthly Net Income: $ _____
[ ]   The income of the obligee is imputed at $ _____ because:

     [ ]   the obligee's income is unknown.
     [ ]   the obligee is voluntarily unemployed.
     [ ]   the obligee is voluntarily underemployed.
     [ ]   other:

The obligor may be able to seek reimbursement for day care or special child rearing expenses not actually incurred. RCW 26.19.080.

3.4   SERVICE OF PROCESS.

SERVICE OF PROCESS ON THE OBLIGOR AT THE ADDRESS REQUIRED BY

PARAGRAPH 3.2 OR ANY UPDATED ADDRESS, OR ON THE OBLIGEE AT THE ADDRESS REQUIRED BY PARAGRAPH 3.3 OR ANY UPDATED ADDRESS, MAY BE ALLOWED OR ACCEPTED AS ADEQUATE IN ANY PROCEEDING TO ESTABLISH, ENFORCE OR MODIFY A CHILD SUPPORT ORDER BETWEEN THE PARTIES BY DELIVERY OF WRITTEN NOTICE TO THE OBLIGOR OR OBLIGEE AT THE LAST ADDRESS PROVIDED.

3.5   TRANSFER PAYMENT.

The obligor parent shall pay the following amounts per month for the following children:

Name	Amount
_____	$_____
_____	$_____
_____	$_____
_____	$_____
TOTAL MONTHLY TRANSFER AMOUNT	$_____

[ ]   The parents' combined monthly net income exceeds $7,000 and the court sets child support in excess of the advisory amount because:

[ ]   If one of the children changes age brackets, the child support shall be as follows:

[ ]   This is a downward modification that has caused an overpayment of $ _____. This amount shall be repaid or credited as follows:

[ ]   This is an upward modification that has caused an underpayment of $_____. This amount shall be paid as follows:

[ ]   Other:

THE OBLIGOR PARENT'S PRIVILEGES TO OBTAIN OR MAINTAIN A LICENSE, CERTIFICATE, REGISTRATION, PERMIT, APPROVAL, OR OTHER SIMILAR DOCUMENT ISSUED BY A LICENSING ENTITY EVIDENCING ADMISSION TO OR GRANTING AUTHORITY TO ENGAGE IN A PROFESSION, OCCUPATION, BUSINESS, INDUSTRY, RECREATIONAL PURSUIT, OR THE OPERATION OF A MOTOR VEHICLE MAY BE DENIED OR MAY BE SUSPENDED IF THE OBLIGOR PARENT IS NOT IN COMPLIANCE WITH THIS SUPPORT ORDER AS PROVIDED IN CHAPTER 74.20A REVISED CODE OF WASHINGTON.

3.6   STANDARD CALCULATION.

$ _____ per month. (See Worksheet line 15.)

3.7   REASONS FOR DEVIATION FROM STANDARD CALCULATION.

[ ] The child support amount ordered in paragraph 3.5 does not deviate from the standard calculation.

[ ] The child support amount ordered in paragraph 3.5 deviates from the standard calculation for the following reasons:

    [ ] Income of a new spouse of the parent requesting a deviation for other reasons;

    [ ] Income of other adults in the household of the parent requesting a deviation for other reasons;

    [ ] Child support actually paid or received for other children from other relationships;

    [ ] Gifts;

    [ ] Prizes;

    [ ] Possession of wealth;

    [ ] Extraordinary income of a child;

    [ ] Tax planning which results in greater benefit to the children;

    [ ] A nonrecurring source of income;

    [ ] Extraordinary debt not voluntarily incurred;

    [ ] A significant disparity in the living costs of the parents due to conditions beyond their control;

    [ ] Special needs of disabled children;

    [ ] Special medical, educational, or psychological needs of the children;

    [ ] The child spends a significant amount of time with the parent who is obligated to make a support transfer payment. The deviation does not result in insufficient funds in the receiving parent's household to meet the basic needs of the child. The child does not receive public assistance;

    [ ] Children from other relationships;

    [ ] Costs incurred or anticipated to be incurred by the parents in compliance with court-ordered reunification efforts or under a voluntary placement agreement with an agency supervising the child;

    [ ] The obligor has established that it is unjust or inappropriate to apply the presumptive minimum payment of $25.00 per child.

    [ ] Other:

The factual basis for these reasons is as follows:

    [ ] Other:

3.8   REASONS WHY REQUEST FOR DEVIATION WAS DENIED.

    [ ]   Does not apply. A deviation was ordered.

    [ ]   A deviation was not requested.

[ ]   The deviation sought by the [ ] obligor [ ] obligee was denied because:

          [ ]   no good reason exists to justify deviation.

          [ ]   Other:

3.9   STARTING DATE AND DAY TO BE PAID.

Starting Date: _____

Day(s) of the month support is due: _____

3.10   INCREMENTAL PAYMENTS.

[ ]   Does not apply.

[ ]   This is a modification of child support. Pursuant to RCW 26.09.170 (9)(a) and (c), the obligation has been modified by more than 30 percent and the change would cause significant hardship. The increase in the child support obligation set forth in Paragraph 3.5 shall be implemented in two equal increments, one at the time of this order and the second on _____ [Date] six months from the entry of this order.

3.11   HOW SUPPORT PAYMENTS SHALL BE MADE.

Select Enforcement and Collection, Payment Services Only, or Direct Payment:

[ ]   Enforcement and collection: The Division of Child Support (DCS) provides support enforcement services for this case because: [ ] This is a public assistance case, [ ] this is a case in which a parent has requested services from DCS, [ ] a parent has signed the application for services from DCS on the last page of this support order. (Check all that apply.) Support payments shall be made to:

          Washington State Support Registry
          P. O. Box 45868
          Olympia, WA 98504
          Phone: 1-800-922-4306 or
                    1-800-442-5437

[ ]   Payment services only: The Division of Child Support will process and keep a record of all payments but will not take any collection action. Support payments shall be made to:

          Washington State Support Registry
          P. O. Box 45868
          Olympia, WA 98504
          Phone: 1-800-922-4306 or
                    1-800-442-5437

[ ]   Direct Payment: Support payments shall be made directly to:

          Name_____
          Mailing Address_____

          _____

A party required to make payments to the Washington State Support Registry will not receive credit for a payment made to any other party or entity. The obligor parent shall keep the registry informed whether he or she has access to health insurance coverage at reasonable cost and, if so, to provide the health insurance policy information.

3.12   WAGE WITHHOLDING ACTION.

Withholding action may be taken against wages, earnings, assets, or benefits, and liens enforced against real and personal property under the child support statutes of this or any other state, without further notice to the obligor parent at any time after entry of this order unless an alternative provision is made below:

[If the court orders immediate wage withholding in a case where Division of Child Support does not provide support enforcement services, a mandatory wage assignment under Chapter 26.18 RCW must be entered and support payments must be made to the Support Registry.]

[ ]   Wage withholding, by notice of payroll deduction or other income withholding action under Chapter 26.18 RCW or Chapter 74.20A RCW, without further notice to the obligor, is delayed until a payment is past due, because:

   [ ]   the parties have reached a written agreement that the court approves that provides for an alternate arrangement.

   [ ]   the Division of Child Support provides support enforcement services for this case [see 3.11] and there is good cause [as stated below under "Good Cause"] not to require immediate income withholding which is in the best interests of the child and, in modification cases, previously ordered child support has been timely paid.

   [ ]   the Division of Child Support does not provide support enforcement services for this case [see 3.11] and there is good cause [as stated below under "Good Cause"] not to require immediate income withholding.

   Good Cause:

3.13   TERMINATION OF SUPPORT.

Support shall be paid:

   [ ]   provided that this is a temporary order, until a subsequent child support order is entered by this court.
   [ ]   until the child(ren) reach(es) the age of 18, except as otherwise provided below in Paragraph 3.14.
   [ ]   until the child(ren) reach(es) the age of 18 or as long as the child(ren) remain(s) enrolled in high school, whichever occurs last, except as otherwise provided below in Paragraph 3.14.
   [ ]   after the age of 18 for _____ [Name] who is a dependent adult child, until the child is capable of self-support and the necessity for support ceases.
   [ ]   until the obligation for post secondary support set forth in Paragraph 3.14 begins for the

child(ren).
[ ]   Other:

3.14   POST SECONDARY EDUCATIONAL SUPPORT.

[ ]   No post secondary educational support shall be required.

[ ]   The right to petition for post secondary support is reserved, provided that the right is exercised before support terminates as set forth in paragraph 3.13.

[ ]   The parents shall pay for the post secondary educational support of the child(ren). Post secondary support provisions will be decided by agreement or by the court.

[ ]   Other:

3.15   PAYMENT FOR EXPENSES NOT INCLUDED IN THE TRANSFER PAYMENT.

[ ]   Does not apply because all payments, except medical, are included in the transfer payment.

[ ]   The mother shall pay _____% and the father _____ % (each parent's proportional share of income from the Child Support Schedule Worksheet, line 6) of the following expenses incurred on behalf of the children listed in Paragraph 3.1:
        [ ]   day care.
        [ ]   educational expenses.
        [ ]   long distance transportation expenses.
        [ ]   other:

      Payments shall be made to [ ] the provider of the service [ ] the parent receiving the transfer payment.

[ ]   The obligor shall pay the following amounts each month the expense is incurred on behalf of the children listed in Paragraph 3.1:

        [ ]   day care: $ _____ payable to the [ ] day care provider [ ] other parent;
        [ ]   educational expenses: $ _____ payable to the [ ] educational provider [ ] other parent;
        [ ]   long distance transportation: $ _____ payable to the [ ] transportation provider [ ] other parent.
        [ ]   other:

3.16   PERIODIC ADJUSTMENT.

[ ]   Does not apply.
[ ]   Child support shall be adjusted periodically as follows:

[ ]   Other:

3.17 INCOME TAX EXEMPTIONS.

[ ] Does not apply.
[ ] Tax exemptions for the children shall be allocated as follows:

[ ] The parents shall sign the federal income tax dependency exemption waiver.
[ ] Other:

3.18 MEDICAL INSURANCE FOR THE CHILDREN LISTED IN PARAGRAPH 3.1.

Unless one or more of the **alternatives** below are checked, **each parent** shall maintain or provide health insurance coverage if:

(a) Coverage that can be extended to cover the child(ren) is or becomes available to each parent through employment or is union-related; and
(b) The cost of such coverage for the mother does not exceed $_____ (25 percent of mother's basic child support obligation on Worksheet line 7), and the cost of such coverage for the father does not exceed $_____ (25 percent of father's basic child support obligation on Worksheet Line 7).

[ ] **Alternative 1:** The parent below shall maintain or provide health insurance coverage if coverage that can be extended to cover the child(ren) is or becomes available to that parent through employment or is union-related and the cost of such coverage **does not exceed** $_____ (25 percent of that parent's basic child support obligation on Worksheet line 7).

[ ] Mother
[ ] Father

[ ] **Alternative 2:** The parent below shall maintain or provide health insurance coverage if coverage that can be extended to cover the child(ren) is or becomes available to that parent through employment or is union-related even if such coverage **exceeds** $_____ (25 percent of that parent's basic child support obligation on Worksheet line 7).

[ ] Mother
[ ] Father

[ ] **Alternative 3:** The parent below is not obligated to provide health insurance coverage:

[ ] Mother
[ ] Father

This parent is not obligated to provide health insurance coverage because:

[ ] The other parent provides insurance coverage.
[ ] Other:

The parent(s) shall maintain health insurance coverage, if available for the children listed in paragraph 3.1, until further order of the court or until health insurance is no longer available through the parents' employer or union and no conversion privileges exist to continue coverage following termination of employment.

A parent who is required under this order to provide health insurance coverage is liable for any covered health care costs for which that parent receives direct payment from an insurer.

A parent who is required under this order to provide health insurance coverage shall provide proof that such coverage is available or not available within 20 days of the entry of this order to the physical custodian or the Washington State Support Registry if the parent has been notified or ordered to make payments to the Washington State Support Registry.

If proof that health insurance coverage is available or not available is not provided within 20 days, the obligee or the Department of Social and Health Services may seek direct enforcement of the coverage through the obligor's employer or union without further notice to the obligor as provided under Chapter 26.18 RCW.

3.19   EXTRAORDINARY HEALTH CARE EXPENSES.

The OBLIGOR shall pay _____% of extraordinary health care expenses (the obligor's proportional share of income from the Child Support Schedule Worksheet, line 6), if monthly medical expenses exceed $ _____ (5% of the basic support obligation from Worksheet line 5).

3.20   BACK CHILD SUPPORT.

[ ]   No back child support is owed at this time.
[ ]   Back child support that may be owed is not affected by this order.
[ ]   The obligee parent is awarded a judgment against the obligor parent in the amount of
       $ _____ for back child support for the period from _____ [Date]
       to _____ [Date].

[ ]   Other:

3.21   BACK INTEREST.

[ ]   No back interest is owed at this time.
[ ]   Back interest that may be owed is not affected by this order.
[ ]   The obligee parent is awarded a judgment against the obligor parent in the amount of
       $ _____ for back interest for the period from _____ [Date] to
       _____ [Date].

[ ]   Other:

3.22   OTHER:

Dated: _____

JUDGE/COMMISSIONER _____

Presented by:

Approved for entry:
Notice of presentation waived:

_____
Signature

_____
Signature

_____
Print or Type Name

_____
Print or Type Name

[ ]   I apply for full support enforcement services from the DSHS Division of Child Support.

_____
Signature of Party

[ ]   Approval required in Public Assistance cases. Approved for entry, notice of presentation waived.

_____
Deputy Prosecuting Attorney/WSBA No.

This page intentionally blank.

SUPERIOR COURT OF WASHINGTON
COUNTY OF

In re the Marriage of:	**NO.**
Petitioner,	PARENTING PLAN
and	[ ] PROPOSED **(PPP)**
	[ ] TEMPORARY **(PPT)**
	[ ] FINAL ORDER **(PP)**
Respondent.	

This parenting plan is:

[ ]   the final parenting plan signed by the court pursuant to a decree of dissolution entered on
                    [Date].

[ ]   the final parenting plan signed by the court pursuant to an order entered on   [Date]
         which modifies a previous parenting plan or custody decree.

[ ]   a temporary parenting plan signed by the court.

[ ]   proposed by   [Name].

IT IS HEREBY ORDERED, ADJUDGED AND DECREED:

I. GENERAL INFORMATION

This parenting plan applies to the following children:

<u>Name</u>   <u>Age</u>

II. BASIS FOR RESTRICTIONS

Under certain circumstances, as outlined below, the court may limit or prohibit a parent's contact with the child(ren) and the right to make decisions for the child(ren).

2.1   PARENTAL CONDUCT (RCW 26.09.191(1), (2)).

[ ]   Does not apply.

[ ]   The [ ] mother's [ ] father's residential time with the child(ren) shall be limited or restrained completely, and mutual decision-making and designation of a dispute resolution process other than court action shall not be required, because [ ] this parent [ ] a person residing with this parent has engaged in the conduct which follows.

    [ ]   Willful abandonment that continues for an extended period of time or substantial refusal to perform parenting functions (this applies only to parents, not to a person who resides with a parent).

    [ ]   Physical, sexual or a pattern of emotional abuse of a child.

    [ ]   A history of acts of domestic violence as defined in RCW 26.50.010(1) or an assault or sexual assault which causes grievous bodily harm or the fear of such harm.

2.2   OTHER FACTORS (RCW 26.09.191(3)).

[ ]   Does not apply.

[ ]   The [ ] mother's [ ] father's involvement or conduct may have an adverse effect on the child(ren)'s best interests because of the existence of the factors which follow.

    [ ]   Neglect or substantial nonperformance of parenting functions.

    [ ]   A long-term emotional or physical impairment which interferes with the performance of parenting functions as defined in RCW 26.09.004.

    [ ]   A long-term impairment resulting from drug, alcohol, or other substance abuse that interferes with the performance of parenting functions.

    [ ]   The absence or substantial impairment of emotional ties between the parent and child.

    [ ]   The abusive use of conflict by the parent which creates the danger of serious damage to the child's psychological development.

    [ ]   A parent has withheld from the other parent access to the child for a protracted period without good cause.

    [ ]   Other:

III. RESIDENTIAL SCHEDULE

The residential schedule must set forth where the child(ren) shall reside each day of the year, including provisions for holidays, birthdays of family members, vacations, and other special occasions, and what contact the child(ren) shall have with each parent. Parents are encouraged to create a residential schedule that meets the developmental needs of the child(ren) and individual needs of their family. Paragraphs 3.1 through 3.9 are one way to write your residential schedule. If you do not use these paragraphs, write in your own schedule in Paragraph 3.13.

3.1   SCHEDULE FOR CHILDREN UNDER SCHOOL AGE

[ ]   There are no children under school age.
[ ]   Prior to enrollment in school, the child(ren) shall reside with the [ ] mother [ ] father, except for the following days and times when the child(ren) will reside with or be with the other parent:

from   [day and time] to   [day and time]

[ ]   every week [ ] every other week [ ] the first and third week of the month
[ ]   the second and fourth week of the month [ ] other:

from   [day and time] to   [day and time]

[ ]   every week [ ] every other week [ ] the first and third week of the month
[ ]   the second and fourth week of the month [ ] other:

3.2   SCHOOL SCHEDULE.

Upon enrollment in school, the child(ren) shall reside with the [ ] mother [ ] father, except for the following days and times when the child(ren) will reside with or be with the other parent:

from   [day and time] to   [day and time]

[ ]   every week [ ] every other week [ ] the first and third week of the month
[ ]   the second and fourth week of the month [ ] other:

from   [day and time] to   [day and time]

[ ]   every week [ ] every other week [ ] the first and third week of the month
[ ]   the second and fourth week of the month [ ] other:

[ ]   The school schedule will start when each child begins [ ] kindergarten [ ] first grade [ ] other:

3.3   SCHEDULE FOR WINTER VACATION.

The child(ren) shall reside with the [ ] mother [ ] father during winter vacation, except for the following days and times when the child(ren) will reside with or be with the other parent:

3.4   SCHEDULE FOR OTHER SCHOOL BREAKS.

The child(ren) shall reside with the [ ] mother [ ] father during other school breaks, except for the following days and times when the child(ren) will reside with or be with the other parent:

3.5   SUMMER SCHEDULE.

Upon completion of the school year, the child(ren) shall reside with the [ ] mother [ ] father, except for the following days and times when the child(ren) will reside with or be with the other parent:

[ ]   Same as school year schedule.
[ ]   Other:

3.6   VACATION WITH PARENTS.

[ ]   Does not apply.
[ ]   The schedule for vacation with parents is as follows:

3.7   SCHEDULE FOR HOLIDAYS.

The residential schedule for the child(ren) for the holidays listed below is as follows:

	With Mother (Specify Year Odd/Even/Every)	With Father (Specify Year Odd/Even/Every)
New Year's Day		
Martin Luther King Day		
Presidents' Day		
Memorial Day		
July 4th		
Labor Day		
Veterans' Day		
Thanksgiving Day		
Christmas Eve		
Christmas Day		

[ ]   For purposes of this parenting plan, a holiday shall begin and end as follows (set forth times):

[ ]   Holidays which fall on a Friday or a Monday shall include Saturday and Sunday.

[ ]   Other:

3.8   SCHEDULE FOR SPECIAL OCCASIONS.

The residential schedule for the child(ren) for the following special occasions (for example, birthdays) is as follows:

	With Mother (Specify Year Odd/Even/Every)	With Father (Specify Year Odd/Even/Every)

[ ]   Other:

3.9   PRIORITIES UNDER THE RESIDENTIAL SCHEDULE.

[ ]   Does not apply.
[ ]   If the residential schedule, paragraphs 3.1 - 3.8, results in a conflict where the children are scheduled to be with both parents at the same time, the conflict shall be resolved by priority being given as follows:

  [ ]   Rank the order of priority, with 1 being given the highest priority:

        school schedule (3.1, 3.2)   vacation with parents (3.6)
        winter vacation (3.3)   holidays (3.7)
        spring vacation (3.4)   special occasions (3.8)
        summer schedule (3.5)

  [ ]   Other:

3.10   RESTRICTIONS.

[ ]   Does not apply because there are no limiting factors in paragraphs 2.1 or 2.2.
[ ]   The [ ] mother's [ ] father's residential time with the children shall be limited because there are limiting factors in paragraphs 2.1 and 2.2. The following restrictions shall apply when the children spend time with this parent:

[ ]   There are limiting factors in paragraph 2.2, but there are no restrictions on the [ ] mother's [ ] father's residential time with the children for the following reasons:

3.11   TRANSPORTATION ARRANGEMENTS.

Transportation costs are included in the Child Support Worksheets and/or the Order of Child Support and should not be included here.

Transportation arrangements for the child(ren), between parents shall be as follows:

3.12 DESIGNATION OF CUSTODIAN.

The children named in this parenting plan are scheduled to reside the majority of the time with the [ ] mother [ ] father. This parent is designated the custodian of the child(ren) solely for purposes of all other state and federal statutes which require a designation or determination of custody. This designation shall not affect either parent's rights and responsibilities under this parenting plan.

3.13 OTHER.

3.14 SUMMARY OF RCW 26.09.430 - .480, REGARDING RELOCATION OF A CHILD.

This is a summary only. For the full text, please see RCW 26.09.430 through 26.09.480.

If the person with whom the child resides a majority of the time plans to move, that person shall give notice to every person entitled to court ordered time with the child.

If the move is outside the child's school district, the relocating person must give notice by personal service or by mail requiring a return receipt. This notice must be at least 60 days before the intended move. If the relocating person could not have known about the move in time to give 60 days' notice, that person must give notice within 5 days after learning of the move. The notice must contain the information required in RCW 26.09.440. See also form DRPSCU 07.0500, (Notice of Intended Relocation of A Child).

If the move is within the same school district, the relocating person must provide actual notice by any reasonable means. A person entitled to time with the child may not object to the move but may ask for modification under RCW 26.09.260.

Notice may be delayed for 21 days if the relocating person is entering a domestic violence shelter or is moving to avoid a clear, immediate and unreasonable risk to health and safety.

If information is protected under a court order or the address confidentiality program, it may be withheld from the notice.

A relocating person may ask the court to waive any notice requirements that may put the health and safety of a person or a child at risk.

Failure to give the required notice may be grounds for sanctions, including contempt.

If no objection is filed within 30 days after service of the notice of intended relocation, the relocation will be permitted and the proposed revised residential schedule may be confirmed.

A person entitled to time with a child under a court order can file an objection to the child's relocation whether or not he or she received proper notice.

An objection may be filed by using the mandatory pattern form WPF DRPSCU 07.0700, (Objection to Relocation/Petition for Modification of Custody Decree/Parenting Plan/Residential Schedule). The objection must be served on all persons entitled to time with the child.

The relocating person shall not move the child during the time for objection unless: (a) the delayed notice provisions apply; or (b) a court order allows the move.

If the objecting person schedules a hearing for a date within 15 days of timely service of the objection, the relocating person shall not move the child before the hearing unless there is a clear, immediate and unreasonable risk to the health or safety of a person or a child.

IV. DECISION MAKING

4.1   DAY-TO-DAY DECISIONS.

Each parent shall make decisions regarding the day-to-day care and control of each child while the child is residing with that parent. Regardless of the allocation of decision making in this parenting plan, either parent may make emergency decisions affecting the health or safety of the children.

4.2   MAJOR DECISIONS.

Major decisions regarding each child shall be made as follows:

Education decisions	[ ]	mother	[ ]	father	[ ]	joint
Non-emergency health care	[ ]	mother	[ ]	father	[ ]	joint
Religious upbringing	[ ]	mother	[ ]	father	[ ]	joint
	[ ]	mother	[ ]	father	[ ]	joint
	[ ]	mother	[ ]	father	[ ]	joint
	[ ]	mother	[ ]	father	[ ]	joint
	[ ]	mother	[ ]	father	[ ]	joint
	[ ]	mother	[ ]	father	[ ]	joint
	[ ]	mother	[ ]	father	[ ]	joint

4.3   RESTRICTIONS IN DECISION MAKING.

    [ ]   Does not apply because there are no limiting factors in paragraphs 2.1 and 2.2 above.

    [ ]   Sole decision making shall be ordered to the [ ] mother [ ] father for the following
        reasons:

        [ ]   A limitation on the other parent's decision making authority is mandated by
            RCW 26.09.191 (See paragraph 2.1).

        [ ]   Both parents are opposed to mutual decision making.

        [ ]   One parent is opposed to mutual decision making, and such opposition is
            reasonably based on the following criteria:

            (a)   The existence of a limitation under RCW 26.09.191;

            (b)   The history of participation of each parent in decision making in each of
                the areas in RCW 26.09.184(4)(a);

            (c)   Whether the parents have demonstrated ability and desire to cooperate
                with one another in decision making in each of the areas in RCW
                26.09.184(4)(a); and

            (d)   The parents' geographic proximity to one another, to the extent that it
                affects their ability to make timely mutual decisions.

    [ ]   There are limiting factors in paragraph 2.2, but there are no restrictions on mutual
        decision making for the following reasons:

V. DISPUTE RESOLUTION

*The purpose of this dispute resolution process is to resolve disagreements about carrying out this
parenting plan. This dispute resolution process may, and under some local court rules or the provisions
of this plan must, be used before filing a petition to modify the plan or a motion for contempt for failing to
follow the plan.*

[ ]   Disputes between the parties, other than child support disputes, shall be submitted to (list person
    or agency):

    [ ]   counseling by   , or

    [ ]   mediation by   , or

    [ ]   arbitration by   .

The cost of this process shall be allocated between the parties as follows:

[ ]   % mother   % father.
[ ]   based on each party's proportional share of income from line 6 of the child support worksheets.
[ ]   as determined in the dispute resolution process.

The counseling, mediation or arbitration process shall be commenced by notifying the other party by [ ] written request [ ] certified mail [ ] other:

In the dispute resolution process:

(a)   Preference shall be given to carrying out this Parenting Plan.
(b)   Unless an emergency exists, the parents shall use the designated process to resolve disputes relating to implementation of the plan, except those related to financial support.
(c)   A written record shall be prepared of any agreement reached in counseling or mediation and of each arbitration award and shall be provided to each party.
(d)   If the court finds that a parent has used or frustrated the dispute resolution process without good reason, the court shall award attorneys' fees and financial sanctions to the other parent.
(e)   The parties have the right of review from the dispute resolution process to the superior court.

[ ]   No dispute resolution process, except court action is ordered.

VI. OTHER PROVISIONS

[ ]   There are no other provisions.
[ ]   There are the following other provisions:

VII. DECLARATION FOR PROPOSED PARENTING PLAN

[ ]   Does not apply.

[ ]   (Only sign if this is a proposed parenting plan.) I declare under penalty of perjury under the laws of the state of Washington that this plan has been proposed in good faith and that the statements in Part II of this Plan are true and correct.

_____
Mother

_____
Date and Place of Signature

_____
Father

_____
Date and Place of Signature

VIII. ORDER BY THE COURT

It is ordered, adjudged and decreed that the parenting plan set forth above is adopted and approved as an order of this court.

WARNING: Violation of residential provisions of this order with actual knowledge of its terms is punishable by contempt of court and may be a criminal offense under RCW 9A.040.060(2) or 9A.40.070(2). Violation of this order may subject a violator to arrest.

When mutual decision making is designated but cannot be achieved, the parties shall make a good faith effort to resolve the issue through the dispute resolution process.

If a parent fails to comply with a provision of this plan, the other parent's obligations under the plan are not affected.

Dated: _____

_____
JUDGE/COMMISSIONER

Presented by:

Approved for entry:

_____
Signature

_____
Signature

Print or Type Name

Print or Type Name

This page intentionally blank.

SUPERIOR COURT OF WASHINGTON
COUNTY OF

In re:	**NO.**
Petitioner,	**RETURN OF SERVICE** (OPTIONAL USE) **(RTS)**
and	
Respondent.	

I DECLARE:

1.　　I am over the age of 18 years, and I am not a party to this action.

2.　　I served _____ [Name] with the following documents:

    [ ]　　summons, a copy of which is attached, and petition in this action
    [ ]　　parenting plan or residential schedule
    [ ]　　child support order
    [ ]　　child support worksheets
    [ ]　　sealed financial source documents cover sheet and financial documents
    [ ]　　financial declaration
    [ ]　　notice of and motion for temporary order
    [ ]　　motion for and ex parte order
    [ ]　　adequate cause notice of hearing
    [ ]　　declarations of _____
    [ ]　　motion for and order to show cause re: _____.
    [ ]　　other:

3.　　The date, time and place of service were (if by mail refer to Paragraph 4 below):

RETURN OF SERVICE (RTS) - Page 1 of 2
WPF DRPSCU 01.0250 (6/2004) - CR 4(g), RCW 4.28.080(14)

Date: _____ Time: _____ a.m./p.m.

Address: _____

_____

4. Service was made pursuant to Civil Rule 4(d):

[ ] by delivery to the person named in paragraph 2 above.

[ ] by delivery to _____ [Name], a person of suitable age and discretion residing at the respondent's usual abode.

[ ] by publication as provided in RCW 4.28.100. (A copy of the summons is attached.)

[ ] (check only if there is a court order authorizing service by mail) by mailing two copies postage prepaid to the person named in the order entered by the court on _____ [Date]. One copy was mailed by ordinary first class mail, the other copy was sent by certified mail return receipt requested. (Attach return receipt below.) The copies were mailed on _____ [Date].

5. Other:

I declare under penalty of perjury under the laws of the state of Washington that the foregoing is true and correct.

Signed at _____, [City] _____ [State], on _____ [Date].

_____   _____
Signature   Print or Type Name

Fees:

Service   _____
Mileage   _____
Total   _____

(Attach Return Receipt here, if service was by mail.)

SUPERIOR COURT OF WASHINGTON
COUNTY OF

In re the Marriage of:	
	NO.
Petitioner,	**MOTION AND DECLARATION FOR**
and	**DEFAULT**
	(MTDFL)
Respondent.	

I. MOTION

_____ [Name of moving party] moves the court for an order of default. Venue of this action is proper as set forth in the Declaration below.

Dated: _____   _____
                                                                             Signature of Moving Party or Lawyer/WSBA No.

                                                                             _____
                                                                             Print or Type Name

II. DECLARATION

2.1   PROPER JURISDICTION AND VENUE.

The court has proper jurisdiction and venue pursuant to the allegations of the petition at the time of filing.

The petitioner resides in _____ [County and State].

The child(ren) reside(s) in _____ [County and State].

Respondent resides in _____ [County and State].
[ ]   Other:

2.2   JURISDICTION OVER NONMOVING PARTY.

This court has jurisdiction over _____ [Name of nonmoving party] because:

[ ]   the nonmoving party is presently residing in Washington.
[ ]   the petitioner and respondent lived in Washington during their marriage and the petitioner continues to reside, or be a member of the armed forces stationed, in this state.
[ ]   the petitioner and respondent may have conceived a child while within Washington.
[ ]   Other:

2.3   SERVICE ON NONMOVING PARTY.

The nonmoving party was served with _____ [Documents] on _____ [Date]:

[ ]   in the state of Washington.
[ ]   in _____ [State or Country where served].   Service within the state of Washington could not be made for the following reasons:

2.4   TIME ELAPSED SINCE SERVICE ON THE NONMOVING PARTY.

[ ]   The nonmoving party was served within the state of Washington and more than 20 days have elapsed since the date of service.
[ ]   The nonmoving party was served outside the state of Washington and more than 60 days have elapsed since the date of service.
[ ]   The nonmoving party was served by mail and more than 90 days have elapsed since the date of mailing.
[ ]   The nonmoving party was served by publication and more than 60 days have passed since the date of first publication.

2.5   APPEARANCE OF THE NONMOVING PARTY.

[ ]   The nonmoving party has failed to appear.
[ ]   The nonmoving party has appeared, but has failed to respond.

2.6   SERVICEMEMBERS CIVIL RELIEF ACT STATEMENT.

The nonmoving party:
[ ]   is on active duty in the U.S. armed forces;
[ ]   is not on active duty in the U.S. armed forces;
[ ]   I am unable to determine whether the nonmoving party is or is not on active duty in the U.S. armed forces;

based upon the following facts:

[ ]   As indicated above, the nonmoving party is on active duty and (check all that apply):

[ ]   The nonmoving party is represented by an attorney.
[ ]   The court has appointed an attorney to represent the nonmoving party.
[ ]   A stay of these proceedings [ ] has [ ] has not been entered by the court.

2.7   Other:

I declare under penalty of perjury under the laws of the state of Washington that the foregoing is true and correct.

Signed at _____, [City]_____ [State], on _____ [Date].

_____   _____
Signature of Moving Party   Print or Type name

This page intentionally blank.

SUPERIOR COURT OF WASHINGTON
COUNTY OF

In re the Marriage of:	
	NO.
Petitioner,	ORDER OF DEFAULT
and	**(ORDFL)**
Respondent.	

I. BASIS

A motion for default has been presented by   [Name of moving party].

II. FINDINGS

The court FINDS that:

2.1   PROPER JURISDICTION AND VENUE.

The court has proper jurisdiction and venue.

2.2   SERVICE ON NONMOVING PARTY.

[Name of nonmoving party] was served with

on   [Date].

ORD OF DEFAULT (DISSO)(ORDFL) - Page 1 of 2
WPF DR 03.0200 (7/2003) - CR 55(a); RCW 26.09.020

2.3   TIME ELAPSED SINCE SERVICE.

[ ]   The nonmoving party was served within the state of Washington and more than 20 days have elapsed since the date of service.

[ ]   The nonmoving party was served outside the state of Washington and more than 60 days have elapsed since the date of service.

[ ]   The nonmoving party was served by mail and more than 90 days have elapsed since the date of mailing.

[ ]   The nonmoving party was served by publication and more than 60 days have passed since the date of first publication.

2.4   APPEARANCE.

[ ]   The nonmoving party has failed to appear.

[ ]   The nonmoving party has appeared but has failed to respond.

2.5   OTHER.

III. ORDER

IT IS ORDERED that the nonmoving party is in default.

Dated: _____   _____
                                                                     JUDGE/COMMISSIONER

Presented by:

_____
Signature

Print or Type Name

SUPERIOR COURT OF WASHINGTON
COUNTY OF

In re:

Petitioner,	**NO.**
and	**MOTION AND DECLARATION TO SERVE BY MAIL (MTAF)**
Respondent.	

I. MOTION

_____ [moving party] moves the court for an order allowing service of the summons and petition by mail.

Dated: _____

_____
Signature of Moving Party or Lawyer/WSBA No.

_____
Print or Type Name

II. DECLARATION

2.1.   Service should be made by mail because:

[ ]   _____ [nonmoving party] is not a resident of this state.
[ ]   _____ [nonmoving party] cannot be found in this state.
[ ]   the moving party is proceeding in forma pauperis and cannot afford service by publication or personal service.

2.2   The moving party has not been able to locate or serve the nonmoving party because:

     [ ]   the nonmoving party has departed from Washington to avoid service of summons.
     [ ]   the nonmoving party has concealed himself/herself to avoid service of summons.
     [ ]   other:

2.3   The facts supporting the above allegations are:

2.4   The following efforts were made to locate the nonmoving party for personal service:

2.5   Service by mail is as likely to provide actual notice as service by publication.

2.6   The mailings should be sent to the following address:

2.7   This address is:

     [ ]   The last known mailing address of the nonmoving party.
     [ ]   The mailing address of the nonmoving party's parent or nearest living relative.
     [ ]   Other:

2.8   Other:

I declare under penalty of perjury under the laws of the state of Washington that the foregoing is true and correct.

Signed at _____ , [City] _____ [State], on _____ [Date].

_____   _____
Signature of Moving Party   Print or Type Name

SUPERIOR COURT OF WASHINGTON
COUNTY OF

In re:

Petitioner,	**NO.**
and	ORDER ALLOWING SERVICE BY MAIL
Respondent.	**(ORRSR)**

I. BASIS

The court has considered _____ [Moving party]'s motion and declaration requesting an order allowing service of the summons and petition by mail.

II. FINDINGS

Based on the motion and declaration, the court FINDS that the summons and petition in this matter should be served on _____ [Nonmoving party] by mail in accordance with CR 4(d)(4).

III. ORDER

IT IS ORDERED:

3.1   The summons and petition shall be served on the nonmoving party by mail by a person 18 years of age or over and competent to be a witness <u>but not the moving party</u>.

3.2   Two (2) copies shall be mailed postage prepaid, one by ordinary first class mail, and the other by certified mail, return receipt requested, showing when, and to whom, delivered, each showing a return address for the sender or an address through which correspondence may be directed to the sender.

3.3   The mailings shall be sent to the following address(es):

3.4   These addresses are:

        [ ]   The last known mailing address of the nonmoving party.
        [ ]   The mailing address of the nonmoving party's parent or nearest living relative.
        [ ]   Other:

3.5   A summons and petition mailed to the nonmoving party in care of parents or other individuals shall be addressed directly to the parent or other individual with a note enclosed asking that the summons and petition be delivered to the nonmoving party.

3.6   The person mailing the summons and petition shall complete a Return of Service form.

Dated: _____   _____
                                                              Judge/Commissioner

Presented by:

_____
Signature

Print or Type Name

SUPERIOR COURT OF WASHINGTON
COUNTY OF

In re the Marriage of:

	NO.
Petitioner,	
and	SUMMONS BY MAIL
	(SM)
Respondent.	

TO THE RESPONDENT:

1.   The petitioner has started an action in the above court requesting:

        [ ]   that your marriage be dissolved.
        [ ]   a legal separation.
        [ ]   that the validity of your marriage be determined.

        Additional requests, if any, are stated in the petition, a copy of which is attached.

2.   You must respond to this summons by serving a copy of your written response on the person
        signing this summons and by filing the original with the clerk of the court. If you do not serve
        your written response within 90 days from the date of mailing of this summons (90 days after the
        _____ day of _____, 20____), the court may enter an order of default against
        you, and the court may, without further notice to you, enter a decree and approve or provide for
        other relief requested in the petition. In the case of a dissolution of marriage, the court will not
        enter the final decree until at least 90 days after service and filing. If you serve a notice of
        appearance on the undersigned person, you are entitled to notice before an order of default or a
        decree may be entered.

3.   Your written response to the summons and petition must be on form WPF DR 01.0300, Response
        to Petition (Domestic Relations). Information about how to get this form may be obtained by
        contacting the clerk of the court, by contacting the Administrative Office of the Courts at (360)
        705-5328, or from the Internet at the Washington State Courts homepage:

                    http://www.courts.wa.gov/forms

4. If this action has not been filed with the court, you may demand that the petitioner file this action with the court. If you do so, the demand must be in writing and must be served upon the person publishing this summons. Within 14 days after you serve the demand, the petitioner must file this action with the court, or the service on you of this summons will be void.

5. If you wish to seek the advice of an attorney in this matter, you should do so promptly so that your written response, if any, may be served on time.

6. One method of serving a copy of your response on the petitioner is to send it by certified mail with return receipt requested.

This summons is issued pursuant to RCW 4.28.100 and Superior Court Civil Rule 4.1 of the state of Washington.

Dated: _____   _____

                                                   Signature of Lawyer or Petitioner

                                                   Print or Type Name

FILE ORIGINAL OF YOUR RESPONSE   SERVE A COPY OF YOUR RESPONSE ON:
WITH THE CLERK OF THE COURT AT:

                                                   [ ] Petitioner [You may list an address that is not
                                                   your residential address where you agree to
                                                   accept legal documents.]

                                                   [ ] Petitioner's Lawyer

[Name of Court]   [Name]

[Address]   [Address]

Date Mailed:_____

SUPERIOR COURT OF WASHINGTON
COUNTY OF

In re:

                                Petitioner,

and

                              Respondent.

NO.

MOTION AND DECLARATION FOR SERVICE OF SUMMONS BY PUBLICATION
(DCLR)

I. MOTION

_____ [moving party] moves (asks) the court, pursuant to RCW 4.28.100, for an order allowing service of the summons and petition by publication.

Dated: _____

_____
Signature of Moving Party or Lawyer/WSBA No.

Print or Type Name

II. DECLARATION

2.1.   Service of summons by publication is justified because:

    [ ] _____ [nonmoving party] is not a resident of this state.
    [ ] _____ [nonmoving party] cannot be found in this state because:

        [ ]   the nonmoving party has departed from Washington to avoid service of summons.

[ ]   the nonmoving party has concealed himself/herself to avoid service of summons.

[ ]   other:

2.2   The facts supporting the above allegations are:

2.3.   The following efforts were made to locate the nonmoving party for personal service or service by mail:

2.4.   [ ]   A copy of the summons (substantially in the form prescribed in RCW 4.28.110) and the petition have been deposited in the post office, directed to the nonmoving party at the nonmoving party's place of residence.

        [ ]   I do not know the nonmoving party's address.

I declare under penalty of perjury under the laws of the state of Washington that the foregoing is true and correct.

Signed at _____, [City] _____ [State], on _____ [Date].

_____

Signature of Moving Party   Print or Type Name

SUPERIOR COURT OF WASHINGTON
COUNTY OF

In re:

　　　　　　　　　　　　　　　　　　Petitioner,

and

　　　　　　　　　　　　　　　　　　Respondent.

NO.

ORDER FOR SERVICE OF
SUMMONS BY PUBLICATION
(If Required by Local Practice)
(ORPUB)

I. BASIS

The court has considered _____ [moving party]'s motion and
declaration requesting that the summons in this matter be served by publication.

II. FINDINGS

Based on the representations made in the declaration, the court FINDS that the summons in this matter
may be served on _____ [nonmoving party] by
publication in accordance with RCW 4.28.100.

III. ORDER

IT IS ORDERED that the summons in this matter may be served on the nonmoving party by publication
in conformity with RCW 4.28.100.

Dated: _____   _____
　　　　　　　　　　　　　　　　　　　　　　　　　　Judge/Commissioner

Presented by:

_____

Signature

Print or Type Name

This page intentionally blank.

SUPERIOR COURT OF WASHINGTON
COUNTY OF

In re the Marriage of:

Petitioner,	NO.
and	SUMMONS BY
	PUBLICATION
	(SMPB)
Respondent.	

TO THE RESPONDENT:

[NOTE TO PUBLISHER: Publish only those boxes which are checked.]

1.   The petitioner has started an action in the above court requesting:

[ ]   that your marriage be dissolved.
[ ]   a legal separation.
[ ]   that the validity of your marriage be determined.

2.   The petition also requests that the court grant the following relief:

[ ]   Provide reasonable maintenance for the [ ] husband [ ] wife.
[ ]   Approve a parenting plan for the dependent children.
[ ]   Determine support for the dependent children pursuant to the Washington State Child Support Schedule.
[ ]   Approve a separation agreement.
[ ]   Dispose of property and liabilities.
[ ]   Change name of wife to:
[ ]   Change name of husband to:
[ ]   Order payment of court costs and reasonable fees.
[ ]   Enter a continuing restraining order.
[ ]   Order payment of day care expenses for the children.

[ ]   Award the tax exemptions for the dependent children as follows:

[ ]   Order payment of attorney's fees, other professional fees and costs.

[ ]   Other:

3.   You must respond to this summons by serving a copy of your written response on the person signing this summons and by filing the original with the clerk of the court. If you do not serve your written response within 60 days after the date of the first publication of this summons (60 days after the   day of   , 20   ), the court may enter an order of default against you, and the court may, without further notice to you, enter a decree and approve or provide for other relief requested in this summons. In the case of a dissolution of marriage, the court will not enter the final decree until at least 90 days after service and filing. If you serve a notice of appearance on the undersigned person, you are entitled to notice before an order of default or a decree may be entered.

4.   Your written response to the summons and petition must be on form WPF DR 01.0300, Response to Petition (Domestic Relations). Information about how to get this form may be obtained by contacting the clerk of the court, by contacting the Administrative Office of the Courts at (360) 705-5328, or from the Internet at the Washington State Courts homepage:

http://www.courts.wa.gov/forms

5.   If you wish to seek the advice of an attorney in this matter, you should do so promptly so that your written response, if any, may be served on time.

6.   One method of serving a copy of your response on the petitioner is to send it by certified mail with return receipt requested.

7.   Other:

This summons is issued pursuant to RCW 4.28.100 and Superior Court Civil Rule 4.1 of the state of Washington.

Dated: _____   _____
    Signature of Lawyer or Petitioner

    _____
    Print or Type Name

FILE ORIGINAL OF YOUR RESPONSE
WITH THE CLERK OF THE COURT AT:

SERVE A COPY OF YOUR RESPONSE ON:

[ ] Petitioner [You may list an address that is not
your residential address where you agree to
accept legal documents.]

[ ] Petitioner's Lawyer

[Name of Court]

[Name]

[Address]

[Address]

This page intentionally blank.

SUPERIOR COURT OF WASHINGTON
COUNTY OF

In re the Marriage of:

Petitioner,	NO.
and	MOTION AND DECLARATION FOR TEMPORARY ORDER (MTAF)
Respondent.	

I. MOTION

Based on the declaration below, the undersigned moves the court for a temporary order which:

[ ]   orders temporary maintenance.

[ ]   orders child support as determined pursuant to the Washington State Support Schedule.

[ ]   approves the parenting plan which is proposed by the [ ] husband [ ] wife.

[ ]   restrains or enjoins the [ ] husband [ ] wife from transferring, removing, encumbering, concealing or in any way disposing of any property except in the usual course of business or for the necessities of life and requiring each party to notify the other of any extraordinary expenditures made after the order is issued.

[ ]   restrains or enjoins the [ ] husband [ ] wife from molesting or disturbing the peace of the other party or of any child.

[ ]   restrains or enjoins the [ ] husband [ ] wife from going onto the grounds of or entering the home, work place or school of the other party or the day care or school of the following named children:

[ ]   restrains or enjoins the [ ] husband [ ] wife from knowingly coming within or knowingly remaining within   (distance) of the home, work place or school of the other party or the day care or school of the following children:

[ ]   restrains or enjoins the [ ] husband [ ] wife from removing any of the children from the state of Washington.

[ ] restrains or enjoins the [ ] husband [ ] wife from assigning, transferring, borrowing, lapsing, surrendering or changing entitlement of any insurance policies of either or both parties whether medical, health, life or auto insurance.

[ ] **(IF THIS BOX IS CHECKED CLEAR AND CONVINCING REASONS FOR THIS REQUEST MUST BE PRESENTED IN THE DECLARATION BELOW.)** requires the [ ] husband [ ] wife to surrender any deadly weapon in his or her immediate possession or control or subject to his or her immediate possession or control to the sheriff of the county having jurisdiction of this proceeding, to his or her lawyer or to a person designated by the court.

[ ] makes each party immediately responsible for their own future debts whether incurred by credit card or loan, security interest or mortgage.

[ ] divides responsibility for the debts of the parties.

[ ] authorizes the family home to be occupied by the [ ] husband [ ] wife.

[ ] orders the use of property.

[ ] requires the [ ] husband [ ] wife to vacate the family home.

[ ] requires the [ ] husband [ ] wife to pay temporary attorney's fees, other professional fees and costs in the amount of   to:

[ ] appoints a guardian ad litem on behalf of the minor children.

[ ] other:

Dated: _____   _____

                                                Signature of Lawyer or Moving Party

                                                Print or Type Name

II. DECLARATION

Temporary relief is required because:

If the surrender of deadly weapons is requested, list reasons:

I declare under penalty of perjury under the laws of the state of Washington that the foregoing is true and correct.

Signed at _____ on _____.
                   [City and State]   [Date]

                                        _____
                                        Signature

                                        Print or Type Name

DO NOT ATTACH FINANCIAL RECORDS TO THIS DECLARATION. FINANCIAL RECORDS SHOULD BE SERVED ON THE OTHER PARTY AND FILED WITH THE COURT SEPARATELY USING THE SEALED FINANCIAL SOURCE DOCUMENTS COVER SHEET (WPF DRPSCU 09.0220). IF FILED SEPARATELY USING THE COVER SHEET, THE RECORDS WILL BE SEALED TO PROTECT YOUR PRIVACY (ALTHOUGH THEY WILL BE AVAILABLE TO THE OTHER PARTIES IN THE CASE, THEIR ATTORNEYS, AND CERTAIN OTHER INTERESTED PERSONS. SEE GR 22 (C)(2)).

This page intentionally blank.

SUPERIOR COURT OF WASHINGTON
COUNTY OF

In re the Marriage of:	
	NO.
Petitioner,	TEMPORARY ORDER
	(TMO/TMRO)
and	
Respondent.	[ ] Clerk's Action Required

I. JUDGMENT/ORDER SUMMARIES

1.1   RESTRAINING ORDER SUMMARY:
  [ ] Does not apply.   [ ] Restraining Order Summary is set forth below:

Name of person(s) restrained: _____. Name of person(s)
protected: _____. **See paragraph 3.1.**

VIOLATION OF A RESTRAINING ORDER IN PARAGRAPH 3.1 WITH ACTUAL NOTICE OF ITS TERMS IS A CRIMINAL OFFENSE UNDER CHAPTER 26.50 RCW AND WILL SUBJECT THE VIOLATOR TO ARREST. RCW 26.09.060.

1.2   MONEY JUDGMENT SUMMARY:

  [ ]   Does not apply.
  [ ]   Judgment Summary is set forth below.

A.	Judgment creditor	_____
B.	Judgment debtor	_____
C.	Principal judgment amount	$ _____
D.	Interest to date of judgment	$ _____
E.	Attorney's fees	$ _____
F.	Costs	$ _____
G.	Other recovery amount	$ _____

H. Principal judgment shall bear interest at _____% per annum
I. Attorney's fees, costs and other recovery amounts shall bear interest at _____ % per annum
J. Attorney for judgment creditor _____
K. Attorney for judgment debtor _____
L. Other:

II. BASIS

A motion for a temporary order was presented to this court and the court finds reasonable cause to issue the order.

III. ORDER

It is ORDERED that:

| 3.1 | RESTRAINING ORDER: |

VIOLATION OF A RESTRAINING ORDER IN PARAGRAPH 3.1 WITH ACTUAL NOTICE OF ITS TERMS IS A CRIMINAL OFFENSE UNDER CHAPTER 26.50 RCW AND WILL SUBJECT THE VIOLATOR TO ARREST. RCW 26.09.060.

[ ] Does not apply.
[ ] The [ ] husband [ ] wife is restrained and enjoined from molesting or disturbing the peace of the other party or of any child.
[ ] The [ ] husband [ ] wife is restrained and enjoined from going onto the grounds of or entering the home, work place or school of the other party, or the day care or school of the following named children: _____
[ ] The [ ] husband [ ] wife is restrained and enjoined from knowingly coming within or knowingly remaining within _____ (distance) of the home, work place or school of the other party, or the day care or school of these children:
_____

CLERK'S ACTION/LAW ENFORCEMENT ACTION:

[ ] This order shall be filed forthwith in the clerk's office and entered of record. The clerk of the court shall forward a copy of this order on or before the next judicial day to
_____ (name of appropriate law enforcement agency) which shall forthwith enter this order into any computer-based criminal intelligence system available in this state used by law enforcement agencies to list outstanding warrants. (**A law enforcement information sheet must be completed by the party or the party's attorney and provided with this order before this order will be entered into the law enforcement computer system.**)

SERVICE:

[ ] The restrained party or attorney appeared in court or signed this order; service of this order is not required.
[ ] The restrained party or attorney did not appear in court; service of this order is required.

(Continued on next page)

EXPIRATION DATE:

This restraining order will expire in 12 months and shall be removed from any computer-based criminal intelligence system available in this state used by law enforcement agencies to list outstanding warrants, unless a new order is issued, or unless the court sets forth another expiration date here: _____(month/day/year).

3.2   TEMPORARY RELIEF.

[ ]   The [ ] husband [ ] wife shall pay the other party $_____ per month maintenance.

        Starting Date: _____
        Day(s) of the month payment is due: _____

        Payments shall be made to:

        [ ]   the Washington State Child Support Registry (if child support is ordered).
        [ ]   directly to the other spouse.
        [ ]   the clerk of this court as trustee for remittance to the other spouse (if there are no dependent children).
        [ ]   Other:

[ ]   Child support shall be paid in accordance with the order of child support, signed by the court.

[ ]   The parties shall comply with the Temporary Parenting Plan signed by the court.

[ ]   The [ ] husband [ ] wife is restrained and enjoined from transferring, removing, encumbering, concealing or in any way disposing of any property except in the usual course of business or for the necessities of life and requiring each party to notify the other of any extraordinary expenditures made after the order is issued.

[ ]   The [ ] husband [ ] wife is restrained and enjoined from removing any of the children from the state of Washington.

[ ]   The [ ] husband [ ] wife is restrained and enjoined from assigning, transferring, borrowing, lapsing, surrendering or changing entitlement of any insurance policies of either or both parties whether medical, health, life or auto insurance.

[ ]   The [ ] husband [ ] wife shall surrender any deadly weapon in his or her immediate possession or control or subject to his or her immediate possession or control to: _____ _____ (Name or agency).

[ ]   Each party shall be immediately responsible for their own future debts whether incurred by credit card or loan, security interest or mortgage.

[ ]   Responsibility for the debts of the parties is divided as follows:

[ ]   The family home shall be occupied by the [ ] husband [ ] wife.

[ ]   Use of property shall be as follows:

[ ]   The [ ] husband [ ] wife shall vacate the family home. You have a right to keep your residential address confidential. [ ] _____ [Name] waives confidentiality of the address which is: _____
_____.

[ ]   The [ ] husband [ ] wife shall pay temporary attorney's fees, other professional fees and costs in the amount of $_____ to:

[ ]   Other:

3.3   BOND OR SECURITY.

[ ]   Does not apply.
[ ]   The filing of a bond or the posting of security is waived.
[ ]   Other:

3.4   OTHER:

Dated: _____   _____
    JUDGE/COMMISSIONER

Petitioner or petitioner's attorney: Respondent or respondent's attorney:
A signature below is actual notice of this order.   A signature below is actual notice of this order.

_____ _____   _____ _____
Signature   WSBA No.   Signature   WSBA No.

_____   _____
Print or Type Name   Print or Type Name

SUPERIOR COURT OF WASHINGTON
COUNTY OF

In re:

                                 Petitioner,

and

                                 Respondent.

NO.

FINANCIAL DECLARATION
[ ] PETITIONER
[ ] RESPONDENT
(FNDCLR)

Name: _____   Date of Birth: _____

I. SUMMARY OF BASIC INFORMATION

Declarant's Total Monthly Net Income (from § 3.3 below) $ _____

Declarant's Total Monthly Household Expenses (from § 5.9 below) $ _____

Declarant's Total Monthly Debt Expenses (from § 5.11 below) $ _____

Declarant's Total Monthly Expenses (from § 5.12 below) $ _____

Estimate of the other party's gross monthly income (from § 3.1f below)   [ ] $ _____

                                                  [ ] unknown

II. PERSONAL INFORMATION

2.1   Occupation:

2.2   The highest year of education completed:

2.3   Are you presently employed? [ ] Yes [ ] No

        a. If yes: (1)   Where do you work. Employer's name and address must be listed on the Confidential Information Form.

	(2)	When did you start work there (month/year)?	_____

b. If no:
	(1)	When did you last work (month/year)?	_____
	(2)	What were your gross monthly earnings?	$ _____
	(3)	Why are you presently unemployed?	

III. INCOME INFORMATION

If child support is at issue, complete the Washington State Child Support Worksheet(s), skip Paragraphs 3.1 and 3.2. If maintenance, fees, costs or debts are at issue and child support is NOT an issue this entire section should be completed. (Estimate of other party's income information is optional.)

3.1 GROSS MONTHLY INCOME.
If you are paid on a weekly basis, multiply your weekly gross pay by 4.3 to determine your monthly wages and salaries. If you are paid every two weeks, multiply your gross pay by 2.15. If you are paid twice monthly, multiply your gross pay by 2. If you are paid once a month, list that amount below.

			Name	Name
			_____	_____
a.	Wages and Salaries		$ _____	$ _____
b.	Interest and Dividend Income		$ _____	$ _____
c.	Business Income		$ _____	$ _____
d.	Spousal Maintenance Received			
	From _____		$ _____	$ _____
e.	Other Income		$ _____	$ _____
f.	Total Gross Monthly Income (add lines 3.1a through 3.1e)	$ _____	$ _____
g.	Actual Gross Income (Year-to-date)		$ _____	$ _____

3.2 MONTHLY DEDUCTIONS FROM GROSS INCOME.

a.	Income Taxes	$ _____	$ _____
b.	FICA/Self-employment Taxes	$ _____	$ _____
c.	State Industrial Insurance Deductions	$ _____	$ _____
d.	MANDATORY Union/Professional Dues	$ _____	$ _____
e.	Pension Plan Payments	$ _____	$ _____
f.	Spousal Maintenance Paid	$ _____	$ _____
g.	Normal Business Expenses	$ _____	$ _____
h.	Total Deductions from Gross Income (add lines 3.2a through 3.2g)	$ _____	$ _____

3.3 MONTHLY NET INCOME. (Line 3.1f minus line 3.2h or line 3 from the Child Support Worksheet(s).) $ _____ $ _____

3.4 MISCELLANEOUS INCOME.

    a.   Child support received from other relationships $ _____ $ _____

    b.   Other miscellaneous income (list source and amounts)

    _____ $ _____ $ _____

    _____ $ _____ $ _____

    _____ $ _____ $ _____

    _____ $ _____ $ _____

    c.   Total Miscellaneous Income (add lines 3.4a through 3.4b) $ _____ $ _____

3.5 Income of Other Adults in Household $ _____ $ _____

3.6 If the income of either party is disputed, state monthly income you believe is correct and explain below:

IV. AVAILABLE ASSETS

4.1 Cash on hand $ _____

4.2 On deposit in banks $ _____

4.3 Stocks and bonds, cash value of life insurance $ _____

4.4 Other liquid assets: $ _____

V. MONTHLY EXPENSE INFORMATION

Monthly expenses for myself and _____ dependents are: (Expenses should be calculated for the future, after separation, based on the anticipated residential schedule for the children.)

5.1 HOUSING.

    Rent, 1st mortgage or contract payments $ _____

    Installment payments for other mortgages or encumbrances $ _____

    Taxes & insurance (if not in monthly payment) $ _____

    Total Housing $ _____

5.2 UTILITIES.

    Heat (gas & oil) $ _____

    Electricity $ _____

    Water, sewer, garbage $ _____

Telephone	$ _____
Cable	$ _____
Other	$ _____
Total Utilities	$ _____

5.3   FOOD AND SUPPLIES.

Food for _____ persons	$ _____
Supplies (paper, tobacco, pets)	$ _____
Meals eaten out	$ _____
Other	$ _____
Total Food Supplies	$ _____

5.4   CHILDREN.

Day Care/Babysitting	$ _____
Clothing	$ _____
Tuition (if any)	$ _____
Other child-related expenses	$ _____
Total Expenses Children	$ _____

5.5   TRANSPORTATION.

Vehicle payments or leases	$ _____
Vehicle insurance & license	$ _____
Vehicle gas, oil, ordinary maintenance	$ _____
Parking	$ _____
Other transportation expenses	$ _____
Total Transportation	$ _____

5.6   HEALTH CARE. (Omit if fully covered)

Insurance	$ _____
Uninsured dental, orthodontic, medical, eye care expenses	$ _____
Other uninsured health expenses	$ _____
Total Health Care	$ _____

5.7   PERSONAL EXPENSES (Not including children)

Clothing	$ _____
Hair care/personal care expenses	$ _____
Clubs and recreation	$ _____

Education $ _____

Books, newspapers, magazines, photos $ _____

Gifts $ _____

Other $ _____

Total Personal Expenses $ _____

5.7   MISCELLANEOUS EXPENSES.

Life insurance (if not deducted from income) $ _____

Other _____ $ _____

Other _____ $ _____

Total Miscellaneous Expenses $ _____

5.9   TOTAL HOUSEHOLD EXPENSES (The total of Paragraphs 5.1 through 5.8) $ _____

5.10   INSTALLMENT DEBTS INCLUDED IN PARAGRAPHS 5.1 THROUGH 5.8.

Creditor	Description of Debt	Balance	Month of Last Payment
_____	_____	_____	_____
_____	_____	_____	_____
_____	_____	_____	_____
_____	_____	_____	_____

5.11   OTHER DEBTS AND MONTHLY EXPENSES NOT INCLUDED IN PARAGRAPHS 5.1 THROUGH 5.8.

Creditor	Description of Debt	Balance	Month of Last Payment	Amount of Monthly Payment
_____	_____	_____	_____	$ _____
_____	_____	_____	_____	$ _____
_____	_____	_____	_____	$ _____
_____	_____	_____	_____	$ _____
_____	_____	_____	_____	$ _____
_____	_____	_____	_____	$ _____
_____	_____	_____	_____	$ _____

Total Monthly Payments for Other Debts and Monthly Expenses $ _____

5.12   TOTAL EXPENSES (Add Paragraphs 5.9 and 5.11) $ _____

VI. ATTORNEY FEES

6.1   Amount paid for attorney fees and costs to date: $ _____

6.2   The source of this money was:

6.3   Fees and costs incurred to date: $ _____

6.4   Arrangements for attorney fees and costs are:

6.5   Other:

I declare under penalty of perjury under the laws of the state of Washington that the foregoing is true and correct.

Signed at _____, [City] _____ [State] on _____ [Date].

_____   _____
Signature of Declarant   Print or Type Name

The following financial records are being provided to the other party and filed separately with the court.
Financial records pertaining to myself:

[ ] Individual [ ] Partnership or Corporate Income Tax returns for the years _____
_____including all W-2s and schedules;
[ ] Pay stubs for the dates of _____
_____.
[ ] Other:_____
_____
_____
_____
_____
_____
_____
_____.

DO NOT ATTACH THESE FINANCIAL RECORDS TO THE FINANCIAL DECLARATION. THESE FINANCIAL RECORDS SHOULD BE SERVED ON THE OTHER PARTY AND FILED WITH THE COURT SEPARATELY USING THE SEALED FINANCIAL SOURCE DOCUMENTS COVER SHEET (WPF DRPSCU 09.0220). IF FILED SEPARATELY USING THE COVER SHEET, THE RECORDS WILL BE SEALED TO PROTECT YOUR PRIVACY (ALTHOUGH THEY WILL BE AVAILABLE TO THE OTHER PARTIES IN THE CASE, THEIR ATTORNEYS, AND CERTAIN OTHER INTERESTED PERSONS. SEE GR 22 (C)(2)).

SUPERIOR COURT OF WASHINGTON
COUNTY OF

In re:	NO.
Petitioner(s),	SEALED FINANCIAL SOURCE DOCUMENTS (SEALFN)
and	
Respondent(s).	**CLERK'S ACTION REQUIRED**

SEALED FINANCIAL SOURCE DOCUMENTS

(List documents below and write "Sealed" at least one inch from the top of the first page of each document.)

❏   Income Tax records.
     Period Covered:

❏   Bank statements.
     Period Covered:

❏   Pay Stubs.
     Period Covered:

❏   Credit Card Statements.
     Period Covered:

❏   Other:

Submitted by:

_____

NOTICE: The other party will have access to these financial source documents. If you are concerned for your safety or the safety of the children, you may redact (block out or delete) information that identifies your location.

Index

A

abandonment, 42
abuse, 42, 96, 102
Acceptance of Service, 58, 90
adultery, 2
age of consent, 4
aid to families with dependent children, 47
alcohol, 4, 42
alimony. *See spousal maintenance*
anger, 6, 7, 14, 60
annuities, 46
annulment, 3, 4
    grounds, 3
appliances, 33, 38
attorneys, 3, 15, 21, 22, 23, 24, 25, 26, 27, 28, 38, 44, 49, 56, 57, 60, 72, 73, 76, 77, 79, 90, 93, 94, 96, 97, 98, 99, 100, 102, 104, 105, 122, 127, 128, 130
    advantages to hiring, 22
    evaluating, 24
    fee, 28
    firing, 28
    referral service, 24
    selecting, 23
    wanting, 22
    working with, 26

B

bailiff, 13, 16, 59, 110, 112, 120, 122, 123
bank accounts, 32, 33, 71, 76
blue book, 37
bonds, 5, 33, 36
bonuses, 46

C

capital gains, 46

caption, 56, 57, 70, 83

cash, 36, 38

cash surrender value, 38

child custody, 94, 96, 115

child support, 2, 4, 5, 6, 7, 13, 15, 17, 34, 43, 44, 45, 46, 47, 49, 50, 52, 53, 62, 63, 66, 68, 69, 71, 73, 80, 81, 82, 83, 88, 90, 91, 97, 105, 113, 114, 115, 116, 117, 118, 119, 122, 128

calculating, 49

determining, 44

schedule, 43, 49, 68

Child Support Guidelines, 49, 63

Child Support Worksheets, 47, 49, 50, 62, 66, 80, 83, 91, 97, 105, 118, 119

children, 2, 5, 6, 7, 13, 15, 16, 31, 34, 40, 41, 42, 43, 44, 45, 47, 49, 50, 52, 53, 67, 68, 69, 70, 74, 78, 79, 80, 84, 86, 90, 91, 95, 113, 118, 122, 126, 128, 129, 130

protecting, 126

church, 3

clerk, 13, 14, 16, 17, 20, 23, 55, 56, 57, 58, 59, 60, 66, 67, 74, 93, 94, 100, 103, 110, 112, 115, 118, 119, 120, 122, 123, 124

filing with, 57

combined income, 45, 48, 49

commissions, 45

community property, 34, 77

companionship, 5

consanguinity, 3

consent divorce, 16, 51, 52, 58, 65, 66, 67, 69, 71, 73, 75, 77, 79, 81, 83, 85

contempt, 32

contested divorce, 22, 51, 52, 53, 93, 94, 95, 97

counseling, 7, 8, 9, 67

courtroom manners, 22, 60, 120

credit card statements, 96

custody, 4, 6, 12, 13, 40, 41, 45, 62, 68

D

dating, 6

Debt Inventory, 39, 40, 95

debts, 2, 5, 16, 34, 39, 40, 52, 67, 68, 72, 73, 77, 95, 114, 115, 116, 117

separate, 40

Declaration, 88, 89, 90, 91, 108, 109, 110, 111, 114, 116, 117, 118, 119, 120, 122

Decree of Dissolution, 66, 70, 71, 72, 74, 75, 78, 79, 80, 88, 90, 91, 105, 121

deeds, 33

defendant, 103

deferred compensation, 45

denial, 6

digests, 19

disability insurance, 46

dissolution of marriage, 2

dividends, 33, 46

divorce, 2

alternatives to, 7

documents, 103

domestic violence, 42

driver's license number, 33

E

emergency, 114, 121

emotional divorce, 5

equitable distribution, 34

evaluating your situation, 31

evidence, 93, 96, 100, 103, 104
ex parte orders, 121
Ex Parte Restraining Order, 114, 115, 122
Ex Parte Restraining Order/Order to
    Show Cause, 115, 122
exhibits, 99, 103, 104, 116

H

hearing date, 16, 17, 59, 60
hearsay rule, 100
hiding assets, 32

F

family law facilitator, 20, 117, 119, 121, 123
filing fee, 115, 125
final pleadings, 90, 105
Financial Declaration, 116, 117, 119, 120
financial divorce, 6
Findings of Fact and Conclusions of Law,
    66, 75, 77, 80, 88, 90, 91, 105
fitness, 96
food stamps, 47
furniture, 6, 33, 37, 76

I

identity theft, 71, 72, 76, 77
income, 13, 32, 33, 45, 46, 47, 48, 49, 80,
    96, 97, 98, 113, 116, 117, 120, 121, 125,
    127, 128
income tax returns, 32, 96
indigent, 125
inheritance, 35, 77
insurance, 4, 33, 36, 38, 46, 50, 82
interest, 46
Internal Revenue Service (IRS), 127, 128
    form 8832, 128
investment papers, 33
irretrievably broken, 2, 3, 15, 67
IRS form 8832, 128

G

gathering information, 31, 32
grief, 6
grievance, 29
gross income, 45, 47, 48
guardian ad litem, 43, 130
guilt, 6, 7

J

jewelry, 38
joinder, 58, 69, 75, 90
judges, 11, 12, 13, 14, 16, 17, 19, 21, 22,
    23, 26, 32, 34, 39, 40, 41, 43, 44, 47, 51,
    55, 56, 59, 60, 61, 62, 63, 66, 67, 68, 70,
    75, 79, 80, 83, 87, 88, 89, 91, 93, 95, 96,
    97, 100, 101, 102, 103, 104, 105, 110,
    112, 113, 114, 115, 119, 120, 121, 122,
    123, 124, 126, 128

K

kidnapping prevention, 126

L

laws and procedures, 13, 14, 16, 55
lawyers. *See attorneys*
legal divorce, 5
legal encyclopedia, 19
legal forms
    form 1, 59, 88, 94, 107
    form 2, 3, 15, 66, 67, 88, 89, 94, 107
    form 3, 66, 70, 88
    form 4, 66, 75, 88
    form 5, 43, 66, 88, 97, 114
    form 6, 41, 66, 80, 88, 96, 115
    form 7, 215
    form 8, 88
    form 9, 88, 91
    form 10, 108
    form 11, 108
    form 12, 108
    form 13, 111
    form 14, 111
    form 15, 111
    form 16, 114, 116
    form 17, 114, 116, 118
    form 18, 116
    form 19, 116, 117
legal research, 1, 15, 17
legal separation, 4
legal system, 11, 12, 13, 14, 15, 17, 19
life insurance, 33, 38
loneliness, 6

M

maintenance. *See spousal maintenance*
marriage, 1, 2, 3, 4, 5, 6, 7, 8, 9, 15, 34, 35,
    50, 57, 61, 67, 74, 76, 77, 78, 79, 80, 84
    minimum age for, 3
marriage counseling, 8
mental capacity to consent, 4
mental cruelty, 2
military, 38, 89, 90
Motion and Declaration for Default, 88,
    89, 90, 91
Motion and Declaration for Ex Parte
    Restraining Order and for Order to
    Show Cause, 114
Motion and Declaration for Service of
    Summons by Publication, 111
Motion and Declaration for Temporary
    Order, 114, 116, 118, 119, 120, 122
Motion and Declaration to Serve by Mail,
    108, 109
Motion/Declaration for Ex Parte
    Restraining Order and for Order to
    Show Cause, 122
motions, 114
    general procedures, 115

N

neglect, 42
negotiating, 61, 62, 63, 96
net income, 45, 47, 48, 49, 80
no-fault, 2
Notice of Intended Relocation of Children,
    130
notifying your spouse, 16, 58

O

oral arguments, 115, 120, 121
Order Allowing Service by Mail, 108, 109, 110
Order for Default, 88, 89, 91
Order for Protection, 122, 126
Order for Service of Summons by Publication, 111, 112
Order of Child Support, 66, 80, 83, 88, 90, 91, 97, 105, 114, 118, 119
orders, 114
    entering, 123
overtime, 46

P

Pacific Reporter, 19
Parenting Plan, 2, 5, 15, 34, 40, 41, 42, 43, 44, 66, 68, 69, 80, 83, 85, 86, 88, 90, 91, 94, 96, 105, 113, 115, 118, 119, 123, 129
    factors to consider, 41, 42
    restrictions, 42
passports, 126
paystub, 33
pensions, 38
    benefits, 46
    papers, 33
    plans, 128
perjury, 69, 91, 109, 111, 117
personal service, 59, 107, 108
Petition for Dissolution, 3, 15, 16, 57, 58, 59, 66, 67, 68, 69, 88, 89, 94, 97, 107, 110, 112, 119
Petition for Legal Separation, 4
petitioner, 103
plaintiff, 103

pleadings, 90, 105, 119, 120, 122
pregnant, 68
prenuptial agreement, 71, 72, 76, 77
primary residential parent, 5, 15, 40, 41, 62, 96
private investigators, 93, 96
Pro Se, 75, 79, 83, 86, 89, 91, 108, 110, 111, 112, 116, 119
process servers, 59
proof of mailing, 59
property, 2, 4, 5, 6, 11, 13, 15, 16, 31, 32, 34, 35, 36, 37, 38, 39, 40, 51, 52, 53, 61, 62, 63, 65, 70, 71, 76, 77, 95, 96, 108, 114, 121, 122, 127, 128
    division of, 38, 127
    protecting, 121
Property Inventory, 35, 61, 95
protecting yourself, 126
publication, 107, 110, 111, 112

Q

Qualified Domestic Relations Order (QDRO), 128

R

real estate, 24, 33, 36, 70, 76
relocation, 129, 130
residency, 15
residential placement, 2
residential time, 40, 41, 42, 43
respondent, 103
Response to Petition, 90, 94, 97
Return of Service, 59

Revised Code of Washington Annotated
    (RCWA), 1, 14, 17, 18, 19, 44
    RCWA 26.09, 17
    RCWA 26.09.010, 17
    RCWA 26.17.075, 44
    RCWA 26.18, 17
    RCWA 26.19, 17
Rules of Civil Procedure, 20
Rules of Court, 20

S

salaries, 45
Sealed Financial Source Documents Cover
    Sheet, 116, 116-117, 119, 120
second jobs, 46
separate property, 34, 35, 39, 40, 77
service by publication, 107
settlement, 94, 98, 127, 128
severance pay, 46
sick pay, 46
social life, 5
Social Security benefits, 46
Social Security number, 33
spousal maintenance, 2, 46, 50, 51, 52, 53,
    65, 68, 69, 71, 73, 78, 97, 113, 114, 115,
    116, 117, 127, 128
stocks, 33, 36
subpoenas, 93, 96
Summons, 59, 69, 88, 89, 94, 107, 108,
    110, 111, 112, 119
Summons by Mail, 108, 110, 112
Summons by Publication, 111, 112
support, 88, 90, 91, 96, 97, 100, 105, 113,
    114, 115, 116, 117, 118, 119, 122, 128

T

tax assessment value, 37
taxes, 45, 47, 48, 51, 127, 128
Temporary Order, 114, 115, 116, 118, 119,
    123
Temporary Order of Child Support Order,
    114
temporary orders, 113, 114, 115, 117, 118,
    119, 120, 121, 122, 123
Temporary Parenting Plan, 115
trial, 93, 97, 98, 99, 100, 101, 103, 105
    general procedures, 100
Trial Brief, 99, 100
trial separation, 9
trust income, 46

U

uncontested divorce, 16, 22, 51, 52, 87, 88,
    89, 91
unemployment, 46

V

vehicles, 33, 37
visitation, 7, 40, 41, 68, 96, 113, 115

W

wages, 45

Washington Court Rules, 20

Washington Practice, 19

Washington State Bar Association, 29

Washington State Family Law Deskbook,
    20

West's Washington Digest 2nd, 19

wills, 33, 96

witnesses, 93, 96, 97, 100, 101, 102, 103,
    104, 120, 121
    expert, 97, 102, 103, 127, 128, 130
    questioning, 104

workers' compensation, 46

worksheet 1, 35, 39, 95

worksheet 2, 39, 40, 95

Sphinx® Publishing's National Titles
Valid in All 50 States

LEGAL SURVIVAL IN BUSINESS

The Complete Book of Corporate Forms (2E)	$29.95
The Complete Hiring and Firing Handbook	$19.95
The Complete Home-Based Business Kit	!4.95
The Complete Limited Liability Kit	$24.95
The Complete Partnership Book	$24.95
The Complete Patent Book	$26.95
The Entrepreneur's Internet Handbook	$21.95
The Entrepreneur's Legal Guide	$26.95
Financing Your Small Business	$17.95
Fired, Laid-Off or Forced Out	$14.95
How to Buy a Franchise	$19.95
How to Form a Nonprofit Corporation (3E)	$24.95
How to Form Your Own Corporation (4E)	$26.95
How to Register Your Own Copyright (5E)	$24.95
HR for Small Business	$14..95
Incorporate in Delaware from Any State	$26.95
Incorporate in Nevada from Any State	$24.95
The Law (In Plain English)® for Small Business	$19.95
The Law (In Plain English)® for Writers	$14.95
Making Music Your Business	$18.95
Minding Her Own Business (4E)	$14.95
Most Valuable Business Legal Forms You'll Ever Need (3E)	$21.95
Profit from Intellectual Property	$28.95
Protect Your Patent	$24.95
The Small Business Owner's Guide to Bankruptcy	$21.95
Tax Power for the Self-Eemployed	$17.95
Tax Smarts for Small Business	$21.95
Your Rights at Work	$14.95

LEGAL SURVIVAL IN COURT

Attorney Responsibilities & Client Rights	$19.95
Crime Victim's Guide to Justice (2E)	$21.95
Legal Research Made Easy (3E)	$21.95
Winning Your Personal Injury Claim (3E)	$24.95

LEGAL SURVIVAL IN REAL ESTATE

The Complete Kit to Selling Your Own Home	$18.95
Essential Guide to Real Estate Contracts (2E)	$18.95
Essential Guide to Real Estate Leases	$18.95
Homeowner's Rights	$19.95
How to Buy a Condominium or Townhome (2E)	$19.95
How to Buy Your First Home (2E)	$14.95
How to Make Money on Foreclosures	$16.95
The Mortgage Answer Book	$14.95
The Weekend Landlord	$16.95
Working with Your Homeowners Association	$19.95

LEGAL SURVIVAL IN SPANISH

Cómo Comprar su Primera Casa	$8.95
Cómo Conseguir Trabajo en los Estados Unidos	$8.95
Cómo Hacer su Propio Testamento	$16.95
Cómo Negociar su Crédito	$8.95
Cómo Organizar un Presupuesto	$8.95
Cómo Solicitar su Propio Divorcio	$24.95
Guía de Inmigración a Estados Unidos (4E)	$24.95
Guía de Justicia para Víctimas del Crimen	$21.95
Guía Esencial para los Contratos de Arrendamiento de Bienes Raices	$22.95
Inmigración y Ciudadanía en los EE.UU. Preguntas y Respuestas	$16.95
Inmigración a los EE.UU. Paso a Paso (2E)	$24.95
Manual de Beneficios del Seguro Social	$18.95
El Seguro Social Preguntas y Respuestas	$16.95
¡Visas! ¡Visas! ¡Visas!	$9.95

LEGAL SURVIVAL IN PERSONAL AFFAIRS

101 Complaint Letters That Get Results	$18.95
The 529 College Savings Plan (2E)	$18.95
The 529 College Savings Plan Made Simple	$7.95
The Alternative Minimum Tax	$14.95
The Antique and Art Collector's Legal Guide	$24.95
The Childcare Answer Book	$12.95
Child Support	$18.95
The Complete Book of Insurance	$18.95
The Complete Book of Personal Legal Forms	$24.95
The Complete Credit Repair Kit	$19.95
The Complete Legal Guide to Senior Care	$21.95
Credit Smart	$18.95
The Easy Will and Living Will Kit	$16.95
Fathers' Rights	$19.95
File Your Own Divorce (6E)	$24.95
The Frequent Traveler's Guide	$14.95
Gay & Lesbian Rights	$26.95
Grandparents' Rights (3E)	$24.95
How to File Your Own Bankruptcy (6E)	$21.95
How to Make Your Own Simple Will (3E)	$18.95
How to Parent with Your Ex	$12.95
How to Write Your Own Living Will (4E)	$18.95
How to Write Your Own Premarital Agreement (3E)	$24.95
The Infertility Answer Book	$16.95
Law 101	$16.95
Law School 101	$16.95
The Living Trust Kit	$21.95
Living Trusts and Other Ways to Avoid Probate (3E)	$24.95
Mastering the MBE	$16.95
Nursing Homes and Assisted Living Facilities	$19.95
The Power of Attorney Handbook (5E)	$22.95
Quick Cash	$14.95
Seniors' Rights	$19.95
Sexual Harassment:Your Guide to Legal Action	$18.95
Sisters-in-Law	$16.95
The Social Security Benefits Handbook (4E)	$18.95
Social Security Q&A	$12.95
Starting Out or Starting Over	$14.95
Teen Rights (and Responsibilities) (2E)	$14.95
Unmarried Parents' Rights (and Responsibilities)(2E)	$19.95
U.S. Immigration and Citizenship Q&A	$18.95
U.S. Immigration Step by Step (2E)	$24.95
U.S.A. Immigration Guide (5E)	$26.95
What to Do—Before "I DO"	$14.95
What to Do When You Can't Get Pregnant	$16.95
The Wills, Estate Planning and Trusts Legal Kit	$26.95
Win Your Unemployment Compensation Claim (2E)	$21.95
Your Right to Child Custody, Visitation and Support (3E)	$24.95

SPHINX® PUBLISHING ORDER FORM

BILL TO:		SHIP TO:	
Phone #	Terms	F.O.B. Chicago, IL	Ship Date

Charge my: ☐ VISA ☐ MasterCard ☐ American Express

☐ **Money Order or Personal Check**

Credit Card Number: ☐☐☐☐☐☐☐☐☐☐☐☐☐☐☐☐

Expiration Date: ☐☐☐☐

Qty	ISBN	Title	Retail	Ext.
		SPHINX PUBLISHING NATIONAL TITLES		
___	1-57248-363-6	101 Complaint Letters That Get Results	$18.95	___
___	1-57248-361-X	The 529 College Savings Plan (2E)	$18.95	___
___	1-57248-483-7	The 529 College Savings Plan Made Simple	$7.95	___
___	1-57248-460-8	The Alternative Minimum Tax	$14.95	___
___	1-57248-349-0	The Antique and Art Collector's Legal Guide	$24.95	___
___	1-57248-347-4	Attorney Responsibilities & Client Rights	$19.95	___
___	1-57248-482-9	The Childcare Answer Book	$12.95	___
___	1-57248-382-2	Child Support	$18.95	___
___	1-57248-487-X	Cómo Comprar su Primera Casa	$8.95	___
___	1-57248-488-8	Cómo Conseguir Trabajo en los Estados Unidos	$8.95	___
___	1-57248-148-X	Cómo Hacer su Propio Testamento	$16.95	___
___	1-57248-462-4	Cómo Negociar su Crédito	$8.95	___
___	1-57248-463-2	Cómo Organizar un Presupuesto	$8.95	___
___	1-57248-147-1	Cómo Solicitar su Propio Divorcio	$24.95	___
___	1-57248-507-8	The Complete Book of Corporate Forms (2E)	$29.95	___
___	1-57248-383-0	The Complete Book of Insurance	$18.95	___
___	1-57248499-3	The Complete Book of Personal Legal Forms	$24.95	___
___	1-57248-500-0	The Complete Credit Repair Kit	$19.95	___
___	1-57248-458-6	The Complete Hiring and Firing Handbook	$18.95	___
___	1-57248-484-5	The Complete Home-Based Business Kit	$16.95	___
___	1-57248-353-9	The Complete Kit to Selling Your Own Home	$18.95	___
___	1-57248-229-X	The Complete Legal Guide to Senior Care	$21.95	___
___	1-57248-498-5	The Complete Limited Liability Company Kit	$24.95	___
___	1-57248-391-1	The Complete Partnership Book	$24.95	___
___	1-57248-201-X	The Complete Patent Book	$26.95	___
___	1-57248-480-2	The Mortgage Answer Book	$14.95	___
___	1-57248-369-5	Credit Smart	$18.95	___
___	1-57248-163-3	Crime Victim's Guide to Justice (2E)	$21.95	___
___	1-57248-481-0	The Easy Will and Living Will Kit	$16.95	___
___	1-57248-251-6	The Entrepreneur's Internet Handbook	$21.95	___
___	1-57248-235-4	The Entrepreneur's Legal Guide	$26.95	___
___	1-57248-346-6	Essential Guide to Real Estate Contracts (2E)	$18.95	___
___	1-57248-160-9	Essential Guide to Real Estate Leases	$18.95	___
___	1-57248-375-X	Fathers' Rights	$19.95	___
___	1-57248-517-5	File Your Own Divorce (6E)	$24.95	___
___	1-57248-450-0	Financing Your Small Business	$17.95	___
___	1-57248-459-4	Fired, Laid Off or Forced Out	$14.95	___
___	1-57248-502-7	The Frequent Traveler's Guide	$14.95	___
___	1-57248-331-8	Gay & Lesbian Rights	$26.95	___
___	1-57248-139-0	Grandparents' Rights (3E)	$24.95	___
___	1-57248-475-6	Guía de Inmigración a Estados Unidos (4E)	$24.95	___
___	1-57248-187-0	Guía de Justicia para Victimas del Crimen	$21.95	___
___	1-57248-253-2	Guía Esencial para los Contratos de Arrendamiento de Bienes Raices	$22.95	___
___	1-57248-334-2	Homeowner's Rights	$19.95	___
___	1-57248-164-1	How to Buy a Condominium or Townhome (2E)	$19.95	___
___	1-57248-197-7	How to Buy Your First Home (2E)	$14.95	___
___	1-57248-384-9	How to Buy a Franchise	$19.95	___
___	1-57248-472-1	How to File Your Own Bankruptcy (6E)	$21.95	___
___	1-57248-390-3	How to Form a Nonprofit Corporation (3E)	$24.95	___
___	1-57248-345-8	How to Form Your Own Corporation (4E)	$26.95	___
___	1-57248-520-5	How to Make Money on Foreclosures	$16.95	___
___	1-57248-232-X	How to Make Your Own Simple Will (3E)	$18.95	___
___	1-57248-479-9	How to Parent with Your Ex	$12.95	___
___	1-57248-379-2	How to Register Your Own Copyright (5E)	$24.95	___
___	1-57248-394-6	How to Write Your Own Living Will (4E)	$18.95	___
___	1-57248-156-0	How to Write Your Own Premarital Agreement (3E)	$24.95	___
___	1-57248-504-3	HR for Small Business	$14.95	___
___	1-57248-230-3	Incorporate in Delaware from Any State	$26.95	___
___	1-57248-158-7	Incorporate in Nevada from Any State	$24.95	___
___	1-57248-531-0	The Infertility Answer Book	$16.95	___
___	1-57248-474-8	Inmigración a los EE.UU. Paso a Paso (2E)	$24.95	___
___	1-57248-400-4	Inmigración y Ciudadania en los EE.UU. Preguntas y Respuestas	$16.95	___
___	1-57248-453-5	Law 101	$16.95	___
___	1-57248-374-1	Law School 101	$16.95	___
___	1-57248-377-6	The Law (In Plain English)® for Small Business	$19.95	___
___	1-57248-476-4	The Law (In Plain English)® for Writers	$14.95	___
___	1-57248-223-0	Legal Research Made Easy (3E)	$21.95	___
___	1-57248-449-7	The Living Trust Kit	$21.95	___
___	1-57248-165-X	Living Trusts and Other Ways to Avoid Probate (3E)	$24.95	___
___	1-57248-486-1	Making Music Your Business	$18.95	___
___	1-57248-186-2	Manual de Beneficios para el Seguro Social	$18.95	___
___	1-57248-220-6	Mastering the MBE	$16.95	___
___	1-57248-455-1	Minding Her Own Business, 4E	$14.95	___
___	1-57248-480-2	The Mortgage Answer Book	$14.95	___
___	1-57248-167-6	Most Val. Business Legal Forms You'll Ever Need (3E)	$21.95	___
___	1-57248-388-1	The Power of Attorney Handbook (5E)	$22.95	___
___	1-57248-332-6	Profit from Intellectual Property	$28.95	___
___	1-57248-329-6	Protect Your Patent	$24.95	___
___	1-57248-376-8	Nursing Homes and Assisted Living Facilities	$19.95	___
___	1-57248-385-7	Quick Cash	$14.95	___
___	1-57248-350-4	El Seguro Social Preguntas y Respuestas	$16.95	___
___	1-57248386-5	Seniors' Rights	$19.95	___
___	1-57248-217-6	Sexual Harassment: Your Guide to Legal Action	$18.95	___
___	1-57248-378-4	Sisters-in-Law	$16.95	___
___	1-57248-219-2	The Small Business Owner's Guide to Bankruptcy	$21.95	___
___	1-57248-395-4	The Social Security Benefits Handbook (4E)	$18.95	___
___	1-57248-216-8	Social Security Q&A	$12.95	___
___	1-57248-328-8	Starting Out or Starting Over	$14.95	___
___	1-57248-525-6	Teen Rights (and Responsibilities) (2E)	$14.95	___
___	1-57248-457-8	Tax Power for the Self-Employed	$17.95	___
___	1-57248-366-0	Tax Smarts for Small Business	$21.95	___
___	1-57248-236-2	Unmarried Parents' Rights (2E)	$19.95	___
___	1-57248-362-8	U.S. Immigration and Citizenship Q&A	$18.95	___
___	1-57248-387-3	U.S. Immigration Step by Step (2E)	$24.95	___
___	1-57248-392-X	U.S.A. Immigration Guide (5E)	$26.95	___
___	1-57248-178-0	¡Visas! ¡Visas! ¡Visas!	$9.95	___
___	1-57248-177-2	The Weekend Landlord	$16.95	___
___	1-57248-451-9	What to Do — Before "I DO"	$14.95	___
___	1-57248-531-0	What to Do When You Can't Get Pregnant	$16.95	___
___	1-57248-225-7	Win Your Unemployment Compensation Claim (2E)	$21.95	___

(Form Continued on Following Page) Subtotal _____

To order, call Sourcebooks at 1-800-432-7444 or FAX (630) 961-2168 (Bookstores, libraries, wholesalers—please call for discount)

Prices are subject to change without notice.

Find more legal information at: **www.SphinxLegal.com**

SPHINX® PUBLISHING ORDER FORM

Qty	ISBN	Title	Retail	Ext.
____	1-57248-330-X	The Wills, Estate Planning and Trusts Legal Kit	$26.95	____
____	1-57248-473-X	Winning Your Personal Injury Claim (3E)	$24.95	____
____	1-57248-333-4	Working with Your Homeowners Association	$19.95	____
____	1-57248-380-6	Your Right to Child Custody, Visitation and Support (3E)	$24.95	____
____	1-57248-505-1	Your Rights at Work	$14.95	____

CALIFORNIA TITLES

Qty	ISBN	Title	Retail	Ext.
____	1-57248-489-6	How to File for Divorce in CA (5E)	$26.95	____
____	1-57248-464-0	How to Settle and Probate an Estate in CA (2E)	$28.95	____
____	1-57248-336-9	How to Start a Business in CA (2E)	$21.95	____
____	1-57248-194-3	How to Win in Small Claims Court in CA (2E)	$18.95	____
____	1-57248-246-X	Make Your Own CA Will	$18.95	____
____	1-57248-397-0	Landlords' Legal Guide in CA (2E)	$24.95	____
____	1-57248-241-9	Tenants' Rights in CA	$21.95	____

FLORIDA TITLES

Qty	ISBN	Title	Retail	Ext.
____	1-57248-396-2	How to File for Divorce in FL (8E)	$28.95	____
____	1-57248-356-3	How to Form a Corporation in FL (6E)	$24.95	____
____	1-57248-490-X	How to Form a Limited Liability Co. in FL (4E)	$24.95	____
____	1-57071-401-0	How to Form a Partnership in FL	$22.95	____
____	1-57248-456-X	How to Make a FL Will (7E)	$16.95	____
____	1-57248-354-7	How to Probate and Settle an Estate in FL (5E)	$26.95	____
____	1-57248-339-3	How to Start a Business in FL (7E)	$21.95	____
____	1-57248-204-4	How to Win in Small Claims Court in FL (7E)	$18.95	____
____	1-57248-381-4	Land Trusts in Florida (7E)	$29.95	____
____	1-57248-491-8	Landlords' Rights and Duties in FL (10E)	$22.95	____

GEORGIA TITLES

Qty	ISBN	Title	Retail	Ext.
____	1-57248-340-7	How to File for Divorce in GA (5E)	$21.95	____
____	1-57248-493-4	How to Start a Business in GA (4E)	$21.95	____

ILLINOIS TITLES

Qty	ISBN	Title	Retail	Ext.
____	1-57248-244-3	Child Custody, Visitation, and Support in IL	$24.95	____
____	1-57248-206-0	How to File for Divorce in IL (3E)	$24.95	____
____	1-57248-170-6	How to Make an IL Will (3E)	$16.95	____
____	1-57248-265-9	How to Start a Business in IL (4E)	$21.95	____
____	1-57248-252-4	Landlords' Legal Guide in IL	$24.95	____

MARYLAND, VIRGINIA AND THE DISTRICT OF COLUMBIA

Qty	ISBN	Title	Retail	Ext.
____	1-57248-240-0	How to File for Divorce in MD, VA, and DC	$28.95	____
____	1-57248-359-8	How to Start a Business in MD, VA, or DC	$21.95	____

MASSACHUSETTS TITLES

Qty	ISBN	Title	Retail	Ext.
____	1-57248-115-3	How to Form a Corporation in MA	$24.95	____
____	1-57248-466-7	How to Start a Business in MA (4E)	$21.95	____
____	1-57248-398-9	Landlords' Legal Guide in MA (2E)	$24.95	____

MICHIGAN TITLES

Qty	ISBN	Title	Retail	Ext.
____	1-57248-467-5	How to File for Divorce in MI (4E)	$24.95	____
____	1-57248-182-X	How to Make a MI Will (3E)	$16.95	____
____	1-57248-468-3	How to Start a Business in MI (4E)	$18.95	____

MINNESOTA TITLES

Qty	ISBN	Title	Retail	Ext.
____	1-57248-142-0	How to File for Divorce in MN	$21.95	____
____	1-57248-179-X	How to Form a Corporation in MN	$24.95	____
____	1-57248-178-1	How to Make a MN Will (2E)	$16.95	____

NEW JERSEY TITLES

Qty	ISBN	Title	Retail	Ext.
____	1-57248-239-7	How to File for Divorce in NJ	$24.95	____
____	1-57248-448-9	How to Start a Business in NJ	$21.95	____

NEW YORK TITLES

Qty	ISBN	Title	Retail	Ext.
____	1-57248-193-5	Child Custody, Visitation and Support in NY	$26.95	____
____	1-57248-351-2	File for Divorce in NY	$26.95	____
____	1-57248-249-4	How to Form a Corporation in NY (2E)	$24.95	____
____	1-57248-401-2	How to Make a NY Will (3E)	$16.95	____
____	1-57248-469-1	How to Start a Business in NY (3E)	$21.95	____
____	1-57248-198-6	How to Win in Small Claims Court in NY (2E)	$18.95	____
____	1-57248-122-6	Tenants' Rights in NY	$21.95	____

NORTH CAROLINA AND SOUTH CAROLINA TITLES

Qty	ISBN	Title	Retail	Ext.
____	1-57248-185-4	How to File for Divorce in NC (3E)	$22.95	____
____	1-57248-371-7	How to Start a Business in NC or SC	$24.95	____
____	1-57248-091-2	Landlords' Rights & Duties in NC	$21.95	____

OHIO TITLES

Qty	ISBN	Title	Retail	Ext.
____	1-57248-503-5	How to File for Divorce in OH (3E)	$24.95	____
____	1-57248-174-9	How to Form a Corporation in OH	$24.95	____
____	1-57248-173-0	How to Make an OH Will	$16.95	____

PENNSYLVANIA TITLES

Qty	ISBN	Title	Retail	Ext.
____	1-57248-242-7	Child Custody, Visitation and Support in PA	$26.95	____
____	1-57248-495-0	How to File for Divorce in PA (4E)	$24.95	____
____	1-57248-358-X	How to Form a Corporation in PA	$24.95	____
____	1-57248-094-7	How to Make a PA Will (2E)	$16.95	____
____	1-57248-357-1	How to Start a Business in PA (3E)	$21.95	____
____	1-57248-245-1	Landlords' Legal Guide in PA	$24.95	____

TEXAS TITLES

Qty	ISBN	Title	Retail	Ext.
____	1-57248-171-4	Child Custody, Visitation, and Support in TX	$22.95	____
____	1-57248-399-7	How to File for Divorce in TX (4E)	$24.95	____
____	1-57248-470-5	How to Form a Corporation in TX (3E)	$24.95	____
____	1-57248-496-9	How to Probate and Settle an Estate in TX (4E)	$26.95	____
____	1-57248-471-3	How to Start a Business in TX (4E)	$21.95	____
____	1-57248-111-0	How to Win in Small Claims Court in TX (2E)	$16.95	____
____	1-57248-355-5	Landlords' Legal Guide in TX	$24.95	____
____	1-57248-513-2	Write Your Own TX Will (4E)	$16.95	____

WASHINGTON TITLES

Qty	ISBN	Title	Retail	Ext.
____	1-57248-522-1	File for Divorce in Washington	$24.95	____

SubTotal This page ____

SubTotal previous page ____

Shipping — $5.00 for 1st book, $1.00 each additional ____

Illinois residents add 6.75% sales tax ____

Connecticut residents add 6.00% sales tax ____

Total ____

To order, call Sourcebooks at 1-800-432-7444 or FAX (630) 961-2168 (Bookstores, libraries, wholesalers—please call for discount)

Prices are subject to change without notice.

Find more legal information at: **www.SphinxLegal.com**